AFTER POLAND

A Memoir Because of Primo Levi

Cheryl Chaffin

Robin & Madeleine —

Cheryl ♡

AFTER POLAND

A Memoir Because of Primo Levi

Cheryl Chaffin

COMMON GROUND RESEARCH NETWORKS 2018

First published in 2018
as part of the New Directions in the Humanities Book Imprint
doi: 10.18848/978-1-86335-009-9/CGP (Full Book)

Common Ground Research Networks
2001 South First Street, Suite 202
University of Illinois Research Park
Champaign, IL
61820

Library of Congress Cataloging-in-Publication Data

Names: Chaffin, Cheryl, author.
Title: After Poland : a memoir because of Primo Levi / Cheryl Chaffin.
Description: Champaign, IL : Common Ground Research Networks, 2018. |
   Includes bibliographical references.
Identifiers: LCCN 2018027187 (print) | LCCN 2018044643 (ebook) | ISBN
   9781863350099 (pdf) | ISBN 9781863350075 (hardback : alk. paper) | ISBN
   9781863350082 (pbk. : alk. paper)
Subjects: LCSH: Holocaust, Jewish (1939-1945), in literature. | Chaffin,
   Cheryl. | Levi, Primo,--Influence.
Classification: LCC PN56.H55 (ebook) | LCC PN56.H55 C53 2018 (print) | DDC
   818/.603--dc23
LC record available at https://lccn.loc.gov/2018027187

Cover Photo Credit: Cheryl Chaffin
Logo for CompLit InterArt book series Credit: Mónica O'Doherty López-Varela

Table of Contents

ACKNOWLEDGEMENTS

Thank you to friends and colleagues who have read this manuscript with care. The gift of your reading has been invaluable: Gustavo Sánchez Canales, who read early and late drafts, David Sullivan, Andrew Fague, and Mary Ann Mayer. Gratitude to Jeanine Mamary, wise teacher, who one day said, "You need to write these things." Thank you to Shelley Armitage for teachings on life writing and theory of autobiography, and our conversations that continued post-doc as I composed this book. Thank you to friend and former student Aboudeh Almalouhi for sharing your story with me. You have taught me the value of interior strength and the will to persevere, qualities you pair with compassionate intelligence. It was at Vajrapani Institute for Wisdom Culture in Boulder Creek, California that I began this manuscript and completed it. The silent retreats on Lama Ridge provided space to attend to the content of this narrative. Thank you to Auschwitz Jewish Center for a fellowship to study Jewish history in New York and Poland, illuminating new passages into contemplating Primo Levi's writing and his life. Thank you to my colleagues at Cabrillo College, David Sheftman, Ekua Omosupe, and Winifred Baer, for assisting with funds for research and travel. Gratitude to Roger Mihara for designing the beautifully contemplative cover photo. Finally, with gratitude to my family—my son, Elias, and my mother, Carolyn, for indefatigable support and love through six years of graduate school followed by a three-year period during which this book has evolved.

I dedicate this book to those who have come before and to those who will come after.

Portions of this book have been published in *Catamaran Literary Reader*, *Ex-Centric Narratives*, and *Porter Gulch Review*.

Memory, like love, gains strength through restatement, reaffirmation; in a culture, through ritual, tradition, stories, art. Memory courts our better selves; it helps us recognize the importance of deed; we learn from pleasure just as we learn from pain. And when memory evokes consideration of what might have been or been prevented, memory becomes redemptive.

Anne Michaels, "Cleopatra's Love"

Preface

I have written this book to explore for myself and hopefully for others what it means to confront history as a human being. For my particular lifetime that signifies a woman of the late twentieth and early twenty-first centuries. More specifically, what does it mean to live in the world given the violence and atrocity of history as I have inherited it, and as it continues to play out in my present and most certainly affect my future? And, finally, what is the process of self and other-knowing through writers I have read and who have influenced me over years? It is from those immediately compelling questions that this narrative has arisen and that as story and critical inquiry it traces. Returning from Poland, where I had ventured mostly to feel the place that Italian Jewish writer Primo Levi had described in his first memoir, *If This Is a Man*, in its American title, *Survival in Auschwitz*, I felt the weight of what had transpired there.[1] The very intention of the place as one of forced labor, mass killing, and daily atrocity reverberated for me in every artifact and every physical structure, in every pore and spore of the acres that composed Auschwitz I (the first buildings of the *Konzentrationslager*), and its extension, the extermination camp, Birkenau (Auschwitz II).[2]

The despair that descended gradually and in the ensuing months after Poland, primarily through exposure to Treblinka and Auschwitz, the underground prison cells and gas chambers, the shooting walls, inside a cell block, now a lecture hall, where once many prisoners had been forcibly held, the showering and tattooing areas, the sites of mass murder in Polish forests just outside of small towns, accumulated in me. I wanted to scream, but there was no place to do it, no space for grieving, as the small group of scholars kept a busy travel schedule and our visits were followed by academic discussions that left little room for confusion, grief, and doubt. Consequently, I sought solitude to process my internal responses. Some of the essays here have resulted of those quiet moments that enabled me to think, feel, and reflect more deeply than I could have in the midst of others. It was at those moments the swirling universe inside me rose to the surface of consciousness.

When I returned home I felt the scream dull under my daily life. The scream seemed to transmute into a vague and distant disassociation, not quite apathy, but a feeling of dullness, not quite depression, but a slight disaffection, even melancholy. It was not something to get over; rather it was just there. I hardly noticed it. I did not want to write, and I did not know if I could write. Friends said I was probably worn out from writing and defending a dissertation, or maybe it was just the denouement of

---

[1] Throughout this book I refer to Levi's first autobiographical work by the English translation of its Italian title, *Se questo è un uomo*, as *If This is a Man*, rather than its American title, *Survival in Auschwitz*. Levi often refers in his writing to Auschwitz and its subcamps as the *Lager*, the German term for camp.

[2] Auschwitz was established on the grounds of a former Polish Army barracks in 1940. The camp held from 15,000 to 20,000 prisoners. Birkenau, the extermination camp, was first built in 1941. It held 90,000 people in 1944. See Auschwitz-Birkenau State Memorial and Museum website.

my graduate career—a vibrant finale that had accordingly fizzled into gray trails of smoke. Fellowship had immediately followed defense, and now it was back to regular life—working and parenting, nothing momentous to accomplish, no arduous endeavors underway. Perhaps, but there was something deeper. I had lost my drive for life, the joy that had been within me previous to visiting sites of genocide. That joy had disappeared; it had slipped quietly under the surface. Instead, I wondered who I was now that I had stood in the historical presence of fellow human beings who had died in surprise and shock and in cruel and demeaning ways. I knew I could not remain the same, but I was left with something that I only vaguely felt and could not directly name.

It is this experience, among others, that I explore in this book, and this experience that lends the book its title. "What is Poland to you?" a friend asked me one evening over dinner. I did not know how to answer. I had gone for Levi. I simply wanted to be where he had been. I wanted to climb inside his story and to inhabit more clearly in my mind his journey and descent into the camps. Shortly after my friend's query, I began to write in answer to the question.

I have chosen to write this book in a particular and perhaps peculiar form. It was in graduate school that I gravitated to the energy generated of various intersections of autobiographical and critical writing. In literary theory this style of writing has been termed autobiographical literary criticism.[3] Feminist literary scholars from the late 1980s through the 1990s were at the forefront in development of the genre. Jane Tompkins in personal essay and Nancy Miller in memoir had addressed their development as thinkers, tracing their intellectual and emotional maturation through the study of languages and literature. Tompkins, tired of a removed and impersonal theoretical voice and yearning for authenticity in her critical writing, began to experiment with frequent usage of an intimate autobiographical and narrating I. Her seminal essay "Me and My Shadow"[4] declared her right to bring elements of personal life into scholarly writing. The essay details a personal experience of self as a subjectivity often omitted from traditional (read, male) modes of inquiry and theoretical writing. Feminist academics like Tompkins were asking why omit personal life from theory and criticism. In fact, didn't theory evolve of real life? I concluded in reading Tompkin's work that the personal provides an entryway into articulation of critical thought, though it is not the purpose of critical thought. Still, I determined to fuse memoir writing with my desire to create literary criticism and scholarly writing. It was Tompkin's impulse, her effort that I made my own.

Fifteen years earlier, I had found inspiration in Anaïs Nin's diaries as a form of literature. The compilation of diaries and the continuity among them culminates in a single compelling narrative of a woman's thinking, her sensuality, and her blossoming as a writer and artist. In Simone de Beauvoir's memoir, *The Prime of Life*, I observed a woman writing with clarity and exactitude the contours of her life—including, memorably, some maniac hiking days alone in the Pyrenees, as she became a

---

[3] See, for example, *Getting Personal* by Nancy Miller, Leigh Gilmore's *Autobiographics,* and *The Intimate Critique: Autobiographical Literary Criticism.*

[4] Tompkins, "Me and My Shadow" in *The Intimate Critique: Autobiographical Literary Criticism.*

philosopher, a short story writer, and a novelist.[5] Critical and imaginative capacities had merged into one rich strand for these women. I felt that weave, too, as I read philosopher and novelist Rebecca Goldstein's book *Betraying Spinoza*, where she details the knowledge gleaned in studying Spinoza's philosophical treatise, *Ethics*, as a high school student.[6] Her critical reading was coupled with a desire for his autobiography as she sought out details of his personal life grounded in historical time and place. Her desire to know Spinoza in a more intimate way than his proofs allowed goes against the grain of good philosophy, which in order to establish its proofs relies on logos and ideas in the abstract, and foregoes the pathos of the personal. Thus, her betrayal of Spinoza. In interviews Goldstein has talked of being one of the first and only female philosophers in the department at Princeton in the 1970s. She has also written novels, an endeavor, she says, her fellow scholars did not consider the work of a true philosopher. Goldstein's example compelled me to return to graduate school a second time. She had shown me that I did not have to sacrifice an imaginative, poetic, passionate voice to critical writing, that, in fact, the two styles infuse and inform each other. I entered doctoral studies with a desire to shape a writer's voice that was scholarly and poetic, where theory and the ordinary events and emotions of daily life merged. It was the women before me who had done the critically creative work that urged me onward in my studies and writing, and whose intellectual and energetic influence threads the lines of this book.

During the years of doctoral study, I began conscious work on a writer's voice that would permit me space to range through personal narrative content in a creative manner complimented by the rigor, and its attendant freedoms, of critical understanding. I read theory and imagined applying the ideas, words, and feelings of the theorist to my life. How did this apply to my way of thinking about and experiencing the world? How would this look in my body-mind as I cooked dinner for my family, in my interactions with students, in the way I carried myself in the world, as I wrote a poem? In academic papers, I sought to include stories of people, turning again and again to narratives. I was drawn to the work of women philosophers asserting truths in the form of social and political philosophy made directly from reflection on their personal experiences. Susan Brison in her memoir, *Aftermath*, recounts her experience of rape in rural France, confronting an antiquated and frequently misogynist legal system to form a responsive ethics in the aftermath of violent crime.[7] Adriana Cavarero in *Relating Narratives* writes about the uniqueness of the single voice as she develops a philosophy of narrative as a mode of relational ethics.[8] These lines of thinking compelled me with their material specificity—the body, the voice, and the intricacies of personal experience writ large into the often abstract and distant voice of philosophical thinking.

Upon my return from Poland I wanted to infuse my autobiographically critical writing with the sensibility of poetry. Poetry represents the ability to look deeply, to

---

[5] de Beauvoir, *The Prime of Life*, 1960.
[6] Goldstein, *Betraying Spinoza*, 2006.
[7] Brison. *Aftermath*, 2002.
[8] Cavarero, *Relating Narratives: Storytelling and Selfhood*, 2000.

listen quietly, to contemplate and to process the insights crystalized in a moment of life encounter. As I emerged from doctoral study and then traveled to Poland, the desire for poetry's eye and its consciousness made itself felt again. Poetry sculpts prose. It makes story a moment, whittled down to its essence. Poet and essayist Gregory Orr writes that poetry contains within its lines a certain logic, while simultaneously those lines release passion, ecstatic and mournful, that undergird all living.[9] The poet finds in crafting her poems both discipline and release. If I could return to poetry after Poland, then I could live with Auschwitz and its realities at every moment; I could live because poetry returned means the ability to continue life in full reality of violence, death, and despair. It is to acknowledge, accept, and embody collective history, and personal history, little by little, accumulating knowledge as a patchwork quilt—rough, woven together, communally created, experiential, even while living forward, creating a life that adds beauty, hope, and love to the collective human situation. The choice of poetry is an alignment with joy in the face of loss and subsequent grief. To live with Auschwitz then is a choice, not for death but for life.

This was the return, and it is to this return that this book attests.

---

[9] Orr, *Poetry as Survival*, 2002.

CHAPTER 1

Reasons for Remembering

1.1 BY WAY OF BEGINNING

I've been unsure about this boredom, this dull despair, this dispassionate removal from life, as if I'm in the stream but just outside it, watching it without curiosity or interest. I've even worried a little about this state. It is as if pallor (is it despondency?) has descended on me and I cannot shake it. It is true that I've entered midlife and am well into that venture, but this flatness has been particularly noticeable after the mid-summer weeks in New York and Poland studying Jewish and Polish history. The pallor stems directly of my time in Poland, for New York distracted me with its buzz and energy, good restaurants, wildly surging streets, and the view of the Statue of Liberty in the harbor just outside the Museum of Jewish Heritage's fourth floor windows. From that fourth-floor room the fellows discussed books and essays we'd read about Polish war history and the life of Jewish communities before and after the Second World War. We listened to Jewish survivors, who are now eighty and ninety years old, tell their stories. Terrence Des Pres, a scholar at Colgate who wrote *The Survivor: An Anatomy of Life in the Death Camps* and *Writing into the World*, hung himself in November 1987 at the age of forty-seven. I think of him and his situation often in these days. I have thought of his death for a long time, since first reading his work in Chicago, where I had discovered his essay collection, Writing into the World, in the mid-nineties. He was obsessed with the history that evolved of events we have come to call the Holocaust, the Shoah. He looked intimately into the connection between art and terror and genocide. How do we live in the world with the knowledge of such terror? Studying the writings of Elie Wiesel, he noted the importance of silence in approaching the Holocaust. "His solution has been to mobilize silence; to use silence as a category of relation to primary aspects of the Holocaust experience; to render silence in ways that make it—and therefore what it embodies—present and meaningful to us to make silence speak."[10] He also revealed that one could write prose and touch into crystalline moments of poetry through the exactitude and beauty of language, noting, "the poet's capacity to respond to the world's beauty is the index of his will to endure."[11] He wrote of the difficulty of studying genocide that has reminded me of an aphorism written by Friedrich Nietzsche in *Beyond Good and Evil*:

---

[10] Des Pres, *Writing into the World*, 28.
[11] Ibid, 40.

"Whoever fights with monsters should see to it that in the process he does not become a monster. And when you look long into an abyss, the abyss also looks into you."[12]

The closer one gets to the violence and death, the harder it is to recover one's daylight life, the normalcy which one must assume in order to go about her diurnal, quotidian activities. Yet, as James Baldwin writes in his 1953 essay, "Stranger in the Village," people who insist shutting their eyes to reality invite their own destruction. Importantly, he adds that a person who insists on remaining in a state of innocence long past the time that innocence has died turns himself into a monster.[13] The reference to the monster implies that in cleaving to innocence, certainly a brand of willed ignorance, we lose not only the possibility and necessity of maturation but the ethical responsibility, our obligation to others, to be fully and complexly human. For humanness is not a natural state, a mere given. Our humanity grows and matures in engagement with the world. It is sculpted with the act of writing, living with the reality that swirls about us and composes who we are, who we might become, and how we will respond to that becoming.

The writer does not bar herself from the world; she consumes and digests it, sleeps and wakes to it. She lives in it with open eyes and attentive ears so that she may let it move, depress, and disturb her. I've taken Des Pres to heart. I want his exactitude and sensitivity in writing to be my own. Baldwin's words course within me and have become mixed with my movements on earth. Neither of these writers escaped the burden of history. To write is to travel in the direction of elucidation. But to know is to suffer. How does one swim in the pulling undertow? There are writers who continue to work and who have not, as yet, succumbed to the harrowing effects of being human in a suffering, calamitous world.

Carolyn Forché, renowned poet and editor of the anti-war and anti-torture poetry collection, *Against Forgetting*, survives and thrives even as she has travelled to places of horror and recorded those moments in her poems and in her editorial work gathered the voices of other poets who have experienced calamity.[14] Forché remarks that the poetry of witness "reclaims the social from the political and in so doing defends the individual against illegitimate forms of coercion."[15] She also comments that the young poet who travelled to El Salvador during the late1970s and early 80s in the last years of a civil war in the country, returned as a poet who wrote what she had felt and seen there. She left the young poet, in her late twenties, behind and came home changed to write poems that addressed the political situation and the human rights abuses in El Salvador. In "Reading the Living Archives: The Witness of Literary Art," she discusses witness as intrinsic to both the act of reading and writing.[16] The closer one looks (into the/an abyss), the more difficult it becomes to realize or grasp the horror of intense violence inflicted on human beings. The one looking has to constantly suppress the tendency to disbelief. The ethical imperative is to believe and to continue

---

[12] Walter Kaufmann, *Existentialism from Dostoevsky to Sartre*, 1975.

[13] Baldwin, *Notes of a Native Son*, 1955.

[14] Forché, *Against Forgetting: Twentieth-Century Poetry of Witness*, 1993.

[15] Carolyn Forché Biography, *Poetry Foundation*.

[16] Forché, "Reading the Living Archives: The Witness of Literary Art," *Poetry*, May 2011.

looking and to be present with compassion and even love in the face of incredible violation and degradation. "You do not have to ingest suffering," my spiritual teacher once told me. She meant that I did not need to swallow collective suffering and hold it inside, as if holding might somehow decrease the world's pain. I wanted to alleviate the pain of human beings through history and, yet my single body was not big enough to contain this collectivity. The Tibetans teach a meditation called *tonglen*. Breathe in suffering and breathe out love. One assumes the suffering of the world and breathes back love into pain. Buddhist teacher Joan Halifax describes the practice as honing "our ability to be present for our own suffering and the suffering of others a practice of great kindness that opens up our whole being to the overwhelming presence of suffering and our strength and willingness to transform alienation into compassion through the energy of mercy and the cultivation of openness." [17] *Tonglen* is a metaphoric exercise. Taken into the body through breath and practiced cultivating the mind through meditation, it manifests benefits of peace, equanimity, and compassion at the level of embodiment. It is in juxtaposition to work for justice in that is encourages mercy, forgiveness, and compassion as a seeing into and momentarily understanding, even feeling, a shared human condition with other beings, regardless of their actions. That is why it is so challenging, hard to conceptualize, and physically impossible to embody.

Drawing ever nearer to the events of the Holocaust through reading and traveling to places of atrocity, one feels tainted and stained by these acts. It is looking into the face of evil itself. The gaze into the abyss might be contained and controlled by the beauty of poetry and prose, by the courage of reason in the face of chaos and violation, and by the human need to speak—even brutally graphic content—in spite of demolition.

No, I have not lost the will or courage to live. Yet, I feel that I am carrying the history of an epic that is not mine and, strangely, is very much mine. Intuitively and intellectually I recognize this state—flatness coupled with low-level despair—as inimical to creating poetry. Have I looked into an abyss? If so, what has been its mark? With what has it left me? I am not the same as I was before Poland. Poetry wants the devoted eye, heart, and mind. Poems arise of noticing, feeling, and thinking. Poetry desires detail. It wants to note the hidden, the unnoticed, the forgotten, and the bypassed. How do I begin to awaken again?

1.2 GRAVEYARDS AND AN INQUIRY INTO THE DEAD

Seamus Heaney writes, "Everywhere plants/Flourish among graves/Sinking their roots/In all the dynasties/Of the dead." [18] I read this and think of the Jewish graveyards in Warsaw and Lodz. It was hard to distinguish if these were woods where cemeteries had taken root or cemeteries where woods had taken root. But, I did not note the relation between plants and graves in Poland, only thought how beautiful was the

---

[17] Joan Halifax, *Upaya*.
[18] Heaney, "A Herbal," *Human Chain*, 35.

green growing with slate slabs and piles of rock and wondered who all these now-dead had been. In Warsaw and Kraków there were walls composed of pieces of gravestones. Many gravestones had been lost, destroyed, and broken through pogroms and wars. Where they were once shattered, now they were salvaged; where ruined, restored. The walls protected graves, giving form to space and containment to visitors. These walls incorporated and drew the gravestones in again—their names and designs, their colors—black and white, the smooth glow of their surfaces. In the middle of one of these graveyards, a woman kneeled in the grass, pulling weeds, wearing a hat. She was lost in verdancy, her work seemingly purposeless, hardly worth the effort amidst ceaseless growth. Who would care? How to determine the line between too much growth and groomed grounds? Surely, the unburdened flowering of plants crushed any attempt to curtail and control them.

The woman gardening around graves in the Jewish graveyard, acres and acres of graves emerging of grass, couched in thick shade of hardwoods, reminds me of my mother's cousin, Esther, taking us for a walk on her Colorado acres, her curved eighty-four-year-old body reaching down, pulling "weeds" on the sloped hillsides red with dirt, rock-scattered, cactus sprawling. Why are these weeds in the middle of all this wild, I wondered, and laughed aloud to watch her gardening the rugged mountainside. Why do we try to manage the unmanageable? What are we doing when the whole world is growing up around us? In Poland there are so few Jews to take care of the cemeteries. The woman works alone. The poet notices and catches the uncertain beauty of these moments along with their pregnant metaphor to write the poem. One has to wonder, to marvel, to hurt, and to desire to write. One has to love the world, to cry for it and because of it to write anything at all. That must be why I want to return to poetry, why I long to read and write it again.

Why are there stands of hardwoods in the middle of cities, in the midst of Warsaw and Lodz? The Jewish cemeteries span many acres behind walls. In Warsaw the Okopowa Street Jewish Cemetery, established in 1806, is eighty-three acres and the largest Jewish cemetery in Europe. The walls are brick, much like the Jewish ghetto walls of that city. The cemeteries are, of course, in once Jewish neighborhoods. They were part of daily life, part of the compound of Jewish living. Children played on and near cemetery grounds. I imagine there were markets and houses at its edges. The dead were close to life, though not directly part of it. Life pulsated around them, as Heaney writes, "Everywhere plants/Flourish among graves." Those plants then are like people who are always living atop and alongside the dead. Their dead? Our dead? The dead are tree roots pushing us, reminding us that we, too, will enter the earth and become nourishment for plants. The ground on which we stand is composed of our past, entirely ancestral. Sometimes it is a site of burial, sometimes of genocide, other times a busy market with flowers and food and children playing. Sometimes the ground cries. It holds us, supports us, and eventually we return to and become it again.

The dead are both present among and entirely absent the living. I have disliked the term "the dead," which marks those who have passed as a group, uniform, and obliterated. In Poland it was hard to feel that the dead had moved on. They lingered in history, in the places we visited. We went to them; we sought them out. In my mind I thought up other terms. I came to prefer a more human phrase, something like "those who have died." Yet, that was awkward, and I could not say it in discussion. Just now I feel "the dead" as a group represents all those millions who have passed on before us living. We are always, every moment, some of us, joining the dead. The dead live among us in memory, but most of them, at least individually, are forgotten. Those who would remember them are gone as well. The dead is an idea, an idea that erases individuality, which is, of course, lost in death. The dead is a thought of that which has come and gone and that remains, in pieces, among us.

Entering those Jewish cemeteries takes time. One travels from their outer edges on paths that lead into their interiors, paths that often become increasingly forested. I had forgotten our small group was in the middle of a city. Once in the cemetery we were inside a forest, under a canopy, gravestones askew and angled atop the tenacious rise and push of tree roots. In Warsaw, I felt I had entered a story, like a child's fairytale, and was the protagonist lost in a wood. Around me dwelled the remnants of many spirits. They were like ribbons haunting my path, circling their energies about my feet and in the air around me. They induced reverence, caution, and attentiveness. Everywhere there were secrets, small spaces and walks that I could not see. The graves and their occupants were in relationship to one another. They had developed their own connections and divergences over the years. They had watched events appear and disappear. They knew temporality, whereas for me it was only an idea, a wish of enlightenment and knowledge. Only the graves by the path were visible. So much existed beyond.

I walked quietly, light of foot and silent among many who had died and whose markers now crowded and competed for space. Long rows of gray stones standing upright at all angles disappeared into trees with arrow-like trunks. There were small iron fences, both inviting and protective, with motif of curlicue, even filigree, brownish with rust, around family plots. Each fence merited a poem. The fences lived in relationship to the grass, plants, and trees. Sometimes the living things completely obscured the graves; the fence was home to an unruly and unabashedly lush band of plants. There were large, artistic, expressive gravestones heavy with sculpture and verbose epitaphs for famous and wealthy people.

Here is the gravestone of Adam Czerniakow, head of the *Judenrat*, the Warsaw Jewish Ghetto Council. He committed suicide on July 23, 1942, the day before the ordered liquidation of the ghetto and deportation of Jews from the ghetto to Treblinka extermination camp. Here is the grave of Esther Rachel Kaminska (1870–1925), known as the mother of Yiddish Theater.[19] These gravestones asserted a command to remembrance, almost forcing it on the visitor. They reminded me how terrible and difficult it is to pass quietly when one has known attention and admiration in life. Others were humble—diminutive, broken, abandoned, their letters erased by time,

---

[19] Kaminska was a stage and film actress. She was also a playwright. In 1913 she and her daughter founded a theater company. The current Yiddish Theater in Warsaw is named the Jewish Theater Esther Rachel and Ida Kaminski (Teatr Żydowski im. Estery Rachel i Idy Kamińskich), after Esther and her daughter, Ida, who served as director of the theater at its founding in 1950 to 1968 when she left Poland.

snow, wind, and vandalism. A Jewish star carved into stone was more impactful and prominent than a name.

1.3 WHY PHILOSOPHY

I decided to get a doctorate because, among other reasons, I wanted to better understand certain books I had read, books to which I return time and again, such as Annie Dillard's *Holy the Firm* and Primo Levi's first autobiographical work, *If This Is a Man*.[20] This second book has become for me a lifetime engagement. It infiltrates every moment of my thinking and my actions in a life practice of ethics in relation to others and to history. The best way to describe the influence this book continues to exert on me is that the text—words, lines, chapter titles, sentences, metaphors, images, and logical arguments—are in my bloodstream.

By the time my son was three he recognized Levi's name and had heard and somehow absorbed into his subconscious the conversations I had with my mother about the book as I went deeper and deeper into the text to be able to understand its context, its allusions to philosophy and myth and literature, and the writer's tone and his approach to the memory of his experience, arisen of his education as a scientist and also of his profound humanism. One day my son asked me, "Mommy, what is Auschwitz?" His question compelled me to write a poem about introducing to a child the fact of human violence and murderous behavior, an introduction that tears at the fabric of one's initial comfort in the world. From the surrounding world (of which I was an element), notions of monsters, ghosts, and the food chain had begun to enter his consciousness. The need to erase isolation and separateness also existed for him, as for every child from the moment of birth.

I have written that one cannot live with Auschwitz at every moment. In fact, a student recently asked why people work against an end to the story. Why do they need to keep telling the story, to keep it open, to make the process of understanding, forgiveness, and inquiry open-ended and indefinite? In other words, how is it that humans in the face of traumatic memory elect to keep story infinitely alive? How does repetition of and addition to memories through written and oral testimony, as well as in cultural productions and artifacts, serve to heal traumatic history and its aftermath? Without memory, of course, there is no history. If Levi's first book is any indication of living with the memory of Auschwitz and its consequences, then I live with Auschwitz and all it represents at every moment. Which is perhaps what Levi wanted, for he stated in "A Self-Interview" his intention that his readers should act as judges of history. He implied that because of his firsthand experience and his closeness to events he experienced at Auschwitz he could not be a judge, but that he would fulfill

---

[20] Annie Dillard's *Holy the Firm* was published in 1977. Her third book constitutes a philosophical and highly poetic exploration of whether God has any influence or feeling toward catastrophic events. This query forms the center of a narrative where Dillard reflects on God's involvement in human affairs in the aftermath of a plane crash on a small island in the Northwest where a young girl has been badly burned and then dies.

his duty, also a dire need, to remember and recount—and he did so in multiple works—in his position as storyteller.

The book then has invigorated and nourished my intellectual life. I've ingested its spirit, its very purpose, the urgency and beauty with which it was written for its author and for his readers. This book stands at the center of my study of the Holocaust, of Poland, of Jews and Judaism, of the Second World War. It has become a life journey for me, embodying all things that matter in my consciousness: a strong sense of ethics; the shame of the survivor and his atonement through his life work to which he dedicates himself for having survived; a steady logic as a method of distance and objective witness, rather than a tone of superior intelligence; and, a clear, poetic faculty of reasoning. Levi's is the cultivated voice of a poet and a man who loves language, sentences, and words. His writing possesses the ability of storytelling, coupled with a love of the human being, even after the experience of atrocity, which is the experience of "the demolition of man" as he named it, as well as the destruction of women and children and old people. Levi's work confronts how anything and everything human and related to humanness was utterly and horribly destroyed in those environments of death imagined and created in ideologies and actions germinated of Germany's National Socialist regime.

To carry this tale is a heavy responsibility. Those emerging from centuries of slavery and their descendants, as well as the first peoples that settled the Americas, have also born the responsibility to narrate and offer ethical responses in the wake and the legacy of genocidal histories and know that a lineage of telling and remembering is vital to the care and nurture of memory. The burden of the Holocaust as we've inherited it in the contemporary world is increasingly shared. Those of us haunted by its legacy, directly and indirectly, pass the story to others and teach the lessons of war and genocide again and again to those newer to the planet and to those coming to the story out of some awakened recognition, even if by accident. In teaching that story, we are learning ourselves. We listen closely to first person accounts. We search paintings and films for meaning, for closeness to the memories of the offense. We travel to be with others who share the passion to look and study, to discover and listen. We humble ourselves. We make offerings. I burn candles and incense. I close the door to my room. I write. Even when I do not know what I will write, or if I am able, I go to space where writing happens as a way to honor the spirit energies, the stories, the hauntings, the emotional resonances history leaves in its wake. This is the ritual—to go, to sit, to ignite a flame, to attend in silence, to record, to feel, and, finally, to speak.

The existence of collective memory reflects in the changing focus at the Auschwitz-Birkenau State Memorial and Museum.[21] The museum administration and

---

[21] In April 1946, the Polish Ministry of Culture and Art in conjunction with a group of former prisoners of Auschwitz, conceived the idea for a museum, with plans for a future memorial. It opened in June 1947. It was planned to present the extermination of the peoples conquered by the Germans and to highlight the fact that the German atrocities were committed on a mass scale, while steering clear of "the macabre" and using only suitable visual elements. It stressed that the killing of the Jews should be presented in a special way, and that it was necessary to cooperate with the Central Committee of Jews in Poland (Centralny Komitet

its guides have begun to educate young generations that will carry the memory and history of the camps and the Holocaust into the future. In this effort, it is personal narratives that override a plethora of facts and numbers as a method of teaching and passing on histories that with time become increasingly remote. It is the pathos of story that once again holds sway over the abstract objectivity of numbers. However, the emotional appeal of story does not make it infallible; it is a creation of its author, embroidered from scraps of memory and formed into a narrative universe issued of its maker's interest in craft, a well-formed story, and his cavernous imagination. Into this developing milieu of memory, Levi's narrative composed of observations and stories of those he met within the camps persists and accordingly grows in significance.

Levi began to write the manuscript that would become the book in 1946, just after his release from Auschwitz. He wrote it with an aching desire and desperation to be heard and to have a story. I've been awed by Levi's experience of having to write a book in order to live. Beyond this awe was a need for me, ten years ago when I started to teach his book to college students, to understand the philosophical underpinnings inhabiting his prose. He related his awful experiences to readers with steadiness and a smart distance gleaned from his classical education that had included philosophy, logic, science, and literature. He begins his account with reference to his pre-Auschwitz self, which would have been a young man in his early twenties just graduated from the university. That university education would have been delayed due to the imposition in 1938 of race laws in Italy that excluded Jews from certain courses of study and from particular classes. Levi attended chemistry lab in the basement of a building in his city of Torino. He relates this in The Periodic Table, an autobiographical work in essays that reflects on his life experiences before and after the camp—his experience of these years being some middle time-space that exists in a unique and separate universe but whose influence bifurcates a single life into categories of before and after.

But to return to that pre-Auschwitz self, Levi tells his reader that largely due to the imposed racial laws he lived in a world of his own making, one of sincere male and bloodless (close, but not romantic) female friendships and one haunted by civilized Cartesian phantoms. Those ghostly thoughts remind Levi that once there was a world where people believed in and practiced ethical behavior in their relationships to one another. Levi learns a radically different reality in Auschwitz from the one Descartes had posited, where sensory experiences in a body under duress often trump the rational mind's ability to determine reality through intellect. The rational world hardly exists in Auschwitz, a time and place without reference or location for Levi, as for many prisoners who found themselves suddenly and violently there. Some came, spilling, sick and exhausted from packed cattle trains, and from the arrival platform were made to form lines that would lead to gas chambers. There is a point in the first pages of If *This Is a Man* where Levi, then twenty-four, refers to the presence of mothers, children, and old people who disappear as quickly as he saw them, "Thus, in

---

Żydów w Polsce – CKŻP) to establish the number of Jewish victims, broken down by country (Auschwitz-Birkenau Memorial and Museum).

an instant, our women, our parents, our children disappeared. We saw them for a while in an obscure mass at the other end of the platform; then we saw nothing more."[22] It feels like an end. The end of the story, and it is. There is nothing if not the finality of loss here.

It is also a beginning. He invokes Dante's *Inferno* throughout his account. The clear metaphor, of course, is the descent into hell, what Maurice Blanchot calls the other night—the one that lures the writer into writing of the unspoken, the dark thing that hides from public view but that is the source of story. A subtle comparison to *Inferno* may find representation in the people that both Levi and Dante meet along the way. Those people on the precipice of death come alive again, as in *Inferno*, in their stories as related by Levi. Here is Jean the Pikolo, walking with Levi. He is a good man, always fair to his fellow prisoners whom he oversees on a work crew. Levi tells readers later, in interviews, Jean survived the camps and subsequent forced labor in mines. On a warmish day in June, Jean and Levi walk to the kitchens to fetch a vat of soup for the prisoners. Levi's work crew has been scraping and cleaning the inside of an underground petrol tank. The early summer air infuses Levi and in a rare moment he relaxes and begins to recite in Italian and explain in French to Jean the lines from Canto XXVI, in which Ulysses reveals his story to Dante. Ulysses recounts how as a storm arises on the sea he reminds his crew that they were not born to live as brutes but to pursue virtue and knowledge. But then the walk is over. They have arrived at the kitchens and must queue for the soup. The chapter ends as Levi remembers, "over our heads the hollow seas closed up."[23]

There is the Polish boy, Schlome, who tells Levi upon his arrival into Auschwitz—through a conversation of Polish, German, French, Italian, and multiple signs conveyed in a sort of charade-like exchange—not to drink the water, for it will cause him to swell. Levi does not see the boy again, but he remembers and thanks him in the present time of his book. He and the boy speak of mothers and their countries, as do Levi and Jean. The mother lingers as a metaphor for home throughout his first book, representative of all things loved and lost and that potentially, barring grave illness, injury, and death, one might return to again. The Cartesian phantoms float around as remnants of a recent education that one is human because he thinks. One exists and knows oneself to be because he has thoughts and possesses intellect, the pursuit of excellence and knowledge of which Ulysses reminds his crew.

In graduate school philosophy and ethics courses, we students did not engage the work of René Descartes. Perhaps he was too early in the lineage of thinking that gave rise to the European Enlightenment, too much a foundational thinker. We began with the late eighteenth-century period of Enlightenment, studying the works of those who had followed from a tradition of inquiry and who had made reason their own according to their times. My philosophy professor and mentor had studied at The New School for Social Research. He assigned us the writings of continental philosophers like Immanuel Kant and Friedrich Nietzsche, and later American pragmatists such as

---

[22] Levi, *Survival*, 20.
[23] Ibid, 115.

William James and Ralph Waldo Emerson, followed by Deconstructionists—Jacques Derrida, Michel Foucault, Jean-François Lyotard, and Communitarians—Jürgen Habermas, Martha Nussbaum, and Nancy Fraser. We read contemporary philosophers concerned with politics, ethics, and aesthetics like Judith Butler, Simon Critchley, and Alexander Nehamas. In a course on feminist theory and identity, we delved into Jacques Lacan and feminist thinkers from Simone de Beauvoir to Jacqueline Rose to Julia Kristeva to Luce Irigaray. In "Writing and Resistance" we moved into the traditions of Black writers working from slavery through the twentieth century, as well as other writers of color, such as Gloria Anzaldúa who used the written word to explore multiple cultural, sexual, and lingual identities to break apart limiting notions of social power.

In "Democracy and Difference," a course on political philosophy, I lit up to the work of Hannah Arendt. It was a single book that compelled me: *The Promise of Politics*, a group of collected talks and essays she composed in the 1950s in the wake of the Second World War and thinking deeply, particularly as a German-Jew, about the significance of public space and politics.[24] One passage (which I discuss in a chapter below) awakened me to the sensuality of thinking. The life of passion, of friendship, love, and the body need not be separate from the life lived in the world. In the paragraph, she described how private spaces are necessary to creating alive and vibrant public spaces. Everything in the private world affects and alters the public world. Normally, we think about society and politics shaping our lives and our freedoms. But, in this case, Arendt says no: things we share in those intimate moments and spaces make a difference for how we believe, act, think, and come together in the public world. Ultimately, those intimate interactions shape the collective world, for better or for worse.

Arendt believed that personal life could positively affect the polis (that space of appearance, as she called it, that the Greeks considered constitutive of the political sphere par excellence). That world is not one made strictly of politicians and others managing the state, but it is composed of ordinary humans living their daily lives and interacting with each other trying to figure out how the political realm needs to serve and recognize them. I loved and responded to the very personal configuration that Arendt assigned to the political realm, how she engaged normal people in that realm and how her thinking, expressed with passionate, modulated, and articulate elegance, opened politics to everyone and to all things. In the process of reading Arendt, I discovered a contemporary Italian philosopher, Adriana Cavarero who has written extensively on philosophy of narrative as formative of selfhood and subjectivity.[25] I sought out thinkers who recognized the value of personal narratives to moral philosophy in order to make the philosophical ideas (rather than ideals) real and present in my daily life, to apply those ideas in particular to my study of literature and the process of writing and in thinking about the value of memory and story.

---

[24] Arendt, *The Promise of Politics*, 2005.
[25] See Cavarero's *Relating Narratives* and *For More Than One Voice*.

Some of my interest in and much of my initial draw to Levi's work stems from my study in college of Italian language and a year abroad in Florence. This early and still lingering interest in things Italian also compelled me to read Cavarero's work, along with the simple but not uncomplicated fact that there are still—even in the early twenty-first century—fewer female than male philosophers, and even a smaller number published and translated into English. I felt hungry for and delighted in the words of an Italian female philosopher. The combination of those two adjectives—Italian and female—with the noun—philosopher and its implied verb, philosophizing, constituted for me an impassioned and nearly paradisiacal universe of reading, study, and thought. Both Arendt and Cavarero consider the personal story primary to how we learn and know history and to how we conceptualize our relationships with one another and express our collective needs and desires in public life. Levi's autobiographical writing on Auschwitz and how the experiences there formed his character, both immediately and over the length of his lifetime, exemplify the significant contribution that personal writing makes to historical and ethical knowledge.

Levi, the chemist, teaches us that we need not limit our thinking to the mind, but that the body—in its resistance to and recuperation from demolition—is a central channel of knowing in the world. Levi also discovers in the *Lager* blurred boundaries between waking and dreaming.[26] These boundaries Descartes strove to delineate and explore. What is the relationship between physical or material reality and the world of dreaming? In Levi's *If This Is a Man*, dreaming appears a space to process the day's occurrences and to work through emotional responses to traumatic circumstances in which he finds himself. The dreams he shares in his account, particularly the dream of returning home to close friends and family who are unable to hear his story because they lack experience that allows them to make sense of his deportation and imprisonment, testify to his terror of social and emotional isolation that ensues for camp survivors. The dream is a nightmare, delivering the sober knowledge that an unheard story is no story at all. A story un-received annihilates the survivor's experience. Story barricades itself, a saw-toothed memory against the walls of the brain. It is the dream that teaches him this as yet unarticulated and subconscious emotional truth of the need to tell story in order to rejoin human community and to live again.

My study probably represents a group of contemporary thinkers to whom Levi had been not exposed. But, my understanding of his reference to Descartes at the outset of his book has deepened. The mind didn't matter for much at Auschwitz. What mattered was the ability of the body to survive. The mind quickly became enslaved to the body's demands, and if it did not, the body soon met its demise, as Levi recognized. He did not believe in the concrete as if it was a philosophy. Rather the concrete was ceaselessly imposed upon him through the war, in the camps, and in the alienating aftermath of war, in the experiences of violence and the witness to death and its repercussions and consequences for humans. Levi loved the material world, its

---

[26] See footnote 1 for an explanation of the term *Lager*.

beauty and harshness and felt attracted to it in chemistry. He wanted to mix elements and discover the outcomes of relations between them. What makes his writing so compelling is his ability to create philosophy—a way of thinking about the world morally, metaphysically—with the beauty and suffering of the material world. In this way he captures the embodied human condition, in autobiographical works as well as short stories and novels. Levi notes in *The Periodic Table*, "The hour of the appointment with Matter, the Spirit's great antagonist, had struck: hyle, which, strangely, can be found embalmed in the endings of alkyl radicals: methyl, butyl, etc."[27] Matter is our truncation, our finiteness, and our bondage. Spirit wants infinity, space without time, to demolish all restraints.

What philosophical arguments does Levi set out to disprove in *If This Is a Man* in the chapter-stories of the camp and the life and death that took place there? What room was there for intellect? What need? This is an underlying inquiry in Levi's book, and I think he sets out to prove that, in fact, the mind counted for very little in the camps beyond its ability to imagine and enact ways for the body to survive. Still, Levi depicts cases of the mind's demise and frequently argues through example and allusion that a mind must operate to assist the body in any bid for survival. He also depicts Elias, a man half-crazed, his mind gone, with incredible strength and physical ability, and asserts that this type of man is most suited to surviving Auschwitz. Elias is an anomaly, for he does not fit into Levi's categories of drowned and saved, subtypes of men within the camp, with which he describes the poles of existence at Auschwitz. Those drowning are the *Muselmann*; man, in the process of capitulating to death and hardly recognizable as human. He melts into thin flesh and protruding bones. He no longer sees; he moves into death, silent or wailing—his sound outside the range of language—without knowing that he moves. The saved man is the one who retains a sense of himself as a human being in relationship with other beings. This is an ethical relationship that exists in an embodied knowledge of civil society, in the necessity and value co-existing with others, and in sometimes sustaining oneself in proximity to others. This material and mnemonic knowledge perseveres even under extreme conditions, if only in vestiges, wherein new perverse laws arise. Relationships with others help the individual man avoid total isolation, an isolation that the camp ceaselessly enforces on him as a harbinger of death. The *Muselmann* is the man alone who due to lethal conditions has released his last tenuous hold on life.

Elias exists in an indeterminate space; he is neither drowned nor saved. The extreme physical conditions of the camp increase his physical strength and prowess. His insanity moves him into a kind of savagery or bestiality in relationship to his environment and those around him. Any energy that Levi directs toward his thoughts, reflections, and memory, toward negotiating the immediate demands of the camp environment are for Elias channeled into physical action. Has this man—stocky, short, like a bull in Levi's description—become a machine, an ideal expression of total domination? Admittedly, Levi's portrait of Elias is crafted, selective, and partial. He appears as a part of a proof that the *Lager* as an expression of and experiment in

---

[27] Levi, *The Periodic Table*, 30.

totalitarianism thrives on the pure bestiality of once-men. Still, these types are ultimately categories that defy the complexity of circumstance and the range of experience that each human within the camps perceived, felt, and responded to— whether with consciousness or in disconnection and dying.

Charlotte Delbo writes of going to a large barrack in the women's section of the camp to find her friend who among thousands of dying women lies on a pallet. When they find her (the author does not see and recognize her friend but the woman with her does) she is gray, covered in lice; pink liquid trickles from her mouth, her tongue is swollen, fever wracks her body. The girl cannot speak or see the friends who kneel beside her. The other woman touches the dying girl and leans to kiss her. This is a last gesture, a goodbye. "Kiss her, Charlotte," her companion insists.[28] But the writer finds herself repulsed, unable to kiss the skeletal being from which all life drains. It is not that she does not care for the girl; rather, it is from death itself that she retracts. Later, recording her camp experiences and having waited twenty years to write her books, she feels shame at resisting the kiss. Yet, who kisses death? The girl is gone, raging, burning, leaving. Who kisses death or looks directly into it? Her friend sees the girl; Charlotte sees something terrifying that may come to take her too, and she must resist here in this place of death, surrounded by thousands of dying beings that she may soon join. One has to resist the *Muselmann* then by reason of survival.[29] But what reason is this? By what reason does one step away into the world of the saved? The saved are damned to a life of shame, to the creeping, killing disease of shame. Delbo reminds her readers that she has returned, even when no one would have expected or wanted her to. "And so I came back/You did not know, /did you, /that one can come back from there/One comes back from there/and even from farther away."[30]

Levi never addresses the matter of Cartesian phantoms again, probably because with the brutal gray reality of Auschwitz they disappeared, or at least were submerged. A few dozen pages into his book he confesses that his body was no longer his and that with dwindling numbers of Italians meeting every Sunday in a corner of the *Lager* the reality of remembering and thinking was too much. "It was better not to think."[31] The few disbanded, not to meet again. Mind as marker of one's existence? The shred of the Cartesian phantom dissipates. Any notion that a man is a man because of his intellect, his mind, and his ability to think and reason was for Levi dispelled once initiated into the ways of the camp. Their bodies are disappearing too, becoming gray, yellow, swollen, and emaciated. "When we do not meet for a few

---

[28] Delbo, *Auschwitz and After*, 314.

[29] The term Muselmann was used in men's quarters of the Auschwitz compound. Concentration and labor camps developed their own harsh and abusive lexicons, as reflective of the unique though similar environment of terror within each camp. In *KL: A History of the Nazi Concentration Camps*, Nikolaus Wachsmann notes use of the names cripple, derelict, and jewel, and that "Most common of all was a term used in Auschwitz and several other camps—*Muselmänner* (sometimes *Muselweiber* for women) (209). See also Hermann Langbein's *People in Auschwitz*. Rather than providing an origin of the term, the author details conditions of starvation and disease that imposed physical and physiological stress to the point that people lost their ability to function and, therefore, to relate to self and others.

[30] Delbo, *Auschwitz and After*, 224.

[31] Levi, *Survival*, 37.

days we hardly recognize each other," he confesses.[32] Ironically, I returned to school to grasp Levi's phantoms, forgetting that ghosts are elusive and ephemeral. Yet, I had to understand what Levi cherished when he entered the camp, so I would better know what he lost for those ten interminable months that marked his life inside it.

1.4 CHILDHOOD

No one explains that

Monsters are fears,

That real people look like that,

Torture, maim, eat others,

that the ghost is the dead,

her anguished moan

the throes of dying we hear.

And, the food chain:

how to explain survival

means eating the other?

The monkey eats the beetle,

the hunter eats the monkey,

who eats the hunter?

Now you are three years old and

lonely in your room.

---

[32] Ibid.

Many times, a night

you return

to your mother's bed

where you knead your toes

into her soft, warm legs,

burrow down, tucked away from fear

while fitfully you sleep.

Whoever implied

childhood was

free of terror?

You hear words: war, fighting,

murder, kidnap.

There's a dead bird

in the garden,

prostrate on winter grass, and

you want to know

what Auschwitz is.

1.5 Phantoms of Western Thought: A Confrontation with Reason

It is far harder to kill a phantom than a reality.

Virginia Woolf, "Professions for Women"

Primo Levi embodies an ethical sensibility in a particular time and place, a juncture in history where the past split from the present and forced a radical reconceptualization of knowledge traditions as they had formed in Europe over several centuries. His phrase "civilized Cartesian phantoms," almost in passing at the outset of his account, provides a crucial element in understanding, at least in part, his descent into Auschwitz.

> I was captured by the Fascist Militia on 13 December 1943. I was twenty-four, with little wisdom, no experience and a decided tendency—encouraged by the life of segregation forced on me for the previous four years by the racial laws—to live in an unrealistic world of my own, a world inhabited by civilized Cartesian phantoms, by sincere male and bloodless female friendships. I cultivated a moderate and abstract sense of rebellion.[33]

Levi's phrase describes who he was, in mind, if not in body, when he entered Auschwitz in 1944. The phrase suggests his continental mind educated in natural philosophy and his scientific training. It also signals his youth and his tendency to fantasy in creating, logically, a safe small world of his own that would support and bolster him (university student and burgeoning scientist) through dislocation and violence of war in Europe. Levi studied chemistry at the University of Torino, but confessed that he might have pursued physics had his education not been disrupted by the imposition of racial laws and a protracted period of war. One often hopes when young that knowledge will triumph over the evils of social and political turmoil that so often erupts in violence and that, accordingly, determines the course of one's life. But Levi finds reason not so neat a construct, or, perhaps he discovers that reason takes many forms and is used to multiple and contradictory ends.

The Cartesian phantoms for Levi were ideas he gave up, or would have to, but they were also ideas from his past that he carried with him into Auschwitz. Those ideas had been embodied in certain behaviors in civil society, a community wherein one operates according to certain moral codes. The ideas and practices of thinking he had acquired in schooling, trailed him through the camp; he embodied this inherited knowledge, both unlearning and revising it in the onslaught of the concentrationary world. Of course, ideas were connected with personhood. René Descartes' order of reasoning conceptualized the person as "an integrated, self-conscious, rational, and autonomous human being who is not simply subject to causal laws of motion and dispositions, but is capable of determining itself to act from the recognition, or a clear conception, of truth and goodness and the right principles and values."[34] This personhood began to erode for Levi in the camp. As such, his story constitutes resistance against this erosion and a shared series of discoveries of how to hold out against it.

Levi's study in *If This Is a Man* provides further investigation into Descartes fundamental or first question, the very ground of his inquiry in *Meditations on First Philosophy*, "What is a man?" Descartes asks, "what is real and true?" and "is a new

---

[33] Levi, *Survival*, 13.
[34] Christofidou, *Self, Reason, and Freedom*, 224.

metaphysics possible?"[35] The natural light of reason for Descartes is "not an arbitrary assumption but a precondition of self-consciousness—it is the guiding light of any inquiry."[36] Levi reveals the purpose of his account. "It has not been written in order to formulate new accusations; it should be able, rather, to furnish documentation for a quiet study of certain aspects of the human mind."[37] Levi's choice of documentation establishes factual arguments based on causal analysis. For Descartes causes are reasons. Causes are both mechanical (based in physics) and logico-rational. *Causa sive ratio*.[38] Each fact has a correlative reason. The corresponding effect is an artifact; it is produced by the cause. Levi writes in his preface that the conclusion that "every stranger is an enemy" became during the war a conviction that "lies deep down like some latent infection," and this conviction did not lie at the base of a system of reason.[39] It was irrational, instinctive perhaps, and dangerous. Levi defines it as an unspoken dogma, an assumption with threatening consequences. Its logical conclusion, Levi argues, manifests in the product of the death camps, the *Lager*. He establishes a causal chain that leads to creation of the *Lager* and evolves directly of man's erroneous beliefs, his deluded thinking. What happens when we use reason towards destructive ends? What effects do we create when we use others as a means to an end? It is these beliefs he wishes to challenge in revealing the illusory nature of assumptions that people take for truth. He wants readers to develop a worldview where we do not suspect others simply on the basis of their difference from or their strangeness to us.

The metaphor of infection is not lost here. This metaphor resides in a group of extended metaphors related to disease that writers such as James Baldwin and Martin Luther King have used to describe the terrors and obfuscations of history. For Baldwin and King that was a particular history that included the institution of American slavery, segregation, and racism characterized by abominable violence, rage and bitterness, and the difficult possibility of change.[40] The infection spreads rapidly and attributes to fever. The fever emerges on both sides of the power struggle as murderous violence, shaming ethical violations that erase all hope of shared humanity. Returned to Italy from Poland, via a ten-month journey through Central Europe, Russia, and then into Western Europe by train and foot, Levi withdraws from the raging world to his writing desk and there embarks upon a quiet study of the human mind. He determines that he will contemplate how that mind thinks and reacts under extreme conditions of violence and fear. What happens to humans there, both those victimized and those perpetrating, including those caught in the boundary between categories, and therefore captured by both categories? Levi arrives at conclusions about human nature, particularly the mind—the realm of cognition—

---

[35] René Descartes' *Meditations on First Philosophy* was first published in 1641.

[36] Christofidou, 9.

[37] Levi, *Survival*, 9.

[38] All phenomena have a reason, cause, or ground. Descartes claims exceptions to this principle when he asserts that God creates eternal truths, the causes of which are not always evident to man.

[39] Levi, *Survival*, 9.

[40] See Baldwin's "Notes of a Native Son," 1955 and Dr. King's "Letter from Birmingham Jail," 1963.

through the study of distinct natures, specifically in his observations of individual people and their responses to situations of violence, injustice, and desperation, so close to death, at Auschwitz. His is a metaphysical inquiry decidedly grounded in the physical world as that world has evolved of the malicious use of human reason and will.

Descartes, too, had phantoms. He begins *Meditations* with the need to confront outmoded ideas and to build thought from new foundations.

> Several years have now passed since I first realized how numerous were the false opinions that in my youth I had taken to be true, and thus how doubtful were all those that I had subsequently built upon them. And thus, I realized that once in my life I had to raze everything to the ground and begin again from the original foundations, if I wanted to establish anything firm and lasting in the sciences.[41]

In the early and mid-seventeenth century he was searching for a way to understand the relationship of the body and the mind in light of freedom and the will to choose. He sought, in part, through his studies to question the Stoic and Thomist philosophies with which he had been inculcated in the French parochial academy. For over thirty years he engaged the fields of math, science, and technology to pursue metaphysical questions in developing and legitimizing a natural philosophy that his biographer, Stephen Gaukroger, points out was "resolutely Copernican."[42] He sought to distinguish, even separate, the mind from the body, so that he could establish a metaphysical foundation to rational science that the Catholic Church could not condemn. In 1633 he was to publish *Le Monde*, which detailed his theories of matter, including perceptual cognition, motion, hydrodynamics, and a mechanistic cosmology that included celestial physics, such as properties of light. But, he withdrew his work from publication when that year Galileo suffered a second condemnation for his work (his first in 1616) from the Catholic Church.

As Descartes begins his series of meditations, he sits (or imagines himself sitting) by the fireplace, in his winter dressing gown, "holding this sheet of paper in my hands."[43] The paper and his hands bring awareness to his body, located in space and time. He notices that his thoughts are contained, as a consciousness, or perhaps a dream, within his body. It is from this space that he will examine the foundations on which his education has been built, much as Levi will examine the basis of his beliefs as he enters and leaves the concentrationary universe of Auschwitz.[44] Why undermine the very basis of one's knowledge on which he has established his whole inner and outer universe? Descartes confesses, "because undermining the foundations will cause whatever has been built upon them to crumble of its own accord, I will attack

---

[41] Cress, 59.

[42] Gaukroger, *Descartes: An Intellectual Biography*, 355.

[43] Cress, 60.

[44] David Rousset's first used this phrase to describe the world of concentration camps in his 1946 memoir, *L'Univers concentrationnaire*.

straightaway those principles which supported everything I once believed." [45] Descartes challenges the Aristotelian philosophy of forms, which argues that the soul is a form of the body and that when the material body dies the soul (mind or spiritual body) must also die. In Christian doctrine of the early modern period the soul could not die. In response, Descartes formulated a metaphysical argument that would be satisfactory to the theological doctrines of his time: the mind is God and thus continues beyond the body. The human mind is a reflection, though imperfect, of the perfection of the divine mind. Thus, the human soul or mind transcends, like God, the material world and is not dependent upon it. "The soul would not fail to be what it is, even if the body did not exist."[46]

Descartes is at pains to establish a metaphysical premise that will allow him to develop his physical system of the world. He established his doctrine of clear and distinct ideas, the clear light of reason that nourishes and guides the mind in the acquisition and understanding of knowledge and the physical world, in and through this metaphysical grounding. Traditional metaphysics (ontology) had dealt with the question of how the world is. Descartes focuses on how the world is independent of a cognitive self that understands subjectivity not as a universal human nature but as a self that has a unique individual identity. As a result, "the locus of knowledge of the empirical world is now something removed from the empirical world."[47] Accordingly, the purpose of doubt in Descartes' epistemology is to create a conscious gap between the perceiving self that sees the surface qualities of objects and the empirical world, the space wherein the mind begins to translate perception into inquiry and ideas. Body and mind each have their own distinct integrity. They are not one in the same but inform each other. It is this schema of cognition that ignites inquiry.

Descartes famously wrote in *Meditations*, "It is impossible that that which thinks should not exist." He affirms that because he is thinking, he knows himself to exist. He is a thinking being, a man of reason. Levi's account of Auschwitz implicitly builds on, questions, and even destabilizes the earlier philosopher's certainty about existence and reason. In response to the demolition of man, he asks: is violence and bestiality existence; if so, what has become of us; and, on a personal note, how do I make this as human as possible for myself; where and how am I able to think and reason so that I can cling to some sense of self, however tenuous; where have I failed to do so; and, what are the results of having existed outside of moral codes that govern civil society? He is not able to answer all of these queries in his first book; however, these questions will form guiding themes for him over the course of his thinking and writing life, and throughout a number of his works published in multiple genres.

Specifically, in that first account, Levi experienced how mind (*res cogitans*) and body (*res extensa*) worked under duress in relationship to one another. He mostly did not have the luxury of time to scientifically doubt and question what he saw. Rather, deception everywhere was part of the environment of the camps, and the immediate future was mired in obfuscation. The prisoner lacked a total picture of the "logic" of

---

[45] Cress, 60.
[46] Gaukroger, 199.
[47] Gaukroger, 319.

the camps and the universe instituted there. In this case, he had to trust his senses as a guide to navigating the environment. He used his sense of smell to detect clean or dirty water. He used his hearing and knowledge of language to translate what he needed to do immediately in the moment. He sought to use his intellect as a method of clarification. He used his training as a chemist to secure lab work at the IG Farben factory, called Buna-Werke, saving him from manual labor in the harsh outdoor elements. At the same time, skepticism would have allowed him to stand, even in the moment, at a distance and to make quick, practical decisions.[48] I don't want to look at my injured foot. I will leave on the boot, he thinks as he marches back from work after a steel beam has sliced through his heel. In the barracks, his foot is swelling. He removes the boot and determines that he must go to the infirmary for risk of infection. In the immediacy of this place, there is little time for the old purposes of doubt—to question antiquated ideas and turn away from habitual opinions. The body signals to the mind what it needs, and the mind must listen. The man must move to attend to the situation, however limited the information and knowledge he has, if he is to live. The educated man has to act in new ways; the former moral codes, ethics and shared humanity and literature and friendship—all these cherished values that allow one to thrive and grow, with which one associates his sense of personhood, have been tossed away. The educated man must make a decision. One needs his feet to work. One must work to guarantee a few more days of life. Levi will find a way to attend to the foot.

Descartes argued that linguistic capacity and adaptability set humans above all other animals. Traces of these values thread Levi's thinking. Throughout his imprisonment he is sensitive to and aware of the many languages with which he is surrounded. He occupies a space wherein peoples from all over Europe have converged. "The Buna is as large as city. . . .forty thousand foreigners work there, and there are fifteen to twenty languages spoken." [49] He knows he must acquire rudimentary Polish and utilize his scholastic knowledge of German (largely acquired from scientific textbooks in Italy) to avoid punishment as much as possible. He also wants to communicate and connect with others—posing questions, trading things, securing a work partner. He recognizes from the outset that people who rely on each other are more likely to survive than those in isolation. Isolation leads to one's demise. Instead, and in spite of the crushing conditions, Levi finds the camp experience to provide brief but distinct moments of contact with and observation and analysis of others. His approach to figuring out his experience and to making his way within the reverse moral codes of the camp expands his perception of the world beyond his native language, his city, his country, and his understanding of Jewishness as he had lived it within Italy. His mind and body work together in learning how to

---

[48] More than forty sub-camps, exploiting the prisoners as slave laborers, were founded, mainly at various industrial plants and farms, between 1942 and 1944. The largest of them was called Buna-Monowitz, with ten thousand prisoners and was opened by the camp administration in 1942 on the grounds of the Buna-Werke synthetic rubber and fuel plant, located six kilometers from the Auschwitz camp. In November 1943, the Buna sub-camp became Auschwitz III, to which up to forty other Auschwitz sub-camps were subordinated. (Auschwitz-Birkenau Memorial and Museum)

[49] Levi, *Survival*, 72.

manipulate the systems of the camp so as to increase his chances of survival in this crazed environment.

In *Meditations*, Descartes melts a piece of honeycomb wax by the fire. He notes that the body of wax changes shape, texture, and density with heat, yet the mind understands the wax as idea, an extended body having certain categorical features, undergoing change. It is not the senses or imagination that we must rely on in noting these changes to the wax, but a methodology of reason, what he calls "an inspection on the part of the mind alone. This inspection can be imperfect and confused, as it was before, or clear and distinct, as it is now, depending on how closely I [the mind] pay attention to the things in which the piece of wax consists."[50] Things change form, but they are also constant, observes Descartes. I know this to be wax, though it undergoes changes in response to, for example, temperature. But it is still wax. Levi turns to categorization, employing both a scientific and metaphoric approach to behavioral changes people underwent with the pressure of camp conditions. Metaphor offers a significant alternative to the demands of scientific rationality while at the same time permitting Levi to use science itself as metaphor: The *Lager* as laboratory, the twisted use of classification to arrange people into social power hierarchies where as they grow increasingly desperate they perpetrate violence upon one another. First he calls out the divisions of "guests" into which the Nazis classified people, "We had soon learned that the guests of the *Lager* are divided into three categories: the criminals, the political, and the Jews."[51] These intricate classification systems were maintained through a series of numbers, each prisoner tattooed with a distinct number on his arm.[52] There were also triangulated stars of green, red, yellow, pink, often in combination, sewn onto jackets that delineated the damning hierarchy of status and power—criminal, political, Jew, homosexual, Roma, Sinti, Jehovah's Witness—within the concentrationary world.

More specifically, Levi describes people according to their methods of adaptation. Among the types that he names are the Drowned, the Saved, the thief, the ethical man, and the brute. In contemplating human behavior, he attests that people used their minds to adapt and survive, the saved. They also lost their minds, their physical abilities diminished by camp conditions, and facing the loss of everything, their mental and spiritual ability and will to survive disappeared, thus the drowned. These seemingly cold categories help Levi remember and record the changes human beings suffered in situations of extreme duress. Readers might perceive the people in Levi's story as one-dimensional, wholly represented by the categories into which he places them. But in relationship to those he encounters in Auschwitz, Levi knows

---

[50] Cress, 68.

[51] Levi, *Survival*, 33.

[52] Tattooing was first introduced into Auschwitz in 1941, used on Soviet POWs. Those who were immediately sent to the gas chambers after deportation were not issued serial numbers. Incoming prisoners sent to work were registered. The tattoo was considered a way to identify bodies of prisoners who had died. First, they were stamped with a needled device into the upper chest. They were tattooed on their left outer forearm, and for a short time in 1943 prisoners were tattooed in the inner left forearm. For more information on the elaborate history and practice of tattooing at Auschwitz, see United States Holocaust Memorial Museum, "Tattoos and Numbers: The System of Identifying Prisoners at Auschwitz."

nothing of people's former lives. Rather he perceives, as if peering through a slim window, what people are becoming in response to dangerous, damaging conditions. Inevitably, these are not full portraits of human beings, but memories of outstanding qualities or moments of total collapse and the loss of one's humanity. Alberto, his close friend, is a model of adaptation. At the same time, "he himself did not become corrupt. I always saw, and still see in him, the rare figure of the strong yet peace-loving man against whom the weapons of night are blunted."[53] Alberto's father was gassed (an experience Levi does not recount in his book). After his father's death, Alberto struggles with despondency and despair. Henri is a young Jewish French man, classically educated, whose brother has died in the camp and since this loss has exploited his gifts of organization, pity, and theft to survive. He is one of the saved among many who drown. Henri's morals and sense of self, as Levi observes, are compromised. Elias, a dwarfish man from Warsaw, becomes symbolic of brute animal strength. He works obsessively, his strength otherworldly. He needs no rest. For Levi, Elias embodies the outcome of *Lager*. This is adaptability taken to its extreme, "For those who have no sound inner resources, for those who do not know how to draw from their own consciences sufficient force to cling to life, the only road to salvation leads to Elias: to insanity and to deceitful bestiality."[54] It is amazing that Elias survives for as long as he does. The Nazis usually murdered those with abnormalities before or upon entrance to the camp. But he shows himself to be an insane workhorse; he would therefore be a valuable attribute to German war efforts and their purpose of using slave labor in establishing empire. Levi attributes his own survival to chance, a few random but vital circumstances. Lorenzo, an Italian bricklayer brings him bread or soup each day, and Levi recognizes in him a man, "not so much for material aid, as for his having constantly reminded me by his presence that there still existed a just world outside our own. . . .a remote possibility of good, but for which it was worth surviving."[55] Even so, all those deported into Auschwitz were drowned, or at least at Levi tells us "baptized." Levi's categories both mimic and work against the categories that evolved of the infernal killing system that was Auschwitz.

At the outset of "Our Nights," an early chapter in *If This Is a Man* Levi details the process of settling into the barracks as the imprisoned men create small spaces with their belongings. Their cramped and dirty sleeping spaces begin to resemble their actions, values, and immediate needs. He uses an entomological metaphor to illustrate man's need to make a place.

> Man's capacity to dig himself in, to secrete a shell, to build around himself a tenuous barrier of defense, even in apparently desperate circumstances, is astonishing and merits a serious study. It is based on an invaluable activity of adaptation, partly passive and unconscious, partly active: of hammering in a nail above his bunk from which to hang up his shoes; of concluding tacit pacts of non-aggression with neighbours; of understanding and accepting the

---

[53] Levi, *Survival*, 57.
[54] Levi, *Survival*, 98.
[55] Ibid, 121.

customs and laws of a single Kommando, a single Block. By virtue of this work, one manages to gain a certain equilibrium after a few weeks, a certain degree of security in face of the unforeseen; one has made oneself a nest, the trauma of the transplantation is over.[56]

The image of secreting a shell evokes Franz Kafka's short story "Metamorphosis," in which protagonist Gregor Samsa transforms from adult man into an insect or rodent.[57] His family houses him in a little room, where they feed and keep him in the dark. Is this shadowy insect what man has become in the camps, even as he displays his unique perception or expression in the process of adaptation? What is Levi saying about the dark habit of adaptation? Humans adapt because the environment (manmade and natural) compels them to do so. To produce a secretion (in this case, a shell) is to make something that serves a useful function for an organism's survival. Here the shell becomes a sort of structure, carapace, or armor that protects and cordons off a space within which the imprisoned man, the ironic "guest," imprints his signature.[58] He makes the space functional, trying to tame its hostility with markers of belonging and uniqueness.

At the same time, subject to these conditions, humans are without choice, acting on instinct. There is no freedom. Subsequently, they come to embody their defenses against the onslaught of an environment that puts life in peril. Humans are then transformed by their very survival mechanisms. This picture might conjure both relief (that humans can and do adapt) and terror when conditions to which people are forced and reduced by others adversely change humans and frequently kill them. Conditions have the power to make humans physically and spiritually unrecognizable to selves they once knew. This is Levi's point. It is in this argument that the terror of his story resides. One such adaptation is avoiding the danger of a fully logical viewpoint in the camps, a view that would obliterate any hope or willfulness to live. Levi is a brand-new arrival to the camp. He and his group ask the seasoned prisoners for how long they will have to work. For how long each day or for how long will this go on, the reader cannot be sure. The experienced men laugh. Once you are in the *Lager* for a while you stop asking questions. Levi realizes this in the moment of reflection, if not there in the actual moment of narrative, "If we were logical, we would resign ourselves to the evidence that our fate is beyond knowledge, that every conjecture is arbitrary and demonstrably devoid of foundation. But men are rarely logical when their own fate is at stake. Here I am, then, on the bottom. . . .already my own body is no longer mine. It was better not think."[59] The recognition that his life represents the lowest depth of the social system and that he can fall no further brings strange relief in preliminary knowledge (a nod to evidence and logic). Questions must disappear.

---

[56] Levi, *Survival*, 56.

[57] *The Metamorphosis* was first published in 1915. The German title of the novella is *Die Verwandlung*, or *The Transformation*.

[58] In an another imagining, I asked: could the shell be an egg, a space in which to protect oneself, a layer laid down within to hold together the fragile human heart, the hope of a life outside those harrowing walls?

[59] Levi, *Survival*, 36-7.

There is not knowledge, it's impossible to apply reason, yet here is a system, here is a rhythm. The mind searches for sense. At this early moment of the story, logic risks futility as the author awakens to the gravity of this situation. Nothing is his anymore: fate, body, thought, reason. All is lost. Logic swirls on the bottom, an undercurrent that threatens to drown.

Descartes employs the first-person pronoun as he reveals how he used his own reason toward discovery. Perhaps, as one contemporary philosopher would have it, he "restores the primacy of the individual and its freedom in opposition to authoritarian theology. The *I* of *Meditations* charts the journey of any open-minded, serious thinker faced with the question 'what is real and true?' It offers an invitation to embark on a rational critique—the very essence of philosophy."[60] However much Levi loses a sense of that individual self, the autonomous educated man, Descartes' first person remains the *I* that Levi employs within the camps and in his written account of the camps. Levi's writing represents rational critique in the face of atrocity, infused with narrative and centered in individual consciousness. Although Levi never overtly employs the term *ethics* in his account, I would call his consciousness an ethical one, grounded in an ontology that reflects what it means to be a human being in relationship with others. A human being who can think and process the world and who has an inner life that allows the smallest of spaces for reflection will retain some semblance of the free and autonomous human being. He will create within a small harbor where the mind can shelter until conditions change. When they do, he will attempt a return to that mind and give it full space for its utmost expression and exploration.

Levi begins his study with a title, hypothesizing with a conditional clause: "If this is a man." He has issued a call to relationship in the form of a phrase awaiting completion, as a statement that can only be answered in thinking toward a future with openness and inquiry into the past. The title phrase must find its other half in the readings of subsequent generations. As such, it is incumbent on readers to conclude with the independent clause of our own making. An ongoing and dynamic work issues from our reading and thinking in response. That response determines our relations with others; it determines our very existence in the world, if we allow Levi's work to challenge and ultimately change us.

> Self-mastery is achievable by the moderation and transformation of passions and instincts. . .by bringing them into harmony with truth and goodness as revealed by the reflective power of reason and proper use of the will. Self-mastery is a transformation that consists in beginning to see matters afresh, not one that results from considering them afresh.[61]

Self-mastery is a form of awakening. Upon his return, Levi turns to his experience anew, for the first time, in reflection. In this effort, he settles at his desk, solitary

---

[60] Christofidou, 7.
[61] Christofidou, 153.

writer, carving out solitude to study "certain aspects" of individual consciousness, even as he studies what occurred to the mind in the camps. His private story becomes a human story of thinking. Levi sitting down to write recalls Descartes little scene sitting by the fireplace in his nightshirt, dreaming a dream, watching his mind think, and questioning how one knows what is dream and what is real as he begins his meditations. There is no moderation in the camps, an environment *in extremis*, nor is there transformation of the passions and instincts into human sensitivity, a sensitivity that is all but annulled. Almost everything in the environment is raw and cruel. The *Lager* is an environment bent toward destruction. Perhaps there is not much place for skepticism either. Doubt? Doubt engages the mind; it asks for comparison and evaluation. Levi applies rationality—struggling to maintain a sense of himself and a connection to his life—in learning how the camp works and in making decisions about survival. His interactions and encounters with fellow prisoners, those who are for the most part his equals, allows him to practice a careful measure of ethical behavior, hence rationality, in relationship with others.

The result of transformation through self-reflective thinking allows one to establish autonomy. "Autonomy is not only self-governance, but presupposes an ability to know which are the right principles, values, and reasons from which a self can act, and to know why they are the right ones. It implies that rational beings have the power to act (affirm or deny, pursue or avoid) out of neither fear of punishment nor hope of reward, which are external sanctions, but as knowers and as agents (this is once again a rejection of religious dogma and theology's authority)."[62] A self-aware subject acts from reason. This highest quality of freedom narrows choice. There is clarity to move in one direction where choice evolves of knowledge readily available and ideally unclouded by intellectual ignorance. "Autonomy secures the unity of reason and freedom in its highest grade; this is the only way in which man can be truly free, despite living in the physical world of mechanical causal determinism. It is by exploring the notion of freedom that we can begin to understand the significance of the real distinction between the essential natures of mind and corporeality."[63]

What would it look like to apply once again Cartesian thought—dissipated for Levi through the months at Auschwitz—to the narrative that was forming in the aftermath of trauma? Descartes described the lowest quality freedom as indifference, a sort of neither here nor there, a lack of passion and clarity, constrained by external conditions. At the end of his imprisonment, the Germans having fled the camp at the approach of the Russian troops, Levi writes, "I wanted only one thing: to stay in bed under my blankets and abandon myself to a complete exhaustion of muscles, nerve and willpower; waiting as indifferently as a dead man for it to end or not to end. But Charles had already lighted the stove, Charles, our active, trusting, alive friend, and he called me to work."[64] He longs to remain in contact with this self who has the will—only with the help of others at this point—to return to work, a self that logically becomes increasingly remote in the camp as he experiences the physical and mental

---

[62] Christofidou, 153.
[63] Ibid.
[64] Levi, *Survival*, 163.

limitations of *res extensa* under depraved conditions. How does Descartes' notion of *res extensa*—extension in space and motion as a body—relate to Levi's physical experience at Auschwitz? Does Levi find something different or similar to what Descartes explored? Levi finds how vital his attention to the body and senses are as a way of knowing, which is ultimately a way of surviving, physically as well as intellectually and morally. His senses and body are assaulted upon arrival and induction into Auschwitz. Immediately his way of life in the civilian world begins to disintegrate to be replaced by an urgent and acute awareness of attending to the physical environment. Of course, the skills of *res extensa* largely help to keep him alive: listening, hearing, looking, intuiting, and figuring things out—how to look stronger than he is at a selection, how to attend to a deep cut at his heel, how to find clean water, how to find a good work partner, how to manage an ungainly bunkmate, and how to attain an indoor work position in a chemistry lab. These skills are never without relationship to *res cogitans*, the life of mind and intellect that employs a measure of judgment and will to navigate the upside-down world of the camps, to make survival possible within limited means.

It is this personal rational critique of what he has traumatically experienced in Auschwitz that he achieves upon writing his story once home in Torino. The new knowledge arises in return to civilian life. For beings in love with the life of the mind, freedom cultivates a sense of identity connected to thinking. For Levi, writing in the 1980s, identity meant dignity. [65] That dignity was not unconnected with his Jewishness. Dignity was vital for Italian Jews in the face of discriminatory race laws, as they were barred from practicing their professions and lived with the impending danger of forced migration and eventual deportation to internment and death camps. Dignity was for Jews of utmost importance during the war as they struggled to survive and faced incredible atrocities.

Does Levi's imposition of rationality onto the German's strangely "rational" plan for elimination of the Jewish peoples of Europe and other "undesirables" say something? If so, can Western thought traditions help him navigate the experiences of trauma induced by the camps? What has his study revealed? In a painful memory of his university self he stands before Dr. Pannwitz, a Nazi official, an educated and "civilized" doctor, who barely sees him, to take a "chemistry exam," an interrogation in the guise of an exam.[66] He wonders as he takes the exam if he is not lying. Was he once a chemist? Does he have, or not have, the knowledge the Germans need? Has he disappeared? He barely remembers his former self. His "quiet study" and its narratives help him to structure his tale, but his employ of them also makes an argument about the truth value of knowledge that European cultures have held sacred: literature, philosophy, science, and ethics. In his written account, he places rational knowledge systems and their disciplines in direct relationship with Auschwitz, allowing rationality and its companion ethicality to wrestle with the dilemmas to humanity that it presents.

---

[65] See Levi's essay "The Intellectual in Auschwitz" in *The Drowned and The Saved*. Here he states, "In order to live an identity—that is dignity—is necessary."

[66] Levi, *Survival*, 106.

Levi has dipped dangerously into the nether realms, only to return again, his knowledge changed in some drastic and perhaps unrecognizable way by what he has experienced there (in body) and by what he remembers (for the mind to remember is to suffer). He tests all the knowledge he has thus far acquired. The knowledge is intellectual, conceptual, abstract, but there are new knowledge/s post-Auschwitz that he carries. How do those knowledge/s interplay with the traditional epistemic inheritances of his schooling, his civilized phantoms of Western thought? What does the new knowledge contribute to his "aspects" of the mind? What does he report back to us in his documentation? People adapt. Some swim to the surface, others sink and drown. There are few reasons—there is randomness, chance, perhaps luck—to who survives and who perishes; however, with the help of others and given certain conditions one might, with careful thought, observation, and planning, find ways to survive and maintain as much as possible a vestige of humanity—a memory of self and a sense, however remote, of dignity. Violence and depravation reduce people to animal levels. The perpetrators have lost more of their humanity than their victims. For Levi, God does not exist. Any reason that remains, for good or evil, is decidedly man's own.

Descartes believed the senses a ground or basis for doubt. Doubt or skepticism was an important tenet in approaching knowledge a method of inquiry. Three hundred years later phenomenologists such as Edmond Husserl, Martin Heidegger, and Maurice Merleau-Ponty explored embodied, sensate experience, particularly human perception of that experience, as one kind of (very valid) truth. Levi did not necessarily draw on ontologically modern concepts of embodied experience. Nor did he have access to knowledge of what clinicians and the public now designate Post-Traumatic Stress Disorder (PTSD), which would have provided him a clinical understanding of trauma's causes and effects and allowed him, as many contemporary writers, to frame their narrative explorations in psychological terms, as well as within current ideologies of identity, ideologies that dovetail into social and political ramifications of the post-traumatized individual in relation to self and others. However, much like his contemporary writer and thinker Jean Améry, Levi resisted psychological explanations for the experience of trauma within and after the camp. He found psychological approaches and cures to pathologize a dynamic lifetime relationship with traumatic circumstances. In resistance, he referred to Auschwitz as a university and wrote that it placed a sample book before him full of varied experiences and people and a food for curiosity. He described the importance of that food as having "contributed to keeping a part of me alive and that subsequently supplied me with the material for thinking and making books."[67] That confession applies equally to the period of his imprisonment and to his life in Torino as a writer, chemist, author, and spokesperson in the aftermath of Auschwitz.

Levi imposed a humanistic and ethical framework onto the strangely ordered chaos of Auschwitz. With this framing, he tamed his mind and attempted to distance the trauma he underwent. Returning to Italy from a two-year journey that included

---

[67] Levi, *The Drowned and the Saved*, 141.

capture, deportation, imprisonment, and, as recounted in his second autobiographical narrative, *The Truce*, repatriation, he slowly regained his physical strength and full mental capacities. He became again an intelligent, thinking, ethical man who questioned, reviewed, and categorized his experiences in order to arrive at some inevitably unfinished conclusions. This was not an immediate or complete transition. As he attests in the final paragraphs of *The Truce*, in the years after his return to Italy he experienced a gray dread that cast him into a bottomless hole of anguish. He would feel the familiar sense of impending threat and would be entirely alone once again in the *Lager*. He was then cut off from beloved others, from his home, and from the natural world. This was a "dream within a dream."[68] What was real? What was imagined? How did the fields of perception and memory in the wake of traumatic experience cross one another between reality and the imagined?

The certainty of reason's line is complicated and confused in the wake of Auschwitz. Descartes first began his meditations with the mind's effort to differentiate dream from reality, but for Levi the work is different. The traumatic nature of his experience, the uprooting from home and dislocation to a site of genocide becomes for the writer a translation of what seems catastrophically unreal into a witnessing language and narrative that will circulate in the ordinary civil world as reality. His broken phrase, "If this is a man," with its implied question courses through his tale, stinging with indomitable inconclusiveness that arose in his confrontation with and remembering of Auschwitz. Knowledge is uncertain; yet, it guides humans through the historical ruptures that shred personal life and the structures that hold it in place. Levi's knowledge quakes with the challenge that Auschwitz delivered to mind and body. He surfaces to join human community in daily life again, returning to knowledge in a way that is now complex, fraught, and matured. His study, enriched as we consider it in context of Descartes' metaphysical study more than three centuries earlier, reveals the gradual power of knowledge to temporarily stitch the torn life together again.

1.6 ITALY, RELIGION, AND A WRITER

My introduction to Levi's work thirty years ago began at the state university when I studied Italian language. My Italian professor suggested that I live and study in Florence. I had also met a fellow student, Blair, in Italian politics with whom I became good friends. His love of foreign films, novels, music, and gourmet food influenced me. We went to Italy to study. He did not know Italian but he had no worry. He had lived in Amsterdam and had managed to learn Dutch; he could learn Italian too. Whereas I had Italian classes every day in Sweeny Hall and for five years my mind lived in Italian. Italy provided, among other things, a route away from my Swiss-Germanic roots, away from the conservative Baptist church into which I had been born and raised. It offered southern European culture, food, love, beauty, and a way of life that celebrated the aesthetic and the sensual. Once in Florence I woke in

---

[68] Levi, *The Reawakening*, 207.

Italian every day. I began to dream in the language, too. My mind was music and efforts to think in Italian a kind of poetry that, at twenty-two, nurtured separation from my old life: the church, the suburbs where my parents had raised me, the angry divorce through which my parents were just then passing. Early in my adult life then my draw to Latin countries and cultures began. Catholic countries where people had managed to temper the stringent moralism of the Church with sensual living: good food and drink, music, visual art, poetry and literature, romance, friendship, beauty, style, and an acknowledgment of death—served as an impetus to my own love of the physical world, especially sensuality as I found myself then in my early twenties, newly a woman, in Italy.

I also met an Italian man during the first weeks in Florence. Blair had introduced my roommates and me to Antonello and Michele. They were students at the University of Florence and wanted to meet American girls, so they waited outside our hotel where we were initially lodged. There they met Blair who promised to introduce them to some American girls. One night the two students came to our flat for dinner. Michele had dark, languorous eyes, slightly stooped shoulders, and long limbs. He wore varying shades of brown: an overcoat, baggy sweater under which a yellow shirt collar was just visible, loose-fitting pants, and slim leather loafers. He walked as if he were permanently in thought. There was an air of preoccupation about him, something intense and distracted but focused and demanding, that I admired and to which I wanted to be close. It was some quality—that bundled together was intellect—that I might have wanted for myself. I did not realize this; I simply wanted to learn and observe and feel it, to be a recipient and thus a participant. It was distinctly European, more specifically Italian with a slight worldliness—the English language (he was so easy and confident with it), the cigarettes, the knowledge of living elsewhere, the long days of studies, voluminous medical books and Latin and English terminology, his love of politics, bordering on obsession, the many newspapers he perused each day, his dedicated membership in the Italian Communist Party (PCI), and, finally, accordingly, his absolute willed ignorance of popular culture. He spoke flawless English and told me—as we were immediately compelled to one another—that he had studied in Orange, New Jersey (living with an aunt and uncle) in the last year of high school and then had attended Columbia University for a year. He was a medical student, studying cardiology, his father, a doctor who made house calls in Calabrese villages. Immediately, within weeks, I was certain he would not return to his little town Tropea in the southern region of Calabria, but would live in Florence or Milan, even Rome, and work as a doctor in an urban hospital. Perhaps he would even come to the United States to work!

Michele introduced me to politics as elemental to everyday life—reading newspapers and political magazines, discussing politics and debating the international scene, which for him centered on Europe and America. He was a member of the Italian Communist Party (PCI), which with its popular (handsome and charismatic) party secretary, Enrico Berlinguer, held thirty-three percent of the popular vote by the mid-eighties. Berlinguer had died in June 1984 and Michele insisted that I write a paper on his life and political career. He brought stacks of political magazines to my flat and together we read in Italian the articles. As a southern Italian, fiercely committed to the developing south, Michele had a consciousness of and for working people. He lived a frugal lifestyle and committed himself to study, to English language study, and to politics. He shunned popular culture though he enjoyed (like most Italians) good food and wine. However, he was never extreme in his tastes. He preferred *trattorie* and *taverne* nestled into Florence's back streets to bright *ristoranti* in the tourist areas and along boulevards. I was being transformed, according to my desire and beyond my knowledge, in these first weeks in Italy. The country created a barrier between the life I wanted, and had ardently began to imagine and live in the world for myself, and the evangelical, Protestant past I had known in my California family and from which I was fiercely determined to free myself. I wanted to be Italian, to think, live, and move in Italian and like an Italian. A young energy of wanting to fashion myself into another girl, a burgeoning woman, took hold of me.

Blair told me about *The Periodic Table*. The book had been published in 1975. It was now 1985, a year and a half before Levi's death. I did not read the work in Italy and it was another ten years before I would read it, twenty years after its publication. When I did read it, I realized Blair had been right. It was a beautiful book. Blair, who comes from a family of Russian Jews, liked the book because its narrative concerned the time before and after Auschwitz. Once I had finished the book I wanted to read about the great event that had ripped Levi's life in two—a couple decades on one side and another four on the other. That enormous silence hovered over the pages of *The Periodic Table*. The presence of Levi's twenty-month journey—from arrest and deportation in February 1944 to his return home to Torino in October 1945—was a story unto itself, one I first dipped into in *Moments of Reprieve*, portraits of various prisoners and authority figures that Levi had encountered at Auschwitz.

In the mid-1990s living in Chicago and teaching creative writing courses at the Newberry Library just off Michigan Avenue, one of my students wanted to work with me to write his memoirs of surviving internment at Auschwitz and then leaving Hungary for the United States where he went to medical school in Oklahoma. I agreed, and we met weekly to work on his book. He would tell me stories and I transcribed them. I embroidered words and sought clarity here and there. Mostly he wanted to tell me stories. He imagined that Steven Spielberg would want to get a hold of his story. We were living in the years just after *Schindler's List* and the Shoah Foundation archival project. There was possibility and energy around sharing his story as he entered into his eighties and found himself alone, mourning his wife's death, and living in the midst of a dynamic city center. Yet, Emery had trouble focusing on the writing task at-hand. It was more that he wanted company, someone to whom he could tell his stories, and with and for whom he could make and share tea, old photographs, and books. His wife, twenty years his junior, had recently died; she had hung herself in the closet upstairs in their bedroom. She had been severely depressed. He said that I reminded him of his wife. We looked alike and had the same zest for life, before depression had hit her. One day he gifted me an old paperback copy of *Survival in Auschwitz* from his shelf. It must have been from early printings of the book that had been translated into English and published in 1959. It was then, ten years after the time that Blair had first introduced me to Levi's writing that I begin to read.

The book baffled me. What was Teutonic? Who was Tantalus? What wa Silesia and Galicia? My studies had never involved German or Polish histo intellectual and sensual passions had taken me to Southern Europe and away fr harsh, ugly sound of German and the cold plains and difficult history of P Levi's Jewishness was important, but Jewishness remained at the edge o consciousness. He seemed entirely Italian. Yet, he had been arrested and deporte Auschwitz not because he was an Italian partisan, but because he was Jew Internment and near death changed him. He realized the preciousness of Jewishness, the threat of it in a hostile world, and after his return to Italy from Polan through Russia, Romania, Hungary, Germany, and Austria, he wrote partly to explor and claim his Jewishness for himself and to others. Given the proclamatory powers o writing in the world, word and language became as integral to who he became in public as oxygen is integral to heart and brain.

In *The Periodic Table* he writes of a growing awareness of the social and political meaning of his status of a Jew as anti-Semitic measures and laws ("in defense of the Italian race") were imposed in Mussolini's Italy beginning in 1938. These laws affected Levi's opportunities and formed the direction of his life to come. He stopped attending classes at the university, went underground to complete his studies in chemistry lab, and became increasingly involved in Torino's Jewish School. There he was exposed through young Jewish activists who came from socialist families to partisan movements and to Jewishness as a form of rebellion and pride rather than the pariah status that the racial laws increasingly conferred on Jews.

My roommate in Florence, Leslie, was Jewish. She had moved from Chicago to Los Angeles with her mother and brother. She was attending Sonoma State University at the time we met and attended the orientation to our year abroad. I had been raised in the San Francisco Bay Area, in a state both at the edge of things and in the center, while also being proudly off-center. My friends through high school and college had been Jewish, but I never thought to ask them the stories of their families. I was Christian and all I knew of Jews was that they did not believe Jesus was the Son of God. For me, a girl raised primarily on the New Testament, Jesus was almost more important than God. At twenty-two, I had been free of the church for just three years. I had been an ardent believer, obedient, female, and passionate in my will to please God. I possessed an impulse to perfection, a need to please, to not offend, to not hurt anyone or anything. I needed to be trained otherwise, especially as a female, for religion, like an immutable father, made me into a "nice girl," and stifled (but only temporarily) my passionate will. My religious practice was unquestioning, absorbing. For what reasons did I read the Bible, sitting at the window, at my desk in my room, underlining scriptural passages, committing to memory the words that I assumed came directly from God? To be a good Christian, to do what the pastors told me, to emulate their model of how to be in relationship to God. Then a break came and I set into the world to make a self beyond the confines of the church. I could have experience without the imposition of God, without my idea of God through the men who mouthed him.

Blair had told me his ancestors were from Russia. One day when Leslie had returned to live in Chicago from California, and I lived in that city, too, she said, "If I

enty years earlier, I would be dead." It was a strange fact
. Her grandmother in Florida has been struck dead by a car
ɔad when Leslie was young. My friend had lost her child the
d birth. He had perished inside of her and she pushed him out.
e said, and showed me a photograph of him. His fingernails and
ιack of oxygen, but he was whole and perfectly formed. Her father
ɡkin's when we were in our mid-twenties. Life swirled about her and
carried those losses and the fact of death with her. "We wouldn't
thought about death all the time. We have to feign ignorance, go on as if
ɹist," she said. These histories carried a weight of sadness, even depression
d into her long, tall body and into her green, distracted eyes. I loved my
whose presence seemed near and whose eyes, distant in thought, would
ιgly move away from our conversation. There was a world she let me into,
ch sometimes I detected and answered, and other times must have missed in my
vn preoccupations and lack of knowledge.

Leslie, as Blair, was a secular Jew. She did not attend synagogue and it was only
in 1988 when she met her future husband (who had moved from Baltimore to attend
medical school at the University of Chicago) through what she jokingly referred to as
"the Jewish connection"—the web of mothers and aunts and female friends who
arrange matches between their sons and daughters—that she began to take a formal
interest in Jewish holidays, rituals, and customs. I'd not known her to have a Jewish
boyfriend, but we had returned from Italy where she dated Florentine men and she
was serious about marriage and family by the time we had reached our late twenties.
I, on the other hand, foresaw neither marriage nor children in my future.

Leslie spoke a beautiful and correct Italian. We spoke together in the streets,
pretending we were not American so that men would not follow and pester us. Blair
sat on the grass of Piazza dell'Indipendenza in front of our third-floor school
classrooms, playing his saxophone (it sounded horrible, but he valued newness
enough that he never minded revealing in public his novice status) and reading novels.
A few years later in my studio in San Francisco he appeared to make me birthday
dinner. He pressed out small squares of ravioli and filled each one with duck. In his
room in an old Victorian house in San Jose, a visitor had to maneuver around piles of
diving equipment—masks and wetsuits, an oxygen tank and a spear for fishing in the
corner, books strewn over the floor. "Have you read this?" he would ask, picking up *A
Confederacy of Dunces*, "or this?" handing me *The Unbearable Lightness of Being*. I
loved his chaotic creative impulses, his hunger for life and art, and his passionate
culinary exploits. I also resisted his charms as much as possible and tried to forge my
own way, find books and novels that mattered to me. Though he was a strong voice
and presence. I read Levi and Kundera because of his introductions. I found him
fearless. I wanted that energy for myself, but as translated through my own personal
preferences and experiences.

Memories of my friends are layered with my desire for Italy and Italian life.
These remembrances, which dwell now in my body, infuse my reading of Levi's
work. Levi's voice, his mind and language are a portal. In his voice I hear the streets
of Italy and the Italian life of thought and passion that occurs in the home, in meetings

with friends, in cafés, and in the classroom. The knowledge of Italy—its sun, its urban rains that pour through Florentine streets, puddle, and fill gutters, its lilting language, and savory food that tastes of the land and the warmth and fullness of life in this country. It was possible to enter the memory of the Holocaust through Levi because of the beauty of my past years in Italy and the years of learning Italian language. Because of Levi and because of my early studies of Italian politics, I also feel the history of Italy's difficult unification, its betrayal of the Jews in the defense of an imagined, Aryan Italian race. When I read, when I travel, when I pass through the defunct gas chamber I know that nothing is sacred, and everything is. I know that I live in the presence of swirling energies, that nothing has passed through and that I keep the company of ghosts. Levi's steady voice travels beside me. His words in English and Italian infuse me. His dedication and desire to write, the talisman of his narratives, buoys me as I stand in the hallways and pathways of Auschwitz and travel the vast expanse of what was once the death camp of Birkenau. If it were not for Levi, I would not be here. I could not be here.

I could not have entered my own relationship with World War II and Holocaust history without the love of a country and a culture, without the introduction of a writer who would open for me the world of Italy in the early twentieth century. With Levi, dwelling inside his narratives, I travelled to Poland, full of terror, hardly breathing through the torturous descent that begins in Fossoli and arrives into Auschwitz. I would change through years of reading and teaching those pages.[69] It would be those pages, that voice, that life, that country that would take me eastward on a journey in retrospect, tracing a history that exists now in books, in memorials, in train cars, in photographs, in strange relics that were once personal items attached to a life, a universe, a world erased, a world that mattered, a life like a whisper, a resounding yell that has passed through and made me an heir of things once unknown.

1.7 WRITING AS PROSTHESIS

Primo Levi, age twenty-five, began writing *If This is a Man* immediately upon his release from Auschwitz in 1945. The memoir's American title is *Survival in Auschwitz*, but the Italian title reflects more accurately the writer's underlying inquiry in the narrative, which is to render in all its horror the process of how humans can, and do, dehumanize their fellow humans. He asks: who am I know that I've emerged from the camps, and carries within the marked burden, the shame and guilt, of the survivor. Levi commented that this first of many books that he published over his lifetime "has worked for me as a sort of 'prosthesis', an external memory set up like a barrier between my life today and my life then. Today, I relive those events through

---

[69] Fossoli di Carpi was an Italian detention camp built in 1942 by the Italian Army. British prisoners of war as well as Italian political prisoners were interned at Fossoli. In September 1943 German occupation forces begin to intern Italian Jews at the camp, as well as Jews from Dalmatia and Libya. On 22 February 1944, deportations of prisoners to the East began, primarily to Auschwitz-Birkenau. Primo Levi, with several friends, and in a group of about 489 Jewish people, was deported in at this time. See Ian Thomson's *Primo Levi: A Life*, particularly "Into Captivity: 1943-4."

what I have written."[70] Levi wrote on the trains as he made the repatriation journey from Poland to Russia through Eastern Europe, Germany, and Austria to his home in Italy. Upon arrival, Levi talked his story to anyone who would listen as he rode the tram about Torino, the northern Italian city where he was born and lived all his life, with the exception of his deportation, internment, and long journey home. The world was in shock after the end of World War II, but Levi had experienced the most notorious German death camp, Auschwitz, and was determined to tell others his story of survival and release.

One of the memoir's major themes is Levi's need to tell others the story of his survival. In "Our Nights" Levi dreams of revealing his story to his sister and a group of friends once he returns home. "It is an intense pleasure, physical, inexpressible, to be at home, among friendly people and to have so many things to recount."[71] But as the dream progresses he finds he is not heard, recognized, or understood: "but I cannot help noticing that my listeners do not follow me. In fact, they are completely indifferent: they speak confusedly of other things among themselves, as if I was not there. My sister looks at me, gets up and goes away without a word."[72] At the very moment that story promises healing it threatens to kill the storyteller. In fact, the Italian publisher Einaudi did not publish Levi's book until 1958. People were not ready to read about the war, the publisher told Levi. Levi persisted, refusing silence, and the book was finally published to worldwide acclaim.

Yet, a larger question in examining Levi's history is does writing, as a form of creativity, help the survivor of trauma to recover? This is a fascinating question in Levi's case because of several factors: he was a survivor of Nazi concentration camps; he was a chemist by trade who valued logic and reason; and, his adult life had been marked by periods of severe depression, which included periodic suicidal feelings. In childhood he experienced sickness and long periods of recovery. He had lost school friends, such as politically active Sandro Delmastro who during the war, escaping Italy on a train to France, had been apprehended for questioning. He was taken by lorry to Fascist Youth headquarters in Cuneo. When he jumped and ran from the lorry, he was shot and killed by a Fascist youth gang member. Levi's was a generation that came of age during the era of Fascism, racial laws, war, and foreign occupation. Over the course of his lifetime, writing infused him with a sense of order. As a trained chemist, science gave him a metaphor to describe his experience. For example, he relates Auschwitz in his memoir as a kind of laboratory in which he discovers truths of human nature, many of them horrifying and others hopeful. One of his biographers, Ian Thomson, relates that in 1970, at fifty years old, Levi feared memory loss and wrote to a friend that he could "feel lots of neurons decaying and shrinking at a tremendous rate" and called these periods of intense, debilitating depression "shipwrecks."[73]

---

[70] Levi, *The Voice of Memory*, 251.
[71] Levi, *Survival*, 60.
[72] Levi, *Survival*, 60.
[73] Thomson, *Primo Levi: A Life*, 348.

It is possible that he committed suicide—a possibility that will never be confirmed but in that the fatal fall from his apartment foyer stairs occurred when he was suffering a bout of severe depression seems likely, as both Thomson and another biographer, Carole Angier, argue. It is also notable that Michele Levi, the author's paternal grandfather, committed suicide in 1888. His Uncle Enrico may have caused his own death as he set fire to a mattress in the nursing home where he resided and died asphyxiated by the fumes. Thomson tells us that the author "was acquainted with eleven suicides."[74] These acquaintances include writer and former fellow Auschwitz internee, Jean Améry, who wrote on his capture, torture, and imprisonment by the Nazis. Whereas Levi confesses "my personal temperament is not inclined to hatred. I regard it as bestial, crude, and prefer on the contrary that my actions and thoughts, as far as possible, should be the product of reason; therefore I have never cultivated within myself the desire for revenge, or as a desire to inflict suffering on my real or presumed enemy," Améry makes of his hatred for the Germans an art.[75] In Améry's final book, *On Suicide: A Discourse with Voluntary Death*, which Levi read after his friend's suicide in 1978, he makes an historical defense of suicide as free choice, referencing the act as self-murder. Suicide becomes a legitimate path to freedom.

Thomson makes the case that Levi did not outwardly disapprove of suicide. On the contrary, he was attracted in his reading and writing to violent, abrupt endings. It is not lost on us here that Levi's own ending was violent and abrupt. More hauntingly, Levi's late poem, "Give Us" reads: "Give us something to destroy/Give us something that burns, offends, cuts, smashes, fouls."[76] Thomson finds the poem suggestive of Levi's break from a lifetime of "exemplary conduct" as depicted in the searing lines of this poem. At the end of life, there appears in Levi space for creation and destruction, rationality and inner dissolution, pain and joy; and, then, he dies. In an interview in 1983 when asked about a virtue and a defect, he commented, "My virtue is that I stick to reality: a debate that Primo Levi the writer owes to Primo Levi the chemist. My defect is lack of courage, fear for myself and for others. What I mean to say is that I am afraid of people, not of things, that my response to raised voices is to take it and then leave, to avoid all argument. And that is not right."[77] It is clear that Levi did not always confront the moments where he felt and perhaps needed to express anger. Rather he walked away from heated arguments. Many writers have found solace and refuge in writing, not just in the act of composing but in the space of solitude and autonomy writing demands. The action of writing allows one to focus, to delve vertically into an interior life that is a response to relationships and to the world.

Certainly, for Levi, writing was a flow activity as described by psychologist Mihaly Csikszentmihalyi, "an optimal experience when things [are] going well as an almost automatic, effortless, yet highly focused state of consciousness."[78] Yet, true to the dream-nightmare Levi experienced in the cramped bunk at Auschwitz, this flow

---

[74] Ibid, 532.

[75] Levi, *Voice of Memory*, 185.

[76] Thomson, 532.

[77] Levi, *Voice of Memory*, 69.

[78] Csikszentmihalyi, *Creativity*, 110.

experience crashes when audience disappears. It is almost that when there is no one to listen one's very self disappears. The writer-storyteller's raison d'être disintegrates. This is a state that sounds remarkably like depression as Kay Redfield Jamison describes it, "depression is a view of the world through a glass darkly."[79] What is the role of creative work in addressing states of depression? "Creative work can act not only as a means of escape from pain, but also as a way of structuring chaotic emotions and thoughts, numbing pain through abstraction and the rigors of disciplined thought, and creating a distance from the source of despair."[80] In creating one commands audience. Someone is listening. Initially that someone lives inside a writer's head. Later, that someone might become a reader waiting for story. Levi might agree with poet Robert Lowell who suffered manic-depressive illness when he writes, "I am writing my autobiography literally to 'pass the time.' I also hope the result will supply me with swaddling clothes, with a sort of immense bandage of grace and ambergris for my hurt nerves."[81] Lowell's "swaddling clothes," and "bandage of grace" recall Levi's prosthesis. There is a sense of being wounded, an amputee; a prosthesis allows use of a limb again, even if not the authentic and original limb; a bandage covers and protects a wound while it heals. Levi have might concurred with Antonin Artaud's view, "No one has ever written, painted, sculpted, modeled, built, or invented except literally to get out of hell."[82] Levi admits that Auschwitz made him a writer.

> if I had not lived the Auschwitz experience, I probably would never have written anything. I would not have had the motivation, the incentive to write. It was the experience of the camp and the long journey home that forced me to write. I did not have to struggle with laziness, problems of style seemed ridiculous and I found the time to write without taking even one hour away from my daily professional work. It seemed as if those books were all there, ready in my head, and I had only to let them come out and pour on to paper.[83]

It has been argued that Levi, as many writers, fashioned a particular public persona. In this case, he is a man who emerged of Auschwitz with a compulsion to write the head full of books he had inherited upon his exit from the camp. It is this confession, in part, that makes his writing so compelling for me, as I surmise it has for many of his readers. I would not have written if it had not been for the horror, he tells us. I had to write, he confesses, and it is to this writing that his reader is also bound.

Elizabeth Leake describes the peculiar phenomenon surrounding scholarship on Levi's work, exaggerated she argues by the fact of his suicide, whereby scholars identify with their particular version of Levi as expressed by various of his biographers and formulated of passages that they selectively highlight and omit from

---

[79] Jamison, *Touched with Fire*, 125.
[80] Ibid, 123.
[81] Quoted in Jamison, 123.
[82] Ibid, 121.
[83] Levi, *Voice of Memory*, 206.

his work.[84] These scholars avoid biographies that do not conform to their personal view of the author. She quotes eminent scholars taking possession of the author and reflecting their notions of "my Levi." I read this criticism with a note of caution. Devoted readers are liable to appropriate a beloved writer to their own purposes and ideas. We make a writer work for us because our literary loves embody what we value. Yet, Levi, too, wanted to appear in a certain way to his readers. He fashioned a persona in the texts to which we continue to respond.

Because we readers listen to Levi, we are charged with an ethical duty: to witness what happened in the camps, to judge those events, and to remember and act responsibly, in a way that embodies that remembering. Newer versions of *Survival in Auschwitz* begin with a poem Levi wrote in 1961 during the war crimes trial of Adolf Eichmann in Jerusalem. The poem is entitled "Shema," after one of the central prayers of the Torah, in Italian "Ascolta," for the command "Listen." The poem shares the tone of Shema: Hear, O Israel, the Lord our God, the Lord our God is One. The meaning of Shema in Hebrew is multiple: listen, hear, obey, understand, and respond. It is in this spirit that Levi begins, in direct and pointed address, his account. You, Levi writes, you who live safe in warm houses. You who find each evening hot food and friendly faces. He commands our attention with the direct second-person pronoun. He then charges us with the duty to consider if this is a man, to consider if this is a woman.[85] He makes evident the conditions by which people have been destroyed in the camps. Then he demands that we meditate. He commends his words to us. He tells us to carve the words in our hearts, not our minds but our hearts. We are to let the words of his poem imprint themselves on us.

In 1986 at sixty-six Levi suffered physical illness and a final descent into depression. He worked comparatively little and admitted to a fellow concentration camp survivor who felt near death in her later years that "*Anche per me i giorni si stanno facendo corti.*"[86] It has not been easy for Levi's readers and admirers to accept that the writer ended his life, especially when it may have been an accident. When a reader experiences Levi's narrative of the camps she feels that indeed logic, reason, creative intelligence, and goodness override atrocity, injustice, and suffering. Yet, in studying Levi's life one realizes the gravity and the pervasiveness of the camp experience. Levi had wanted to tell his two children of his deportation experience. He tried to talk to each of them around the time each turned fifteen. He thought his daughter, Lisa, had read *If This Is a Man*, but when he attempted to talk with her about his past she ran from the room in tears. His son, Renzo, at age three had asked his father of the number, 174517, tattooed on his arm and Levi had replied, "I was a prisoner once that's what they used to do to us."[87] On Renzo's fifteenth birthday his

---

[84] Leake, *After Words: Suicide and Authorship in Twentieth Century Italy*, 2011.
[85] Levi, *Survival*, 11.
[86] Thomson, 523. "For me, too, the days are getting short." [Translation mine.]
[87] Ibid, 358.

father tried to talk to him of Auschwitz and, as his sister had done, he left the room crying. Levi felt he was never able to reach his children.[88]

His flat may have been permeated with Auschwitz and that encounter with death. But, does Levi's possible suicide annul the body of work in which he beautifully gives form to the experience that was Auschwitz and its subsequent fallout? Does it cast in dubious light the writer's ability to survive and thrive in and through writing? It does not; yet, one must admit that the demon twins of Auschwitz and depression haunted Levi, and their relationship, whatever that may have been, did work toward entropy and disintegration against Levi's experience of flow as he wrote over the years a prodigious body of work.

Levi developed what, according to Csikszentmihalyi in *Flow*, is a discovered life theme, a "reaction to a great personal hurt suffered in early life."[89] The script for one's actions arising out of a discovered life theme is one of awareness and choice. This means that trauma becomes a means to self-efficacy. Csikszentmihalyi goes on to say that "What matters is the interpretation that one places on suffering."[90] When there is a sense that traumatic experience can be controlled and shaped in a way that is beneficial to us, a life theme develops. Life theme appears to be a marker of health, and, by extension, some sort of healing. The external event did matter to Levi, to the extent that the camp experience formed the trajectory of Levi's work, his very purpose in writing. Yet, Levi adopted the role of writer-witness to history. This gave him a special task in the present to bring knowledge to others: "if understanding is impossible," he wrote, "knowing is imperative, because what happened could happen again. Conscience can be seduced and obscured again—even our consciences. For this reason, it is everyone's duty to reflect on what happened."[91] The role of writer-witness provided Levi meaning and purpose. A negentropic life theme is rarely formulated as the response to solely a personal problem but becomes generalized to others, to humanity as a whole.[92]

Importantly, discovered life themes are fragile as they are "products of a personal struggle to define the purpose of life, they have less social legitimacy; because they are often novel and idiosyncratic, they may be regarded by others as crazy or destructive."[93] Through a developed set of goals a new identity is developed. This can be both a form of salvation for the writer and a potential stumbling block if the writer forgets that he is more, and less, than the identity role he has assumed through his writing. Levi's relationship with writing changed at various points in his life. Just after his release from Auschwitz he writes at a nearly frantic pace just to log his memories on paper.

---

[88] There is a body of literature by and about second-generation Holocaust survivors. See, for example, *After Such Knowledge*, by Eva Hoffman. Victoria Aarons has been researching and writing on third-generation Holocaust narratives and representations.
[89] Csikszentmihalyi, *Flow*, 233.
[90] Ibid.
[91] Levi, *The Voice of Memory*, 204.
[92] Csikszentmihalyi, *Flow*, 233. Negentropic describes a living system that works to minimize its entropy.
[93] Ibid, 231.

But I had returned from captivity three months before and was living badly. The things I had seen and suffered were burning inside of me; I felt closer to the dead than the living. I was writing concise and bloody poems, telling the story at breakneck speed, either by talking to people or writing it down, so much so that gradually a book was later born: by writing I found peace for a while and felt myself become a man again, a person like everyone else, neither a martyr nor debased nor a saint: one of those people who form a family and look to the future rather than the past.[94]

Writing returns Levi to normalcy. Here, as he writes it in 1975, his desire to return to the life of a person "like everyone else" pulsates on the page. He wants nothing more than to be fully human, making and raising children, loving, living among others. Initially, he experiences writing as a kind of purification. There is speed in his process, a need to get it all down and exteriorize and exorcise the trauma that is Auschwitz. In that Levi feels deadness more than life, the writing becomes a route back to life, a passage out of Dante's *Inferno*, a text to which Levi likens his own journey into Auschwitz. In the first pages of his memoir he describes his surroundings and the circumstances of the camp: "This is hell. Today, in our times, hell must be like this."[95] Levi's awakening to the journey through hell parallels Dante's description of finding himself on the lip of the inferno, virtually the bottomless hole of grief: "Breaking the deep sleep that filled my head,/A heavy clap of thunder startled me up/As though by force; with rested eyes I stood/Peering to find where I was—in truth, the lip/Above the chasm of pain, which holds the din/Of infinite grief: a gulf so dark and deep/And murky that though I gazed intently down/Into the canyon, I could see nothing below."[96]

Several months later Levi meets a young woman and immediately falls in love. He writes that he "in a few hours we knew that we belonged to each other, not for one meeting but for life, as has in fact been the case."[97] The new love, Lucia, vivifies him and helps to exorcise the death of his friend, Vanda Maestro, interned with him at Fossoli and gassed on October 30, 1944 in the women's camp at Birkenau. In February of that same year, he and Vanda, along with two other friends, had been deported to Auschwitz. Despite the haunting that Levi experiences in Vanda's death, readers sense that with new love comes a measure of renewal.

Alongside the liberating relief of the veteran who tells his story, I now felt in the writing a complex, intense, and new pleasure, similar to that I felt as a student when penetrating the solemn order of differential calculus. It was exalting to search and find, or create, the right word, that is, commensurate, concise, and strong; to dredge up events from my memory and describe them with the greatest rigor and the least clutter. Paradoxically, my baggage of

---

[94] Levi, *The Periodic Table*, 151.
[95] Levi, *Survival*, 72.
[96] *Inferno*, Canto IV, 1-8.
[97] Levi, *The Periodic Table*, 73.

> atrocious memories became a wealth, a seed; it seemed to me that, by writing, I was growing like a plant.[98]

Whereas Levi's first attempts at writing arose after grave loss, love now infused him as he composed. He began to enjoy the process of writing, the search for a word, the intimacy with language. He recognized his blossoming, even comparing himself to a flourishing plant, as Dante flourished in his imagined love for Beatrice, a young Florentine woman whom he admired from afar and whom he made the poet's muse and advocate. Memories of the camp became a seed that nourished writing. Writing became exaltation, an affirmation of Levi's embodied, mnemonic humanness. However, the terror of the camp always lingered.

What was it really like for Levi to be at home once again? In 1962 Levi concludes his book, *The Truce*, narrating his return home to Torino from Poland by way of Russia. He reaches his home on October 19, 1945, traveling with two Italians with whom he was originally deported. He comments that of 650 Italians deported from the internment camp at Fossoli three of them return. At the door to his home Levi is swollen, sick, bearded and in rags. He finds his family warm, welcoming, full of life. He knows that for deportees "on the threshold of our homes, for good or ill, a trial awaited us, and we anticipated it with fear."[99] The gap between the camp and home yawns. It seems as if Levi will fall into its nothingness. He finds the bed yielding softly beneath his weight. For months he walks "with my glance fixed to the ground, as if searching for something to eat or to pocket hastily or to steal for bread; and a dream full of horror has still not ceased to visit me."[100] In the dream he sits at a table with family or friends. They are in a bucolic setting, yet Levi feels "a deep and subtle anguish, the definite sensation of an impending threat."[101] Then everything solid disintegrates around him and he is once again in the *Lager*. There exists nothing true outside the *Lager*; only hell remains, and the sense of love, nature, family, home, and peace is not real.

The inner dream of peace dies, and the *Lager* comes to life, obliterating everything else. Levi ends this second book with the German's dawn command of the camp prisoners, "Wstawàch," wake up. He must wake to the nightmare. Everything else illusion. Here Levi confirms the repetitive nature of trauma. He continues to create book after book in which he works through the impact of Auschwitz. Polish poet Adam Zagajewski writes of his sadness that there are few words that Levi remembered in Polish. The word that stood out among them—rooted in the historical period of the camps, in particular heard in Auschwitz with violence and horror at three and four in the morning through the cold, the eternal command to get up, to leave one hell for another—was *Wstawàch*.[102]

---

[98] Levi, *The Periodic Table*, 153.
[99] Levi, *The Reawakening*, 206.
[100] Levi, *The Reawakening*, 206.
[101] Ibid, 207.
[102] Zagajewski, *Another Beauty*, 2002.

Not only does Levi bear his own traumatic history, he bears the ancient captivity and release story of the Jewish people into and out of Egypt. In addition, he carries within him the stories of those who did not leave the death camps. Trauma constitutes an intimate experience shared in relationship with others. Relating personal trauma experience consists of more than an individual's narrative of past events but is "the story of the way in which one's own trauma is tied up with the trauma of another, the way in which trauma may lead, therefore, to the encounter with another, through the very possibility and surprise of listening to another's wound." [103] When we contemplate the historical witness inherent to Levi's autobiographical texts we understand that the content and purpose of his writing extends well beyond his own sense of self and his single autobiography. His writing revolves around relationship with others, in the camps, on the trip home, in the world before and after the descent into Auschwitz. A conclusive thought in his account is that "part of our existence lies in the feelings of those near to us." [104] As an example, his writing celebrates connection to others in rare moments of safe space and abated hunger at Auschwitz. In this passage he shares the joy of intellectual conversation with Jean, a co-worker of the Chemical Kommando: "We spoke of our houses, of Strasbourg and Turin, of the books we had read, of what we had studied, of our mothers: how all mothers resemble each other! His mother too would have been amazed if she had known that he had found his feet, that day by day he was finding his feet." [105]

The moments of human connection, relived in his writing, express Levi's need for relationship in order to maintain humanness amidst hellish conditions. With Jean, the author relates a sense of commonality around mother, home, language, and literature. It is in the same scene with Jean that Levi recites verses from Dante's *Inferno*. His ability to teach the French-speaking Jean some Italian and to exchange with him their common love of the mountain ranges that flank each of their cities provides momentary and, over Levi's lifetime, unforgettable sustenance in the midst of severe deprivation. When with Jean he begins to remember the mountains of Torino he experiences a wave of emotional pain and he confirms in writing the longing for home within all beings and the torture of displacement from what we most love and that, accordingly, defines who we are. In this expression of love and suffering, Levi is in relationship with the nameless dead as well as the remembered living.

Flow experience pales in the author's confrontation of this post-Auschwitz burden. Can flow stand up to the atrocities of the death camps and the repetitive nature of trauma's post-memory? Flow is a condition around which the self organizes. Csikszentmihalyi details some of conditions for flow: concentration; curiosity; lack of self-consciousness; freedom to choose; enjoyment of mental processes; love of challenge; and, ideally, access to personal and social environments that support these qualities. The psychologist asserts in his work that when adversity arises we often reorganize to create conditions that allow the self to realign. We generate psychic

---

[103] Caruth, *Unclaimed Experience*, 7.

[104] Levi, *Survival*, 172.

[105] Ibid, 111.

energy that allows the inner self to find a new direction outside the dictates of external forces. Levi does this in the camps to the degree that he is able. A trait of survivors is a strongly directed purpose that is not self-seeking. Once released from the camp, writing provides Levi an internal experience that bestows order and demands focused, intelligent attention. However, the survivor may not see himself as helpless. Levi has detailed the survivor's legacy when he exposes the shame in facing the deaths of a multitude.

> The 'saved' of the Lager were not the best, those predestined to do good, the bearers of a message: what I had seen and lived through proved the exact contrary. Preferably the worst survived, the selfish, the violent, the insensitive, the collaborated of the 'gray zone,' the spies. The world survived, that is, the fittest; the best all died.[106]

Writing allows Levi nearly forty years of flow experience. Auschwitz and its repercussions become an organizing experience from which Levi's sensibility, his work, and his thought were shaped. When we consider Levi's possible suicide in this light, many questions arise. Does flow inhibit experiences of depression, ill health, aging, and emotional distress? Does it keep at bay "the memory of the offense," as Levi refers to the survivor's burden in his final book? The clear answer is no. Flow offers no solution or end to human suffering. In fact, it seems to occur regardless of suffering. It is a private, personal experience that the creator sometimes feels when absorbed in the act of creating and that allows him to meet challenges in a satisfactory way. As such, flow is temporal. It allows the creator to put aside, for a limited period of time, the daily cares and embedded traumas of human life. Practices that give rise to flow may delay or stall painful experiences, some of which are mentioned above, but flow is hardly a curative for the suffering that comes with human embodiment.

In a powerful exploration of Levi's death, Diego Gambetta queries the conclusion that the writer planned his own death.[107] In April of 1987 Levi was on anti-depressants, which can lower blood pressure and cause dizziness. Fewer than three weeks earlier he had undergone prostrate surgery. Gambetta hypothesizes Levi's recurrent episodes of depression did not result in suicide. Nor were the memories of Auschwitz responsible. Rather, he postulates on the basis of highly convincing evidence that Levi accidently fell to his death. Levi had gone out in the late morning to the stairwell to say something to the concierge who had just delivered his mail. He may have accidentally fallen over the banister, which came well below his waist. His cardiologist friend, David Mendel, comments, "I think that on the point of fainting, he reached for them [the banisters] to steady himself and fell."[108] Levi left no will and no suicide note. One biographer, Myriam Anissimov, writes that Levi in casting himself

---

[106] Levi, *The Drowned and the Saved*, 82.
[107] Gambetta, "Primo Levi's Last Moments." *Boston Review*, April 1999. Gambetta made an addendum to this article in 2005, in which he confirms his view that Levi's fall was accidental.
[108] Ibid.

over the stairwell, "appears to have succumbed to a sudden violent impulse."[109] Cynthia Ozick has referred to Levi's final book *The Drowned and the Saved* as his "suicide note."[110] Yet, against the tide of biographers, journalists, and writers who affirm the suicide, Gambetta, a professor of Sociology at Oxford University, resists. He notes Levi's energy for life and stresses that "A few days before his death, he canvassed the wonders of using a personal computer for word-processing with his publisher, Giulio Einaudi; Levi promised to tutor him if he decided to buy one."[111] He was working on a novel. The day before his death he had promised to resume conversations with a journalist writing a biographical piece on him. He had scheduled an interview with a journalist from *La Stampa*. He was making plans, engaging a future. These actions appear to run contrary to a suicide attempt.

Why is the question of suicide important to readers and scholars of Levi's work? The way in which he died says something about the nature of his work and his relationship to Auschwitz, particularly his encounter with death in and through writing. The central question in readers' minds appears to be: Did Auschwitz finally kill Levi, despite his enormous efforts at writing post-trauma memory as a form of recovery? If we know his fall was accidental, then we can say that Auschwitz and its tide of evil as expressed through human beings did not defeat Levi. We can even extend this belief to assert that no matter how grave the offense, no matter the degree of "man's inhumanity to man," it is still possible for human beings to survive, even thrive in the aftermath of severe (collective and historical) trauma. Levi's work acts as evidence against any case to the contrary, that human beings cannot recover from grave trauma.

Levi has become a renowned and beloved writer in his native Italy and in the world beyond. His work has been a source of hope to readers in the immediate and long-term aftermath of the physical, social, political, and economic consequences rooted in the occurrence of World War II. Gambetta writes that Levi's possible suicide haunts readers. "Levi's generation, and that of his children (my generation), perceive his writings, rightly or wrongly, as continuous with his life. Their immense value sprang from that fusion: his life seemed to exemplify the possibilities of human decency explored in his books, and to stand as evidence that those possibilities were not mere wishful thinking."[112]

What does Levi's suicide mean to his readers? What died along with Levi in his supposed suicide? Metaphors abound. John Leonard writes that on April 11, 1987 Levi "killed our wishful thinking."[113] Whether suicide or accident, Leonard states that Levi "lost his balance and balance is what we needed from him," along with what other writers have termed his "equanimity" and "moral poise." He postulates that Levi's translation of Franz Kafka's *The Trail* contributed to the writer's unmooring.

---

[109] Anissimov, *Tragedy of an Optimist*, 12.
[110] Ozick, "Primo Levi's Suicide Note," *Metaphor and Memory*, 1989. Originally published in *The New Republic* as "The Suicide Note" in March 1988.
[111] Gambetta, *Boston Review*.
[112] Ibid.
[113] Leonard, "The Drowned and the Unsaved."

Levi, as a child of the Enlightenment's worship of logical reasoning and ordered philosophical inquiry, found Kafka disturbing in his narrative of nonsensical, chaotic, and falsely lawful worlds. Of Kafka, Levi remarked, "I fear him, like a great machine that crashes in on you, like the prophet who tells you the day you will die."* Leonard's exploration suggests that Levi utilized writing to impose a degree of order and sense where there appears to be none. Levi excels at ferreting out revelatory insights into the messiness of human nature where there appears to be nothing but death, pain, violence, and lawlessness. In reason's lucid light that casts a glow over the chaos and pain intrinsic to our human condition, the grave letdown of a writer's suicide becomes existential angst for his hopeful, charmed readers. Many have read the writer's work as a sign of human tenacity, ethicality, and brilliance under duress. His writing reveals (among other qualities) a will to live and his success in doing so, an audacious endeavor over a lifetime.

The idea that Levi succumbed to depression, to illness, to fatigue and fear indicates that we cannot, do not, always survive to finish our lives to their very natural end. Perhaps, for Levi, this *was* the natural end. Perhaps not. But, whatever the case, those of us who have been drawn into his work, have doubtless been changed by his words, his mind and the language that evolved of it. To write one book, the first, *If This Is a Man*, would have been a significant act of courage, but Levi wrote memoirs, short stories, two novels, poems, plays and scripts adopted for radio, television, and theatre, science fiction, articles, essays, translations, and participated in, even conducted with himself, interviews. Clearly, he dedicated his life to writing; and death, whatever its cause, cannot annul the power of his will to create in flow, to communicate with others his experience and view of the world.

Traumatic experience may have been integrated into Levi's sense of self as he created experience anew through memory in narrative. It is also highly possible, despite experiences of flow, that the shattered self that emerged of Auschwitz may have determined the remainder of Levi's forty-some years of life. In returning to Levi's fellow writer, Jean Améry, resolution and comprehension appear but faulty concepts in the midst of trauma and its aftermath. "Clarification would also amount to disposal, settlement of the case, which can then be placed in the files of history. My book is meant to aid in preventing precisely this. For nothing is resolved, no conflict is settled, no remembering has become a mere memory."[114]

Narrative with its qualities of solidity and immortality becomes for Levi a prosthesis that mediates between waking reality and the chaotic, base, inhumane, and terrifying experiences of the past. In language Levi attempted to confer sense onto these experiences, "living and then writing about and pondering those events, I have learned many things about man and about the world."[115] Yet as Améry courageously asserts, language and the rationality it imposes on experience fail to signify that trauma recovery is even partial. To leave hell behind, to construct a world in which

---

[114] Améry, *At the Mind's Limits*, xi.
[115] Levi, *The Voice of Memory*, 206.
* Leonard, "The Drowned and the Unsaved."

we are for a time the creating gods, may be our temporary prosthesis that replaces the damaged part of our souls so that we can walk, talk, and continue, for a while, to live.

1.8 A Turn to Narrative

The reason I had come to Auschwitz, even to Poland, was because of a passion for reading and teaching Primo Levi's memoirs. His memories channeled into narrative motivated my desire to apply to the Auschwitz Jewish Center Fellows Program and to visit the sites about which he wrote, sites that had drastically influenced his life course, his thoughts, and his writing career. He had even admitted, bravely, I thought, that if he had not lived his Auschwitz experience, he probably would have never have written anything. So, it was Levi's words and his need to write that emerged of his camp experience that I carried with me into Auschwitz, even as I visited a place that I understood has become a tourist site, a memorial drastically changed from the killing and labor camp it was from 1940 to 1945.

In visiting Auschwitz, I believed that narrative offered a way to navigate the camp space. It had allowed Levi, as a survivor, to do so, and it would allow me as a visitor to be present to and feel the place that had been Auschwitz when Levi had been interned there seventy years earlier. Over my three days at Auschwitz I learned that hearing, seeing, and imagining individual and community stories of those deported to the camp opens to the visitor space for acknowledging the horror and loss implicit in a visit to these charnel grounds. Yet, there were challenges to these affective ways of experiencing the historic camp sites. The narratives I sought out came for me in the form of photographs, written accounts of survivors—both those remembered from my personal reading and those our guide read to during our camp visits, and in museum artifacts. In speaking of survival, Levi wrote that he felt his steadfast interest in the human spirit and his determination to "recognize in my companions and in myself, men, not things."[116]

It was in this spirit that I encountered the ground of memory. Narrative mattered to me intensely at that moment. Such narratives help visitors to connect to the tenacious continuity of human experience that existed within the camp and its sub-camps. Finally, the attuned visitor may discover several small stories, or the possibilities of such stories, in documentation and artifacts (Levi called these artifacts "relics") in the exhibits at Auschwitz. However, such narrative discovery is not made explicit to visitors, nor is it encouraged. I was to find the pace through the museum and the historic grounds of Auschwitz-Birkenau—even with an intellectual guide and a small group of scholars—rapid.

Auschwitz-Birkenau is a state museum funded by the Polish government. Several former prisoners who wanted to create a memorial at the site established it just after the war in 1946, the same year Levi began to write his account. Gradually, the memorial developed into a museum. Under Communism the emphasis on

---

[116] Levi, *The Voice of Memory*, 207.

memorialization was on those "martyred" in the Second World War, with less emphasis on the genocide of specifically Jewish prisoners. In fact, Levi felt disgust for what he viewed as a Polish tendency to memorialize camp prisoners within a nationalistic framework. With the emphasis on nationalism as recourse to traumatic memory, he perceived the loss and annihilation of Jewish experience and genocide in the camps. [117] Since the early 1990s with Poland's transition to democratic government, there has been exponential growth in the preservation of artifacts, including buildings, as well as in the scope of the museum's educational programs and global digital presence. At peak periods—from April to October—up to 15,000 people visit Auschwitz in a single day. Individuals must visit the camp in tours, between 10:00 a.m. and 3:00 p.m., with a specially trained guide so that they stay together, learn the history, and visit camp areas deemed to be of particular historic value. Our guide was Paweł Sawicki, a journalist and writer with the Press Office for the Auschwitz-Birkenau Memorial and State Museum. Paweł noted that in visiting the camp "it is individuals who are a problem; people must take tours."[118] Individuals sometimes venture into areas not open to the public or under renovation.

The emphasis on groups deters individual exploration of Auschwitz. Yet, when individuals experience the camp in groups they have little space for their own emotional experiences of the place. This loss of individual experience constitutes the very reason that stories should comprise a core element in shaping the visitor's time there. However, due to sheer numbers of visitors, people must move quickly through exhibits housed in the former cellblocks of the Auschwitz I compound. Keeping a steady pace through narrow hallways that open into crowded exhibit rooms, a summer crowd ahead and behind, the visitor may try to comprehend the enormity of atrocity and the total loss for individuals, particularly for Jewish people, as they arrived to the camp from transport trains. The effect of such absorption is stupefying. Cases of hair, shoes, glasses, prosthetics—extensions of one's very self and one's ability to function in the world—form decaying mountains of intimate things that never should have become relics of genocide.

The museum's visitation policy implies that how one conducts oneself is important to the maintenance of the place as memorial and one's experience of it. This is a museum after all. Yet, some fellow visitors' faces betray horror and disgust. A restless silence periodically befalls us. In the long narrow room with suitcases, hair, and children's shoes there is a tangible atmosphere of disbelief—in confronting the space and its remains. We visitors must confront the evidence that systematic cruelties happened right here and how, if at all, we respond. Sighs puncture the space, small words between intimates, people who have known one another over time and who can, perhaps without misunderstanding, confess their horror to one another. The sighs

---

[117] In *The Voice of Memory* Levi says, "I'm rather angered by the fact that the Poles, the Polish government, have taken over Auschwitz and turned it into a memorial to the martyrdom of the Polish nation" (217). However, Levi does not acknowledge that history was overly determined under Communism by Russian historicization of the Second World War as it occurred in Eastern and Central Europe.

[118] From the author's personal notes, July 2014.

seem to surge into one sustained out-breath of injury and mark a particular heaviness of repressed emotion in response to these artifacts.

In the exhibits at Auschwitz I, the original camp buildings that had once been a Polish army barracks, there are placards, dates, numbers, statistics, reports of transports, and historical photos. But the visitor must glimpse these artifacts, rather than linger and invite a potentially emotional response to them. In this first museum space we enter, I stop to hear Paweł's voice explain photos, documents, and artifacts. Rare official photos of the 1944 transports of Hungarian Jews arriving into Auschwitz and disembarking cattle trains are now imagistic banners covering entire lengths of museum walls. Independently, and overwhelmed by these first introductions to artifacts, I search for relationships in the photographs. These isolated images move me. I gravitate toward a man dressed in prison garb and seemingly well fed with a woman, newly arrived, talking, saying something urgently, last words, counsel for survival, an almost passionate moment on the train ramp. What could their relationship be? I take a picture of the picture so that later I may revisit it in contemplation. My eyes search the canvas again. I notice a boy holding a woman's hand—perhaps his mother—surrounded by children and women hurrying along with apprehension, exhausted. Those photos will catalyze poems. I will return to them in search of vaporous specificities of personal histories never available to me, never narrated and remembered to anyone, but somehow shared with all of us. In those photos from 1944 what stands out are instances, vitally important, between people on the ramps as they were driven from trains and corralled and ordered into lines that led towards gas chambers. I imagine moments of fear and love, clinging to one another in the face of grave uncertainty, each adult subsumed with hope and desperation and aching need.

"We must be disciplined now," Paweł tells our group, "in order to get through this tour and see certain things." We move slowly, lingering over documents and relics. He may lose us in the hallways. We will not have time to finish the tour. Disciplined, orderly. Is this how we visitors are to behave at Auschwitz? Yes, there are lines, streams of people channeling through halls and stairways. Yet, even as we hurry and attend to our guide, we see so little of the camp. Past the shooting wall, through Block 11, in a line past cells—one of starvation, another of standing, into which four men bent and crawled and stood for days. I rub the Buddha charm at my neck. "How do you do this?" I ask Paweł just in front of me. He grimaces. "Do you get used to it? It's your job." He steels himself. He erects an interior wall. "Yes," he says, focused on moving us through. We enter the innards of a gas chamber for a minute. We move through. Perhaps moving through is a glimpse, a memory with intention to return to full life, an entry into and surfacing from these once murderous grounds.

Back at Auschwitz Jewish Center (AJC), the fellows gather in the art gallery on the cool first floor, its high paned windows at street level. We sit in chairs in a circle. Paweł begins, explaining that at Auschwitz "the tour suppresses a need for internal narrative and also prevents emergence of such a narrative."[119] The museum's aim, he continues, is not to encourage an emotional experience of the place but to impart historical knowledge of the camps. I resist the idea that one can or should suppress an internal narrative, but upon further reflection imagine the problems germane to a museum space of sobbing and shaking, horrified, grief-stricken, enraged, or overwhelmed people. The priority is to recognize the place and the things within it that point to an historical understanding over and above an all-consuming emotional response to the histories with which it confronts us.

At home with books and solitude, a quiet afternoon, a garden at the window, I listen. I turn to songs and voices, to poetry with its pleas for forgiveness, for life, its grief and understanding. I grapple with what Father Manfred Deselaers at the Center for Dialogue and Prayer called the lifelong wound of Auschwitz. In dialogue with the fellows, Fr. Dr. Deselaers had said, "The task is to try to understand and to take this wound seriously. It touches us, and we think it has to do with us, but what?"[120] Such a lifetime inquiry brings one into an ethical engagement with the place of Auschwitz and the words that remain among humans because of that place. Auschwitz began with the killing of relationship, says the Father. Who is this us? Poles or international visitors and/or Catholics in particular? Certainly, Jews do not question what the wound of the Holocaust has to do with them. Although, I think, Jews may very well question and offer answers to what the wound of the Holocaust has to do with all of us who share the human condition.

My turn to narrative, both in visiting the camp and once home, reflects my desire to mend relationships across time, place, and event. One such text that nourishes that longing is Charlotte Delbo's *Auschwitz and After*, written twenty years after her repatriation to France. She describes this no-place where she has landed from her native France, "We arrived on a morning in January 1943. The doors of the cattle cars were pushed open, revealing the edge of an icy plain. It was a place from before geography. Where were we? We were to find out—later, at least two months hence; we, that is those of us who were still alive two months later—that this place was called Auschwitz. We couldn't have given it a name."[121] Seventy years later, its name has burned itself in our consciousness. Of our contemporary relationship with the camp, Paweł says, "We have only the place and words," neither of which Delbo and her compatriots had upon their arrival. Nor did they have geography. It would be the work of survivors, of writers, artists, photographers—in short, of documentarians—to give us that place in the words and images of their work. Perhaps words persist and flourish against violence, against forgetting history.

The modest, even minimal, remains of buildings, monuments, exhibits, and words structure humanity's current relationship with the camp. For example, just three to five percent of original documents and records in the camp remain intact. Most were destroyed, others confiscated by camp liberators, the Russians. In a contemporary context, the loss of objects through war makes potent the gradual shift

---

[119] Author's personal notes.
[120] Ibid.
[121] Delbo, *Auschwitz and After*, 167.

to narrative as a means of processing and feeling one's visit to the camp. Such a shift indicates that this memorial-museum space has begun to relinquish a focus on historical facts and a lingering political ideological narrative (of Communist Poland) that speaks of martyrdom over the uniqueness of individual lives for a personal, narrative-driven guidance through the camp. Such a turn manifests in an exhibit at Birkenau of 2,400 photos found in suitcases and discovered after camp liberation in 1945.

This turn is also reflected on the second day of the tour when at Birkenau Paweł reads to fellows from testimonies he has carefully chosen. He wants us to have a feeling for camp conditions and how those who lived and survived here experienced the place. At the edge of a stand of birches, near the crumbling bricks of former gas chamber five he reads to us from Henryk Mandelbaum's recounting of his experience as a Sonderkommando. Mandelbaum describes the process of killing within the gas chambers, the extraction of hundreds of bodies and the subsequent cremation of bodies. We are in Birkenau, the death camp, built to house increasing numbers of prisoners and the gas chambers to kill them. At capacity, the extermination camp held 90,000 people. Ironically, the vastness of Birkenau ("birch" in German), the spaces between structures and the paths through woods and along marshy waterways, allows more time to think and feel. In the former barracks, many of these buildings undergoing restoration, Paweł reads a woman prisoner's careful record of the disease, filth, and dying that developed in female camp quarters.

The narrative readings are new for our guide. He holds in his hands white sheets of paper of laser jet words. He wants us to hear firsthand accounts of the places we stand. Does narrative add to our sense of the place and what transpired here? He seems tentative, alert to our responses. As I leave the camp and consider prisoner memories given over to visitors, I contemplate what a turn to narrative implies for historians, curators, educators, and press officers at the Auschwitz-Birkenau Memorial and State Museum—employees who preserve, present, and create the memorial-museum and its space for those who visit. This turn constitutes risk. First it signifies that they make narratives essential to the visitor's tour of the camps, so that narratives hold the rich potential to figure prominently in one's post-visit recollections of the camps. Narratives constitute a vital element in imagining the camps as they once were, not simply as historical markers of criminality and genocide, but as terrible and unforgettable spaces wherein people lived, loved, struggled, and died. It is life that must be honored, not en masse but as a unique and idiosyncratic expression of each individual. It matters that the guide feels the same way. That he believes reading a narrative memory is a way of remembering and feeling. Perhaps it makes the guide as emotionally vulnerable and as human as are his visitors. His turn to story validates all our stories in this place. This is not just his place of employment, an everyday routine for him; it is a place of words, and through him we listen.

Narratives mean that visitors need time and space to respond quietly as an interior process to the experiences of others. The importance of visiting resides in feeling the texture of life from the perspective of another human who experienced the camp. The connection to narrative facilitates a particular and simultaneously enlarged perspective of the camp once inhabited by individuals. Delbo writes that when she returned home she met men who had been prisoners of war. She listened to their stories and "took the measure of the incommunicable."[122] Now, in the presence of many untold stories it is the incommunicable one must attend to at Auschwitz. Levi confessed that when he visited in 1965 he could feel nothing there.[123] Because he gave me his story I felt something large and moving, something with which to wrestle for life. So, it is that narratives affirm our humanness in the places made to annihilate that humanity.

1.9 THE RAMP

Several thousand people—Hungarians in the final transports—

fell out from cattle car trains. They, the last few living,

soon extinguished.

Some would survive, but not without stories

to fill abysses that would open oozing wounds

dangerously festering with losses

of everyone and everything that mattered.

I sought a center, a story to guide me into this world

to take with me in the struggle

a moment

in the midst of killing fields.

In a photo spread across an Auschwitz museum wall,

---

[122] Delbo, *Auschwitz and After*, 167.
[123] Levi visited Auschwitz in 1965 and again in 1982. Ian Thomson's *Primo Levi: A Life* recounts the details and impressions of his return visits.

a woman and a man standing together, her duffel

between them. Hair kerchief-wrapped

after three hundred miles by train.

The man in stripped prisoner's jacket, pants, and hat.

Well fed, not without privilege.

Urgent with listening or asking, does she dare speak?

Right shoulder angled toward him. His toward her.

A diagonal space encapsulating a universe

where he tells her a necessary secret.

She is young enough and can work. Or,

all is well. Food and showers just beyond

barbed wire.

He is one of her—a prisoner, forced here.

Soon the war is over.

It is May or October

1944, cold snakes through her coat.

People sort through bags,

stand in lines according to harsh command.

He knows there will be selections.

She's not speaking. She's listening.

Every word he quietly says—he has

stopped after all—to tell her something—

will map her possible future.

A small section from a larger photo of the selection ramp in May 1944 at the arrival of Hungarian transports into Birkenau. The photos were likely taken by camp officials tasked with documentation of arriving transports.
Source: Auschwitz-Birkenau Memorial and Museum. Author photo, 2014.

1.10 LOOKING FOR BUNA-MONOWITZ

I had to understand Levi's experience to the point that I felt compelled to see and experience, granted in a removed, remote way, the ground that is Auschwitz. I had to understand that this ground could in no way resemble anything Levi had experienced. But I wanted to be there, to know what remained. The grounds that once housed the charnel grounds and forced labor camps of Nazi Germany have returned to Poland, to the ordinary and daily lives of Polish people, particularly those who live in and around the town of Oświęcim.

All around Auschwitz I and Birkenau (Auschwitz II) there were now modest houses with gardens. People had always lived here. Beginning in 1940 homes and farms were demolished to build the death and labor camps and their extensive network of sub-camps. One of the first experimental gas chambers at Auschwitz II had been a Polish farmhouse—the little red house—from which the owners had been evicted. The space that became the camp grew as the Germans ravenously devoured the Polish country in and around Oświęcim for their killing purposes. Yet, life returns, even and especially after war, to cover the scarred and torn earth.

Eva, my roommate, and I rode bikes through the hamlets around Oświęcim on a hot Saturday in July. We could have gone back to the camps for another day. It was a free day and the fellows, some of them, had returned to spend time in the national exhibits and halls at Auschwitz I. We had barely walked Birkenau's vast expanse where we had walked through the hot, buggy marshes around the camp and then the sky darkened to a bruised purple and it had begun to rain. Escaping the deluge, we sheltered with our guide in a crowd of visitors on the railroad tracks and under the guard tower, that ominous icon, to the camp's former entrance. How ironic, I thought in those moments of downpour, that we are seeking refuge where transports arrived.

I could have gone back. But, I was sick. I felt sick there. By the third day at the camps, sitting in a lecture room in the former Auschwitz I barracks, listening to a man drone on about documents (only three percent of former documents remain found), my stomach hurt.[124] I felt despondent, exhausted, unable to tolerate a lecture, a study of documentation and archival records, sitting in a theater seat on the very spot of genocide and every kind of imaginable torture. I felt that people's spirits surrounded me, or at least the memory and tangible suffering of their presence. I felt the historical suffering—not a knowledge, but a feeling of being part of, inseparable from, the people who had seen this ground, felt its great imposing wound in their lives, and recoiled and then, sometimes, asserted themselves as possible in these surrounds.

It was not solely the methods by which people were physically and psychically murdered that sickened me, but the humanness of which people were systematically raped that made me ill. I needed to beat the ground and wail at humanity, the very curse of it. It was a feeling, more than a knowledge, a shared sense of being human, of having a human wholeness in body and in mind and sensation, through time, a continuity and assuredness of this humanness and then an absolute and total violation, an erasure of it, as a fact that made me ill. I wanted to run and knew—intellectually— that I could not. I knew that my humanity meant, at this very moment, not running. I knew I had to listen to the lecture with embodied knowledge of horror and the existential acknowledgment of material knowledge, the endless recounting of facts, the review of history, the review of the archive that must happen ceaselessly in an effort of retrospective sense-making.

---

[124] Author's personal notes, July 2014.

Those feelings were not academic, as feelings rarely are, and I did not care. By Saturday, I felt I should go back. There was so much more; yet, I could not. I chose not to. I wanted to ride a bike in the Polish sunshine and humidity. I wanted a day with pale blue sky and burning sun and Polish traffic and a green river, now clean, and the sound of families swimming, in view of picnics, and people out in the streets for groceries and in their yards for gardening and socializing. I wanted life.

At the Museum of Jewish Heritage in New York, in an old black and white photo, almost sepia tone, of the time—there was a line of prisoners, working, carrying things, in the ubiquitous striped uniforms. The air was sooty, dense with coal, the metal of industry, the ash of burned bodies. The ground was trodden, no living plant visible, everything smashed to dirt. Prisoners' feet blazed paths into the ground. The camp in one space and then a line of fuzzy humans to a work area, the prisoners carrying things to a designated spot. I remembered Levi had carried, with another man, a steel beam. He had not shouldered it successfully and the beam fell and opened the back of his foot. A foot injury meant death. He did not remove his wooden shoe. He did not want to look, to know. When he did he found his sock drenched in blood. He spent days in the infirmary. Was Levi there in the photo? I knew that at some point, beyond February 1944, he would have been there, somewhere. I looked closer. An abyss—the true hell that Levi had described; another world, something unreal. Had that world existed here in Oświęcim, somewhere along the bike paths edged in high green grass? Yes, it had.

I was looking for the remains of Buna-Monowitz. To explain the camp name, Butadiene is a chemical made from the processing of petroleum, a colorless gas with a mild gasoline-like odor, used to make synthetic rubber. Natrium, Latin for sodium. Monowice is the Polish town, adjacent to Oświęcim, where the plant was erected. The labor camp had been complex III of Auschwitz and was located a few kilometers from the main camp. Levi had worked there as a young man in his mid-twenties, a chemist, a slave laborer of the Germans in the IG Farben plant. In the end, just before the Germans fled and as the Russians approached, the Allies bombed every day. He writes of those final days in the camp, "The Russians were knocking at the door. Allied planes came to shake apart the Buna plant: there was no water, steam, or electricity; not a single pane of glass was intact; but the order was to begin producing Buna rubber, and Germans do not discuss orders. To work was as impossible as it was futile; our time was almost entirely spent dismantling the apparatus at every air-raid alarm."[125] Even then, Levi inside the factory trying to work, the place was being destroyed. What did I expect to see but fragments, some skeletal structures of the past?

The green Polish earth was past full blossom. Humidity hung in the air, the sky a dullish high white. Eva rode ahead of me. High on the bike path, I looked left to old, abandoned structures. In the end, for Levi, it was January, a Polish winter I would never know, a cold I could not fathom. His hands were so cold it was hard to work. He continues, "every so often some inspector burrowed through the rubble and snow

---

[125] Levi, *The Periodic Table*, 214.

all the way to us to make sure that the lab's work proceeded according to instructions."[126] The picture he provides his reader is darkly comic. The local militia and German civilians burrowing through rubble and snow to check on rubber production as Levi and his fellow chemists dismantle and reassemble lab equipment, the deluded Germans demanding their orders and instructions fulfilled in freezing temperatures under bombardment from the air!

The Buna camp ruins are not on the guided Auschwitz tour. I had read online that the camp was walled off, not open to visitors. There was a stone monument in Monowice to workers who had labored and died there at the Buna Werke. But, Eva and I did not find the town. My roommate was patient with my obsession with the writer and his life as it was lived those months in Poland, but, I realized, she also could not have been terribly interested in retracing Primo Levi's steps from Auschwitz to Buna-Monowitz on a humid Saturday at high noon.

I relaxed into the heat and humidity, riding along—Eva somewhere behind me or ahead of me—the confluence of the Sola and Vistula Rivers and over a busy bridge, under shelter of shaded trees. We stopped. I did not think we were close. Then, we set out in the other direction, back along the river, and over railroad tracks, through small towns, to a reservoir where teenagers swam and dove. I begin to doubt myself. Why did I so desperately want to find the ruins? Everywhere Poles were living—happy, out in the heat, swimming, making their homes, buying their groceries, riding bikes, and tending their gardens. From the raised bike path along train tracks I could see beautiful little gardens—chickens, grass, tool sheds, fruit trees, and vegetable beds. We ended up in Babice, a village where there had been small subunit of the Auschwitz camp, a forced labor camp, maybe an agricultural farm. On a winding residential street, we spotted a pair of storks nested high upon a telephone pole. Eva and I stopped to take their picture. Why, after three days at Auschwitz, on tours and in various seminars, did I want to find the place that Levi had worked in a laboratory for several miserable winter months of his otherwise full and satisfying life? Eva and I stopped at the reservoir and watched boys jump from a cement edge into the water below. We shared chocolate, a granola bar, a piece of fruit, and some water.

On the bike trail, heading once again in the direction of Oświęcim, I could see old factory ruins. The Allies had repeatedly bombed the factory in late 1944 and Levi had been through those bombings, narrowly missing explosions. Seven months after my return home from the fellowship, I inquire of Maciek who had been our guide those weeks in Poland about Buna-Monowitz. He informs me that the Monowitz camp is not there anymore. "Most of the grounds are now a private factory called Synthos," he writes, "Hence it's not part of the official Auschwitz museum tour. The factory was partly bombed by the Allies, and after the war it continued to operate. It's been a key workplace for many Oświęcimians since, including some Holocaust survivors."[127] A few survivors of Auschwitz worked in the chemical factory in Oświęcim, years after the closure of the camp. The factory was remade, rebuilt, renamed multiple times, in

---

[126] Ibid.
[127] Maciek Zabierowski in personal communication with the author.

short, leveled and reimagined. The skeleton of its memory remained. One of the few remaining Jewish survivors of Oświęcim, Szymon Kluger, worked at the factory. He lived alone, a recluse in the town, working and living on grounds where once his demise had been intended. He remained: tenacious, living, working, going on against every intention that had been planned otherwise for his present and future. His home, in disrepair, was purchased and renovated in 2013 by the Auschwitz Jewish Center. It is now Café Bergson, one of the most beautiful cafés in Poland. There we spent many hours as fellows discussing our time in Auschwitz and talking about the small, formerly Jewish towns we had visited where synagogues were either restored or remained in ruins.

The Kluger Family House, situated behind the Chevra Lomdei Mishnayot Synagogue, was built in the early twentieth century. After the Holocaust, Szymon settled in Sweden and later returned to Oświęcim where he worked for the chemical factory.[128] The current chemical manufacturer on the former grounds of Buna is a major employer in Oświęcim. The factory has been through multiple transformations since the Russians liberated Auschwitz-Birkenau on January 27, 1945.

> Synthos PLC was founded on September 1st, 1945, as the Factory of Synthetic Fuels in Dwory. In 1946, the company was renamed Państwowe Zakłady Syntezy Chemicznej w Dworach (State-owned Chemical Synthesis Plants of Dwory). In 1948, the name was changed to: Zakłady Syntezy Chemicznej w Dworach (Chemical Synthesis Plants of Dwory) One year later, the company was renamed Zakłady Chemiczne Przedsiębiorstwo Państwowe Wyodrębnione w Oświęcimiu (Chemical Works, Separate State Company of Oświęcim).[129]

Maciek explains, "There are some leftovers of the camp structure outside of the Synthos factory, anti-aircraft bunkers and single barracks, converted into sheds on private grounds. But they're scarce."[130] Synthos. Synthesis. Synthesize. History has been synthesized, its horror and terror, into the present life of pastoral, industrial, communist, and now democratic Poland. The factory was somewhat of a watershed for Levi. Strangely, once selected to work there, he was, as his biographer Ian Thomson explains, "now among a privileged caste of specialist slaves who were destined to live a few months longer than their fellows."[131]

One has to sometimes look for history, for evidence of past events, and, naturally, given change and growth, one is often unsuccessful in finding it. What one lives of the past—whether through material experience or vicariously in narrative, art, music, and film—is mostly not what one finds in the present. My adult life has been pocked by travels to find the energetic presence of authors and artists who have moved me. In Concord, I walked around Walden Pond, imagining Thoreau, and visited the house of

---

[128] Auschwitz Jewish Center, "Café Bergson," 2017.
[129] Synthos, 2017.
[130] Personal communication with the author.
[131] Thomson, *Primo Levi: A Life*, 192.

Ralph Waldo Emerson; in Amherst, the house of Emily Dickinson. In New Mexico, I sought Georgia O'Keefe's lodgings, landscapes, and paintings. In Chile, the houses, cities, and beaches of Pablo Neruda. In Canada, in the paintings of Emily Carr, I sought to know the confluence of First Nation and European cultures. Levi has written that perfection belongs to narrated events, not to those we live.[132]

So it was that I did not find Buna-Monowitz. I found a river, a pair of nesting storks, a village of gardens, boys swimming, and a late afternoon meal with Eva and other AJC fellows near to the places where Levi had once suffered and had physically escaped, and that through corporeal memory he continued to carry over his lifetime. He gave his memories to readers so that they would become our own. He asked us to be judges for him, to shoulder the burden of history. How could I read Levi and not be haunted by what he had left me? Poland was a way to bring that haunting into the world, and so I rode with it that day on the bike, my own burden lighter, exposed to sun and air. I will ride with those memories, fragmented, foreign, fuzzy, even lost, for the remainder of my life.

1.11 PRIMO LEVI, ITALY, AND SYRIA

In my youth I was drawn to international students. I befriended Bita and Cee-Cee, two Iranian girls, and Benjamín, a Colombian whose father was a diplomat and had a penthouse in Miami. They were lovely friends—real, kind, and attentive in ways that my American friends and fellow students were not. They were obviously from wealthy families, as they had left their embattled countries during times when many of their compatriots could not have, and in some remote way I recognized that they knew things about the world, about politics, and refuge and exile, that I did not. I don't know that I even had names for these things when I was seventeen. But, I remember the admiration I had for their gravitas.

They were not international students, however. Bita, Cee-Cee, and Benjamín were refugees, however privileged, from wars: political wars, drug wars, political instability and the social chaos and confusion and camaraderie that arise of such wars. But, in my mind, they were grouped under the idea of "foreign exchange," people as a sort of commodity, because that's what countries of privilege did—exchanged students who would act as cultural ambassadors. Those were, I imagined, the students who came to Saratoga High School, an economically privileged, mostly white bedroom community in South Bay, an hour from San Francisco. Benjamín told me his family could not stay in Bogotá and had gone to Miami, that shelter for Latin Americas of all backgrounds, to escape the violence there. He was migratory, as were Bita and Cee-Cee, two sweet girls, whose trauma I neither noticed nor inquired into. But they hardly spoke of their background. Maybe they wanted to forget. Maybe there was shame. Maybe they hadn't seen much as it was only 1980 and the war between Iran and Iraq had just begun. What they felt might have been closer to homesickness and concentrated efforts to adjust and acclimate to their new home than any trauma of

---

[132] Levi, *The Periodic Table*, 215.

war, violence, or political unrest. I knew little then of the world, knew little when I should have known much more. I liked them for their difference, their complications, for things I could not find but wanted, for things I did not know how to name. So, it was that I failed to ask them if they missed home.

Older now, decades past that time, I recognize that we harbor home within. It is not so easy to talk of home; often it is inexpressible—what kind of language is that of home—and frequently painful. At home, the thought of home barely arises, but away it erupts with insistence. My friends surely missed their homes. Perhaps I recognized this longing in fleeting moments. Moments so quick I did not realize they existed.

Levi writes of his longing for home. Deported to Auschwitz, he is nine hundred miles from his native Torino in Italy's northwest. Auschwitz was situated at the outskirts of a small town, Oświęcim, in southern Poland at the meeting of the Vistula and Sola Rivers. Levi does not know where he is geographically. He knows he is in Poland, but he cannot really situate himself. He has been arrested in the Valle d'Aosta as a partisan and held and questioned over a period of several weeks in jail.[133] As a Jew in Nazi-occupied Italy, he is then put on a third-class Pullman from Aosta with several other young Jewish friends and interned for several weeks at Fossoli di Carpi, a detention camp not far from Modena in Emilia-Romagna province. The internees gradually come to realize that they will likely not live. They are en route to the extermination camps in the East, specifically to Auschwitz.

Once in the camp, Levi's relationship to home becomes an increasingly complex territory that comprises desire and suppression. He wants to remember home. It gives him a feeling for who he has been and reminds him that in the life outside the camp he can return to himself again. He dreams that he tells his story to his sister and his friends. "It is an intense pleasure, physical, inexpressible, to be at home, among friendly people and to have so many things to recount."[134] This dream turns to nightmare when none of the people at the table hear him, as if his story is too strange to be understood, or perhaps the people are so distance in time and space from his bunk in Auschwitz it is as if he is speaking from the dead. He wakes to hear fellow prisoners dreaming in their bunks, chewing, and gnawing as if eating ever-allusive food.

Aboudeh is a Syrian student in my summer English course. It is the summer just before I leave on a month-long fellowship to Poland. We are reading Levi's *If This Is a Man*. Some of our discussions center on missing home and the meaning of home as a metaphor for situatedness in the world, for a sense of one's self in community with others, and for familiarity, food, love, culture, and sustenance. When I teach this book, the students need breaks, periods to eat and refresh, to stretch and move into light and sunshine. One day at the break, Aboudeh was clearly tired. "Are you doing okay?" I asked him. He looked defeated, deflated, even exhausted. I felt ashamed, concerned. Why was I teaching the Holocaust when here was a young man whose

---

[133] See Sergio Luzzato's *Primo Levi's Resistance: Rebels and Collaborators in Occupied Italy*, Metropolitan Books, 2016. Luzzato relates Levi's experience in Italy under German occupation in late 1943 and early 1944, including his arrest and deportation to Auschwitz.

[134] Levi, *Survival*, 60.

country had been destroyed? I was cognizant of his recent experience of war and dislocation. His family was now in Beirut and he had been sent to the United States, to live with an uncle and attend college and eventually medical school.

We stood together at the classroom door, he on exterior side and I on the interior side of the threshold. He tells me he sees no need to live in the past. He must be telling me it's hard to live in the past (Auschwitz) when the present (Syria) is horrible enough. Then, he tells me about his friend, getting groceries, walking on a Damascus street, murdered by a missile launched from somewhere outside the city. The talk of violence, the very intimacy of it, makes me want to lose my body, like I don't want to be in a body at the moment of hearing. But he tells me about his friend's passing and the needlessness of it. I remember a friend sharing with me that his sister had driven off a cliff into the Pacific. Cops found her washed up in the waves on a beach up Highway 1. He kept her ashes in his office at school. I wanted to ease his loss and bitterness. I thought he lived with her ghost. He felt he did not want to live. Are we not always living with ghosts? How does the near and distant past not haunt us? Can we live in the face of this haunting?

Who am I to talk to ghosts? To talk with those already haunted? Sometimes without speech, I am shaking, absent language. Sometimes writing feels unforgiveable in the face of atrocity. Levi calls homesickness a pain. Of his fellow deportees he writes, "We know where we come from; the memories of the world outside crowd our sleeping and our waking hours, we become aware, with amazement, that we have forgotten nothing, every memory evoked rises in front of us painfully clear."[135]

Leaving Syria, his family, coming alone to the United States, Aboudeh already knows something of homesickness. It is wiser to stay in the present than ask unanswerable questions of the past. His country is shredded by war. He does not know where people—teachers, friends, and neighbors—are, even if they are alive. He does not know when or if he can return. In part, the homesickness is longing, a need for what is known, to be among the familiar, to dwell in that which makes one recognizable to himself. It is language, culture, food, daily habits, created space, parents, especially when young, warmth, and safety. Home is equivalent with humanness. The migrant, unsettled, transitory, longing for roots is steeped in the absence of a home, searching for it in a place, a person, or perhaps moving constantly, frenetically, so as to forget absence and the persistent, nagging longing it brings.

There is little possibility of return. When one's family home is destroyed, country inhospitable and increasingly uninhabitable, one must make a home again—from Syria to Lebanon, from Poland to Israel. One must focus on attaining his education, delayed, changed, and fragmentary due to uprooting. One must create again a life. One may also return, someone new, a memory of his former self, to repair what has been damaged, if repair is possible. That is Aboudeh's intention. Of Syria, he has forgotten nothing and too much, all at the same time.

---

[135] Levi, *Survival*, 55.

We shared lunch before he headed to UCLA.[136] He was cautiously happy about his journey to the university. Again, he was leaving. It had taken him two years to settle into Santa Cruz, to build a community of friends and make a life. In that time, he had learned a fluent English, had attained the highest of grades, had earned two Associates degrees, and had determined his major at the university. But, he was departing—again—to a world that was entirely new and that he did not know. The struggle was to get his scholarship money for school, as the application process always requires records from previous schools. He does not have those. He repeatedly explains this to the administrators he encounters. My country is destroyed, my schools and the people who worked there probably do not exist, at least they are gone, dispersed, in exile. But the administrator cannot hear this. "The records are necessary," they say to the refugee of war. "Since I was a child, my father told me life was hard," he explains to me.

So, he knows. He does not expect an easy time of things; yet, the persistence and the fortitude to attain what he needs in order to sustain his education threaten to wear him down, even at twenty-one, especially at twenty-one. "Do you remember Auschwitz?" he says, recalling our summer class in which I taught Levi's first book. I do. "My country is an Auschwitz." People are entrapped within its boundaries, seeking passage out, many dying, surviving under the physical dangers and psychological traumas of war. One migrant child dead on the beach—that is one child. There are so many. Many we will never see or know—who are dying now, and now, and now. I sip my chai. Aboudeh eats his lunch. He's going to UCLA. That is one life, a new one, and there is another one—the one he should be living, if not for war, in his country, with his people. He does not allow feeling. He hardly talks to his family in Beirut. Feeling would be too much. For now, he says, he focuses on the tasks at hand.

---

[136] In June 2017, Aboudeh graduated from UCLA with highest honors in Biochemistry. My son and I attended his graduation as his parents were unable to travel to the United States due to "travel ban" restrictions placed on citizens from Iran, Libya, Somalia, Sudan, Syria, and Yemen entering the United States.

CHAPTER 2

Lives of a Writer

2.1 THE POET'S HOUSE

In college, studying in Florence, I fell asleep on my bed reading Henry James' *Portrait of a Lady* for a course on English writers in Italy. The serpentine sentences confounded rather than dazzled me. No one taught me to attend to where, when, and how I read—the times of the day and night I read or the spaces most conducive to reading. No one asked me to reflect on and describe my physical, mental, or emotional experiences of reading. There was a literate universe that I had not yet mined, rich with intersecting streams of knowledge acquisition, ignorance, will, and desire. I had no sense of how to approach a complicated text and sustain reading as I waded through a forest of dense ideas and complex sentences constructed of multiple and accumulating clauses.

A young child, I sought out meaning in the quiet spaces below bookshelves. There I would make a space in a dark corner, my legs curled under me, and leaf through books, absorbing their illustrations and reading their complex and dense text as much as I could. I gravitated to pictures, so much easier to read and more vivid than words. Mine was not a world of books. The bookshelves were spare in our house, not filled with novels and poems and essays. There were encyclopedias and volumes of illustrated Bible stories, from the Old Testament mostly, and *Reader's Digest* abridged novel collections. There was Roald Dahl's *James and the Giant Peach* and *Charlie and the Chocolate Factory*. James was orphaned, raised by two horrible aunts, loved by insects, and was living wildly inside a peach after the death of his aunts—by that very peach! Charlie was poor, and his four grandparents shared one bed, where they lay like sardines, head-to-toe. These were unfamiliar worlds and I was entranced, even stupefied by their difference.

As an English professor, I now study reading pedagogy to address reading challenges and surface reading strategies with my students. I recognize that students have often been assigned reading with the assumption that they could read difficult texts without any instruction in how to do so. At some point in my own development as a reader, I felt inept and fearful as I tried to engage longer texts, even complex shorter ones, and eventually realized through steady reading across genres and fields that I would have to teach myself to read well and thus build the confidence that good readers need to thrive and excel in a literary world. This process was slow and often painstaking, but with each year of dedicated reading and personal study—logging new words in journals, recording life changing passages from books, rereading a section until I learned to make sense of complex sentences or could garner the meaning from what we now call "context clues"—I taught myself to become a skilled reader.

My love of literature deepened when I studied for my Master's degree. It was 1995 in Chicago. This was the first time I considered that I had enough money and time to begin buying and building a collection of serious, even scholarly, books in earnest. It was also the first time I had enough knowledge of literature, literary and cultural theory, and philosophy to begin buying weighty books. These were for me extravagant purchases of vital books that cost upwards of fifteen and twenty dollars in the mid-1990s. I stood in the aisle at the newly opened Barnes and Noble on Clark Street in Chicago and pulled from the shelf *The Hélène Cixous Reader*.[137] Published by Routledge, the volume was heavy with slick pages, dense with content, and contained twenty essays by Cixous. The foreword had been authored by Jacques Derrida, whose work I did not know, but I did know that he was a philosopher, mentor to Cixous, French Algerian and Jewish, a poststructuralist. I was interested in philosophy, exposed to it mostly through philosophical literary writers, but had no background or introduction to the field to help me effectively decipher its thick abstractions; my reading of feminist thinkers and writers had led me here, and I was ready for whatever the volume contained. I knew it was heady.

In the aisles I touched the smooth glossy cover with a lovely photo of a very French-looking woman, her hair cropped short like a man's, her white shirt unbuttoned in a relaxed fashioned, her grin lined with pleasure. She looked in the middle of her life, happy, confident. This was her mind in these pages. I wanted it; I wanted to know what she thought about writing, particularly writing from and in a woman's body, and about politics of every kind—national, colonial, gendered identity. My partner was doing well financially, so I had time to write, read, and spend in bookstores selecting books, perusing them in the bookstore café, and writing titles and quotes in my journal. I recognized keenly the luxurious pace of my life, the manifold opportunities afforded by my situation. I felt hungry for knowledge, enamored of the new city, and gratitude for an avenue that had opened in my life— both by my own choices and dedication and by inherited benefits of position and place in society. I recognized the privilege of knowledge and the difficulty of acquiring space and time to accumulate, integrate, and produce knowledge. It would be a five-year period of my life where I would form a reader's identity for myself and begin to understand that becoming a thinker and a writer was a long-term project, much like construction of a building, solidifying and adding to the structure in sections and layers.

Somehow, perhaps through my graduate studies in the writing program, maybe in reading Simone de Beauvoir, I had happened upon knowledge of Merleau-Ponty's work.[138] My discovery of phenomenology satisfied in me a need to link thought with experience in the world. Merleau-Ponty privileged sensory experience as a vehicle of perception, and therefore of knowledge. He explored how knowing arises through sensing and happens in the condition of embodiment. I bought the book. The cashier exclaimed, "I haven't met anyone before you who reads his work!" Around me there was a quiet community of fellow readers and scholars. Once in a while we would

---

[137] Cixous, Routledge, 1994.
[138] Merleau-Ponty's *Phenomenology of Perception* was first published in 1945.

meet; delight and joy arose in our brief recognition of one another, in a temporal union of minds.

The relationship with the man in Chicago ended through a hard period of mental health issues. At thirty-seven I moved home to coastal California. A little over a year later, I travelled to the end of the South American continent to know Pablo Neruda's houses. I wanted to occupy the spaces that had been intimate to him, and to love the Chilean central coast and the cities—Santiago and Valparaíso—that had given him meaning and infused his poetry with land forms, ocean, a woman he loved, wine, socks—"beauty is twice/beauty/and what is good is doubly/good/when it's a matter of two/woolen socks/in winter, and onions—Onion/clear as a planet/and destined. To shine/constant constellation/ round rose of water/upon/the table/of the poor"—precious but ordinary things of everyday life.[139]

Literature allows the reader to experience through the mind of another a renewed way of knowing the world. It is a sensual experience with the writers that most move me. I experienced Neruda's poems, as I read *Twenty Love Poems and a Song of Despair* in my room in Hosteria La Candela, the foggy night swirling around the borders of my private space, the wind blowing, waves thumping the beach, my heart longing for my absent lover. But my lover at those moments was poetry, specifically the voice and energy of Neruda. It communed with me, and I with its lines and breaks and rhythms and visions and awakenings, more than any human. The largest love I would find in life would be in words, in intimacy with the writers whose minds I loved. Neruda's odes gave reality to feelings and the world pulsed with life in a river of words' caresses. I went to sleep with longing, the ghosts of Neruda's presence lingering in the Isla Negra night.

With poetry, things not imagined were suddenly possible. I was single, childless, momentarily in love. Soon I would meet him in Lima where I would also meet his family. But he refused my invitation to travel for two weeks in Chile. He did not know Chile, but he did not like Chile. "Chile and Peru have old animosities," he said, referring to a war between the two countries that had occurred in the mid-nineteenth century. I'd read to him poems from *The Heights of Machu Picchu*. He did not understand the poems; they did not hold any interest for him. I was alone in love and my need to seek language in the place a writer had lived and written. It was because of Chile and because of the poetry that infused my limbs, my heart, and my thoughts as I walked, ate, slept, and took in the sights that I wanted a child. I did not realize this is what I wanted. Lovers kissed on a bench, they held one another tightly, she sat on his lap. In Santiago people drank wine, ate small plates of food, and listened to jazz. The bar was dark, close, intimate. I sat with a couple from New Zealand who had invited me to eat and listen.

In Isla Negra at the inn, two children, Pablo and Caterina, also guests, whose parents had come to celebrate New Years' with their friends Hugo, a filmmaker, and Charo, a folksinger during Chile's politically tumultuous 1970s, the owners of La Candela, played cards by the fireplace and climbed rocks and collected shells on the

---

[139] Neruda, "Ode to My Socks" and "Ode to the Onion," in *Full Woman, Fleshly Apple, Hot Moon.*

beach with me. The boy told me he, too, was in love. He shared the girl's name and I shared the name of the man I would soon meet in Lima. He knew and liked Neruda's poems. "You share a name," I said.

I liked these children, noticed them in ways I had not noticed children before. Perhaps because I was alone with the poems, with my longing, in a culture of love and emotion, in a new land, my heart was vulnerable to life. Perhaps because an old life had just ended with the man-of-eight-years and I felt the loss of unity in possible marriage, the bungalow we had sold, and, now, the absence of the new man and the reading of poems alone, the child appeared as a possibility. Yet, he did so quietly. Never forcing the fact of his eventual appearance—within eleven months he would be born—but someone emerging of the poems, the odes, and the joy of living expressed in Neruda's praise and notice of small things. I contemplated for him the name Pablo; I decided instead on Elias, which had a strong cadence to it and seemed a name that would happily transcend national borders.

Literature is tied up in these life complications, these losses, and appearances. Writing, language, the craft involved in giving mind and heart to someone else in words has sent me packing to places in search of others' inner worlds. It is through narrative that I've known the world. It is through language I've come to love the world. I write my story through the stories of others—my child, Pablo Neruda, Primo Levi, Charlotte Delbo, Jean Améry, Poland, the history of a war, through violence and cruelty, love and forgiveness, through memory and the need to live a life through language. My life has run to writing. My heart pumps to the sounds of voices and thoughts that nourish my own. There are times I have read another's line and midway through felt the awe of awakening, the sliver of new insight, a unity merging consciousness with all life here and now.

The world will not be the same again since having read that line.

2.2 THE COURAGE TO WRITE

During my pregnancy I quit writing in my journal, a practice I had engaged in for some fifteen years. I felt angry with myself for wanting a child. I had worked so hard to create a life where I was a writer and thinker. I was independent, unmarried, and could come and go as I pleased. Yet, at thirty-nine an inner force had hit me hard. I wanted a child. With my lover at that time, I had become pregnant. Seemingly against my will, but I recognized that there had been a strong unconscious will. Something was pulling me toward the new life of parenting, of knowing and experiencing myself in relationship to and with a child. I was terrified. Only remotely did I think that over a lifetime I would now be responsible for another human being's life and well-being. I felt queasy, just having started my teaching career, trying to establish a stable income, living with my mother, and, suddenly, pregnant. Eighteen months earlier I had departed Chicago where I had lived with my partner of eight years. After the death of his father, he went through nearly two years of depression and maniac episodes coupled with insomnia and periods of anxiety bordering on paranoia and delusion. Our life had fallen apart, we had lost our house, and finally one day, exhausted, I told him I was moving back to California.

I returned home and lived with my mother while I decided what to do with my life. I knew I wanted to teach and had just begun to build a career teaching English and literature in the community colleges. I avoided writing. I was afraid, but also slowly accepting the new life ahead, my ego giving in to the desire to mother and nourish a life. However, the few times I wrote in my journal self-judgment emerged with force. I did not want to subject the pregnant self to that old, self-castigating voice. That self was like God, like father, like some inner man standing over me as my own personal judge. It even carried the tone of my mother who had herself not finished college, married young, raised children early in life, and wanted much more for her daughter than she had experienced.

A part of my subconscious had wanted a child. It was that part that I had listened to one evening in mid-February of 2003. In late November 2003 I embarked on the lifelong endeavor of mothering. I put my journal aside and waited out the pregnancy without writing. Perhaps I should have written. Might it have been a palliative? But I could not bear to reflect upon my condition in words. I did not know myself pregnant, nor did I want to. Native American writer Leslie Marmon Silko writes in her memoir *The Turquoise Ledge* of her refusal to log a difficult time. "I lost my mother on July 11 [2001], and two months later, I lost my country. I was not able to write about this period of my life for a long time, and then when I did, I chose to write fiction."[140] I regret my silence now. Yet, when I read Silko's confession of inability to write during a specific time, even her turn to another genre in which to express her grief, I recognize the power of events to determine our articulateness or muteness at any given time. This recognition is coupled with another: that the journal always reveals something about a time, no matter how hard it is to look—either in the moment or in retrospect. The writing I admire often represents a period when the writer struggled, when it was hard to look at events and respond to them steadily and with unflinching honesty. My capacity was limited then. Instead, I felt, watched, and listened to my body. In the evenings, hand on my belly to feel him move, I began to read to the baby within me, wanting him to hear and recognize my voice. I sat and meditated, chanting to Tibetan monks, centering my consciousness and lowering it from head to belly.

In the two years after Elias was born I began to write poems in earnest. They were mostly poems about the need to love and join with another as I raised my baby into a young child. I felt hungry for sex and intimacy. I wanted to share the demanding and joyous burden of raising a child with a beloved, someone who knew, heard, and understood me. It took me three or four years to drop the idea that I had to raise my child in the company and with the collaboration of a loving man. I learned how to raise him as cooperatively as possible with his father who would visit his son every other weekend and sometimes care for him at his apartment seventy-five miles from our home. Still, things were good. I had full custody and my mother was a second parent in the form of a strong grandmother. There were times I felt my bodily and psychic space constricted with the demands of a young child, and my mom's presence helped in providing me a measure of space and some quiet time for rest.

---

[140] Leslie Marmon Silko, *The Turquoise Ledge*, 99.

In one of the essays I wrote when Elias was an infant and toddler I explored the experience of hatred. At that time, I participated in Diamond Heart, a spiritual school with detailed and developed teachings developed on Buddhist contemplative practices and Western psychotherapeutic modes of inquiry. One of the main teachers, Hameed, who had studied physics at Berkeley and then studied extensively with Tibetan Buddhist teachers, taught that hatred, which is a frustrated desire that builds to anger and sometimes rage, lives within each one of us and rises up with strength in moments of desperation. Hatred includes self-hatred as well as hatred of another as an object that stands in our way and blocks our desire. He did not use the word "desperation" to describe hatred, but thinking about the constraints I felt during that time desperation captures a truth of my experience. It was not so much depression and despair as rage that arose in those days, a sort of edgy panic that bordered on angry outbursts laced with the toxic residue of needing to clear everyone and everything out of my space. I was angry that I had lost the life I had created for myself: the life of a writer, reader, creative person, and independent woman thinker. I felt this life particularly rare and precious given that my mother had not fully achieved it and had encouraged me from my teens and twenties to seek out education and create my own path in the world. It followed I was then angered by the frustrating and sometimes lonely parameters of caretaking for an infant; the life was one of constant tending and cleaning—pumping milking before work at 5:00 in the morning, holding my child down so I could change his diapers while he wrestled and struggled against me (I learned quickly that if I waited for two to five minutes, it would not be such a struggle), scrubbing soiled diapers, scraping from the floor petrified peas and hotdog pieces that had rolled under the refrigerator, washing baby dishes, bibs, sheets, and clothes. My hands were raw and red. My mother talked to me, wanting my companionship and attention, the old relational bond we had once shared. But it was no longer possible. At the same time, my child was crying or fussy, sometimes calling out. He needed me. I wanted to write or even read a sentence in a book and I could not. (Though over time a first sentence grew to two, then a paragraph, and, after a few years I could absorb whole books. I felt my world changed but partially restored. I wrote poems at the bathtub while he splashed and played.) I missed raising my child with a lover, that fathers were helping to raise their children and in an intimate love relation at the same time, that parenting could be shared and wanted as a couple, that if I had an equal partner to share childrearing burdens then I could pick up a pizza while he stayed with our child. Then, I was angry, at the choices I had made: to raise a child as a single parent, to give up my writing and thinking life for childrearing, that I lived with my mother, that I was just developing my career and had limited financial resources.

It was the life I had worked hard to make for myself, the life of quiet mornings drinking coffee on the patio and writing in a notebook, a novel or memoir at-hand, of evening writing groups and salons—of ten to twenty students—that I facilitated at libraries, retreat centers, and in my home. It was winter mornings in my office, bookshelves just behind my swivel chair, looking out over a blanket of crisp glistening snow that covered what in Evanston's early summer would be our bright green lawn. It was the memory of the whole quiet bungalow and time stretching in a day before me when my partner had taken the train into the city for his workday. This life, I knew, represented the idea of the room of one's own that Virginia Woolf had counseled for women in her book of that title. This was the life of the free mind, the creative experimentation, and the psychic exploration that Anaïs Nin had modeled and urged for other women in her diaries and novels. I had heeded the intellectual reasoning and poetic warnings in Adrienne Rich's essays where she had related her harrowing work to find herself as poet, thinker, and activist outside the institutions of motherhood and marriage.[141] I intended to be part of that four percent of women who for whatever reason had not given birth to a child. The ninety-six percent would make their choices for whatever life they wanted, while I chose to create something outside of motherhood's imposition, which was yet another social and economic limitation under which women suffered. Most of the world had given away that life of the room, the creativity or freedom to choose, or had little means to make it. I had the opportunity, the space and time to create a life where I could write and teach. How would raising a child take away that life and its opportunities from me? That question was more rhetorical than anything else. I knew the answer and lived in fear of the possibility that I could in a moment lose all that I had worked to establish for myself as a woman.

Now the lovers were gone. I had chosen to be alone. There was the life not with a lover but living with my mother, with whom I had lived several times over the years of my adult life. My notions of a sustainable, interactive love relationship had dissipated. The real work of being present to myself, steady in my goals and desires, and raising a child and attending to his needs became my most immediate life projects. It wasn't that my reading went out the window—I still heard Woolf, Nin, and Rich. I just had to figure out how to steady my emotions, get some sleep, and slowly bring writing and reading back into my life. For the time being my choices would be limited by the situations and endeavors I had chosen, among them, however ironically, motherhood.

Most of the time I repressed my anger, its antisocial nature, and the simmering undercurrents of psychic and physical space constraints that made me roar and sob with frustration. When the desperate feeling arose, I sought out a quiet corner away from the social interactions of the house and spent a moment or two deep breathing, centering myself, letting go any irritant that had inadvertently become enflamed. But sometimes I erupted. One time I fled from the house crying and drove to a road edged by a flower farm. I parked under enormous pine trees and sobbed, tears merging with a blurry purple field of heather. Another time, I threw pillows at the Buddhist altar I had arranged on a bookshelf across from my bed. There were candles, postcards of Buddhist deities and American poets, prayers beads and soft remains of burnt incense. The pillows hit the statue of Tara, Tibetan goddess of compassion. She remained steady, a slight smile on her lips. Perhaps a candle fell and broke, and some of the stones and the incense fell to the floor. Energy wound up inside sought release. Running away, crying, throwing, yelling were not necessarily mature behaviors but were forceful ways of handling energy and channeling hatred into less destructive and

---

[141] See Adrienne Rich, *Of Woman Born*, 1977.

caustic paths. As my child grew, space opened up. I felt life return and some of the intense focus on him, his needs, his movements every second, loosened. I learned how to better manage competing conversations when my mother and my child were both talking to me and I had to tell one to wait—usually my mother—while I attended to the other. My head would spin. I would lie down at night or for a short nap while my child slept. The world pressed darkly against my eyelids.

With time other avenues opened to me. It was 2008 and I returned to school when my son was nearly five to begin doctoral work. After three years of coursework and another three of writing the dissertation, the degree was conferred. I had, with my mother's help, finished my dissertation while teaching and parenting. I felt newly capable. The committee approved the manuscript, and I sent it off to be published and listed with a database service. I felt entirely done with it, for the time being. The dissertation focused on women writing memoirs to further their political causes and to bring awareness and change to intolerable situations—the war in Afghanistan and government corruption and foreign occupation, child prostitution in Cambodia, and the war in Somalia and the struggles of young women to thrive in conservative Muslim countries full of social and political strife.[142] I wanted to know how women world-over utilized the forms of autobiography to make their lives and struggles real and known to a global public. How were women who had been in disadvantaged positions in their societies using memoir as a forum for argument, and, more importantly, what were they saying? By what channels did they gain access to the power and privilege of publishing and the production of memoir into the global marketplace? What leaps did they have to perform? I was, and remain, interested in these personal stories, increasingly common in the West through the global publishing industry, as valuable, urgent, and complicated statements of ethics and as a wakeup call to social change and political action. Such study also stemmed for me from preliminary research on how writers use writing to work through and confront trauma. In much less difficult circumstances, writing had helped me to know myself and to navigate difficult periods in life. Now, I turned to woman working in all parts of the planet who had turned to writing to express and share their personal and political struggles.

The three women activists whose memoirs I studied had put their lives at risk by acting and speaking publicly against violence and injustice. As I engaged their personal narratives, I marveled at their courage to step into public view and to risk their privacy, their families, and their safety in a commitment to global activist work and publication of their memoirs. There were many things at risk for each woman. Yet, through a three-year engagement with their writing, I heard them telling their readers that they fought against the very invisibility and quietness that I, a woman who has lived in the Western hemisphere her entire life, have prized. I heard Somaly Mam saying, "my safety did not come in invisibility and separateness. In fact, those

---

[142] In *Speaking from Memory: Writing and Reading Women Activist Memoirs* I explore three contemporary memoirs—Somaly Mam's *The Road of Lost Innocence* (2008), Ayaan Hirsi Ali's *Infidel* (2007), and Malalai Joya's *A Woman Among Warlords* (2009)—as testimonies that influence public space in their call for collective response.

things imprisoned me. Those things were the very impetus for my activism. Women and girls in prostitution in Cambodia are entrapped, isolated, and silenced. I have fought against those situations. I have fought for girls to be noticed and for their needs to be attended to and addressed." Their public presence as activists and writers meant they would no longer be their own people—not that these women ever felt their lives were their own—but public spokeswomen for certain viewpoints and actions. People would hate them, to the point of trying to hurt and kill them. Other people would revere them, and want to reward and elevate them to the position of heroines. Courage would make them more than human. But, for them, courage would make them fully human. They would feel themselves as distinct and unique beings through their courage. They had to seek out like-minded others who supported their ideas and their work. There were only a few people, maybe just one person from time to time, they could trust. They would become public figures, public property. Readers, reporters, news agencies, organizations, politicians, activists would feel they knew and possessed them. Sometimes parents or trusted others would try to punish, ostracize, and silence them. Each of these women had moments of feeling entirely alone and isolated. Their distinct lives would become void, except to substantiate and dramatize their stories. People would check them for error. People would want to find fault in them, their presentation of self in the world, their words.

Their photos, larger than life, spilled across the covers of their books. Those images appeared under dramatic titles—*The Road of Lost Innocence*, *Infidel*, *A Woman Among Warlords*, titles determined by Western editors and publishers to attract readers through sensational words and tantalizing narrative promises, implying, a gendered drama—a girl loses her innocence, a young woman is unfaithful, a woman advocates for change among violent men. These women chose publicity. They chose to enter, however willingly, usually at the suggestion of a journalist who perceived the outlines of an intriguing and, probably, marketable story, the public life. They became objects of activism, particularly alluring in that they were from countries where women had struggled for recognition, rights, and social and political power, sometimes at a high cost to their personal lives.

They became subject to public scrutiny, to public disfavor, and sometimes to abandonment by the very journalists who had propositioned them for their stories. In 2014 Somaly Mam's story in *The Road of Lost Innocence* was questioned and disproved in certain—still unsubstantiated—aspects by a *Newsweek* reporter. Journalist Nicholas Kristof, had authored the preface to her memoir and written glowingly and with great care about her work and her person in books, in a documentary film, and in *The New York Times* opinion pages. However, in the aftermath of the *Newsweek* story he was initially silent and then questioning and ambiguous about her truthfulness.[143] He had been a friend, supporter, and colleague of

---

[143] See Simon Mark's cover story in *Newsweek*, "The Holy Saint (and Sinner) of Sex Trafficking," 21 May 2014. See also Nicholas Kristof, "When Sources May Have Lied," *The New York Times*, 7 Jun. 2014. Mam lives in Cambodia; she has also lived and worked in France and has traveled worldwide in her work for AFESIP (Acting for Women in Distressing Situations) and the Somaly Mam Foundation (SMF), the

Mam's. Yet, after the *Newsweek* report, he said Mam was not someone he had known well but rather someone he had mistakenly trusted. I stopped reading his reportage and lost a foundational trust in his work and viewpoints. He had failed in his due diligence, failed to stand by a friend, and failed to clearly and with conviction articulate his views through a charge of deceptive storytelling. Could he not have elucidated his own experience in relating with Mam and investigating the facts of her story? He writes about other issues in Asia, and Africa, with compassion and a call to action, but I no longer trust his reportage. When will he fail to support, even turn against, the next woman, the next friend who needs him through difficulty? When will he risk vulnerability and public criticism to confront and address charges of inauthenticity and even lying placed on his friend Somaly Mam, whom after the exposé he called an "acquaintance"? If she had fabricated details of her past to make her story more dramatic and interesting for global audiences, could they have brought forward together the reasons she felt compelled to invent and embroider a story? Such investigative and exploratory journalism might tell us something about the dangers of needing to create story to "sell" a movement for social change.

In studying the works and lives of those women activists, I found myself asking if in writing I wanted to expose my inner life. Because that, I have felt, is what good writers do. I feel that I know certain writers—Primo Levi, Terry Tempest Williams, Leslie Marmon Silko, for example—because I so gravitate to and admire their writings.[144] Yet, I've never personally met or talked with any of them. Writing, and the printing and publishing technologies that accompany it as forms of distribution, is a kind of modern miracle: a way of drawing near through the ages of loneliness.

How does our personal story reflect what we believe in? How does it evidence what we want to believe in? How does that belief struggle to find its way into practice? Psychoanalyst and scholar Jessica Benjamin asks, how do we begin to believe that our actions, if we act in concert, can make change?[145] We don't really believe that, she says, and consequently we often fail to act. There is not a foundation of love or goodness that allows for us to act from our hearts. However, Benjamin asserts that such a response to the world develops as we continue to act, visualize, and create it. The activists I studied manifest that idea: that what we want, what we work towards, no matter how others try to disrupt and discourage our efforts, can materialize, and can make waves of influence that stir movement to change. Even if we don't know that what we are doing will have any impact, we still have to act from what matters to us, from our hearts and our own personal ethics.

---

funding arm of the organization in the United States. Mam resigned and SMF was dissolved in October 2014. A new organization, Together1Heart, was then formed.

[144] Williams is a memoirist and essayist. She writes of her native Southwest, primarily focusing on human relationship with nature and the land, as well as the value of family, community, and place. She is author of *Refuge, Leap, The Open Space of Democracy*, and *When Women Were Birds*, among many other books. Silko is a Native American novelist and essayist who grew up on the Laguna Pueblo in New Mexico and currently lives and writes in Tucson, Arizona.

[145] Interview with Jessica Benjamin in "The Changing Face of Feminist Psychology," a project of Psychology's Feminist Voices, 2014.

Where there is negativity and intrigue and conflict, it often trumps love and collaboration. Yet, it is possible to live life in resistance to these truths of power and pain; otherwise, the spirit would not survive. Dread, nihilism, and despair would conquer life. The women activists whose writing I studied have acted as if they believed that actions and values could change things. Such behavior constitutes an enormous risk, and for these women that risk has been physical, mental, social, and political. A successful autobiography guarantees nothing. The women on whose work I wrote my dissertation still exist at the edges of institutionalized power. They have frequently been ostracized and relegated to silence; yet, they are fighters and I don't think any of them will disappear so easily. Maybe that's what their speaking means— not so much what they are saying, but how they are saying it and that they are speaking anything at all.

2.3 WHO I WILL BECOME

Attending an academic conference in Vancouver, Canada a few months after my travels to Poland, I take some time away from panels and seminars. I sit on a stool at a café bar facing a side street and reading *The Globe and Mail*. Writer Eve Joseph narrates how a stroke has changed her way of living in the world. She suggests that gratitude and grief are languid and accepting.

> In my first month's post-stroke, I ricocheted between anxiety and gratitude; between feeling vulnerable and mortal and experiencing an intense awareness of what it was to be alive. Gratitude has a languid quality not dissimilar to grief. I felt like a traveller arriving in a new city—even the ordinary looked extraordinary. It wasn't that things were suddenly infused with a new radiance but that my gaze—wherever it happened to fall lingered longer. 'Now I am ready to tell how bodies are changed into different bodies,' wrote Ovid in *The Metamorphoses*. I have been altered—no longer exactly sure who I was but not yet sure who I will become.[146]

Joseph's writing inspires me to write my own early memories of a family trip to Vancouver when I was nineteen. Who was I then, and who had I become? How was Vancouver, this city on the water shrouded in a bay of fog, different for me now and then? I finish Joseph's article and complete the last lines of my poem. I close my journal and walk to Vancouver Art Gallery.

What most captures my gaze is Emily Carr's self-portrait from the middle years of the 1920s. She reveals the back of her head, her arm, brush in hand, shoulders, the blue top of a chair in which she sits, the canvas, and palette of paints. The curator's plaque describes a possible sense of isolation, particularly as a woman painter in a

---

[146] Joseph, *The Globe and Mail*, 9 Jan. 2015. Eve Joseph is a Canadian writer and poet from British Columbia. Her book on her experience of recovery after stroke is entitled *In the Slender Margin: The Intimate Strangeness of Death and Dying*.

field dominated by men. I perceive her world in that picture sheltered and closed, reflecting intimacy between brain, heart, and canvas. The viewer stands outside. Carr allows me to view that intimacy, to sense and perhaps know it, if I want to, but just in case I reject or misapprehend it, she keeps me at a distance. It is only from my own experience—as an artist, a woman, a female in relationship to males—that I understand. "Look," she says, "love me and understand," or "Hate me and go away. I keep you out anyway." She invites and rejects. I so deeply know this predicament that also contains a generous rationality. If we enter that space, we enter Carr's home space. She checks us discreetly at the door.

Carr was born in 1871 on Canada's Pacific Northwest Coast on Victoria Island. She found her style in relationship with Canada's native, or First Nation, peoples and in physical time on the land, the wooded spaces and mountains of the coast. She stopped or slowed painting from 1913 to 1927, from ages forty-two to fifty-six. Discouraged after a failed project when she had hoped the province of British Columbia would purchase her documentary paintings of First Nations peoples but did not, she found other ways to make a living. The middle period. The doldrums. The life half-lived, coming ever closer to death. Struggling to survive financially. Taking in renters, breeding dogs. Painting, the space, the materials, the demands put aside and returned to in later years. She produced much of her artistic work at the end of the 1920s and into the 1930s. She was in her late fifties, then her sixties. As she began to paint again, emerging from a period of fourteen years away from art, she was no longer certain of who she was but not yet sure who she would become.

2.4 VANCOUVER

At the bottom of mountains

snow-capped, ocean-towering

the bay Coal Harbour

Vancouver cold and opaque

below.

Memory returns now: Tahoe's lake, blue jewel

in my mind, of my childhood, to the Vancouver

of my young womanhood. Times when my parents

were married, long ago, times of thick snow,

toboggans, high mountains, copper lakes, and

domed trains sliding quietly through Canadian Rockies.

Forty years, thirty, remote and present

quickly gone lingering in my body.

Permanent grief has taken up residence

loss a lived reality,

gratitude a vast quality

I can write.

Yet, this intemperance

developed of long association

with trauma and violence

years of reading watching listening

vicarious, yet lived engaged

ever present

in Poland, in stories, with students

in loss of former lives,

in daily existence with the dead.

Aging, beautiful difficult body

beloved

disintegrating body.

Wine, dance, music,

literature, love,

time,

space, food,

speech, silence—these things

make a life.

2.5 OUTSIDE OF WRITING

Each person needs something to love. Emily Carr had painting; Primo Levi had chemistry. Rebecca Goldstein is a philosopher, as was Simone de Beauvoir—both writers who turned to writing novels and other creative works infused with philosophy. Writing has been the way I've created meaning and work for myself. I am a teacher because I write. I'm in good company. There is Annie Dillard and Alice Walker. There's Anaïs Nin and Virginia Woolf. There is George Orwell and Henry Miller and Zbigniew Herbert and James Baldwin. These are people who have lived for writing and written to live. These are the artists. They are committed to writing. Many of them also taught. Yet, the entirety of their lives were, and are, dedicated to writing—to seeing, living, and thinking like writers.

Levi moved more and more into the writer's life and the space it requires. He would have become a physicist. But there was the war and the lack of space and the race laws. He was unable to follow that trail of study. He picked chemistry, more practical, easier to attain to in those hard times of condensed spaces and limited choices. He worked in a paint factory after the war and through his life. As he aged, he wrote more and more frequently. The paint factory was secondary, pushed to a place of decreasing significance through his life as he wrote, eventually retired, and won recognition and fame for his writing. He was more a writer, because he was a thinker, than anything else. It is the same for the writers whose names I've included here. They came into the world to be thinkers, to live thinking and to reveal their relationship with the world on the page, in printed word.

Writing is the expression of living. It becomes the poem of seeing, of senses, of embodiment in the world—never apart from it but shot through with its worldliness. Writing is metaphysics too, the feelings, the intuitions, the senses of things, the world of metacognition, knowing about knowing, and delving into that awareness of what it is to be a knowing being. Because we see, feel, sense, and know we must write. There are these secondary things: chemist, director, teacher, politician, activist, poet, philosopher—but the central thing here, the drive to live, is writing. Our job titles capture the basic thrust of activity. Contained in those nouns is writing. The central reason these other jobs exist for the writer is to support and to make a way for her writing in the world. For me, it's teaching. I enjoy teaching, creating courses, working with students in developing their thoughts and refining their writing techniques. However, the moments when I feel most energized are when I write. Even the tiredness after an arduous writing session is good because I've done what I loved— I've engaged in the activity (giving written form to thinking) that most fulfills me and has become my purpose in the world.

Writing allows me to be curious about the world, to question it, to query and look closely at the actions we take and the human moments we have in relation, in response to, and because of those actions. How is it that we know ourselves? How is it that we float amidst the chaos of our actions, confused, isolated and then, suddenly, we find one another—one or two others, a whole group of us—with whom we have encounters and for whom those encounters can change our outlook, our actions, our understandings? Even then, we must start all over again, constantly. The starting happens over and over through the day, all over the planet. We wound, we kill, and then we suffer, and we forgive, or we die, or we embrace. We find our ways, and, oftentimes, we do not, and the starting does not come. The starting becomes an end.

2.6 HER CAMERA AS WEAPON

Julia Pirotte's self-portrait, taken in 1942, moves me. I return often to her sad reflectiveness, the camera there as her eye, an eye that both protects her from and opens her to the world. She is already vulnerable, quietly internal, and, simultaneously, so entirely immersed in and made of and by the world. This is during the war. She has seen so much, maybe too much, more than a human should see. Should we be forced to look? Now an inner refrain, Charlotte Delbo's words haunt me: look, just try to see. It's impossible, truly impossible to look. Yet, Julia trains her camera. She trains it on herself. She cannot look directly into the mirror. The camera is her eye. It becomes her way of seeing, meditated through technology, imprinted like a tattoo, the image, the moment of life on her eye. She chose photography, or it chose her. She shows herself not seeing, not seeing the self in the mirror, with an inward focus, away from direct contact with the camera, catching herself in relationship with the past and its haunting of the present. Hers is an indirect gaze. The focus of her portrait the edge of mirror, hands, camera, even apron, scarf, collar. For me, she embodies how one sensitively approaches devastation—never directly and with great care, fully aware that devastation is much greater than her single being, beyond her full capacity of witnessing or understanding, and that if faced can swallow her whole. As the book mediates devastation for the writer, so the camera mediates for Pirotte the photographer. She wrote in an essay, "I like sadness: it's more photogenic than joy."[147] She knows sadness more than joy; it's strangely familiar to her. Sadness has devoured her face. She has become her own most beautiful photograph.

She lost her brother to typhus in a Gulag camp, her sister was guillotined by Gestapo in Breslau (1944), her father and stepmother were murdered in death camps, and her first husband, mobilized in the war, she never again saw. Her mother had died when Julia was nine. She came from a small town in Poland called Końskowola. In post-war Poland she formed the WAF, the Military Photographic Agency. She was sent by the agency to document the Kielce pogrom in July 1946. Many of her photos of that event the Polish police confiscated and destroyed. There are some remaining. I have a collection of these photos in *Faces and Hands*, as well as in Jan Gross's book, *Fear*, where I first discovered Pirotte's photos in the interleaves of the book and felt compelled by this Polish-Jewish woman's documentation.[148] She called the camera a potential weapon—as she learned when she used it in the wrong circumstances and others, also in the midst of war, felt threatened and exposed by the camera's eye. After that, she turned it into an "instrument of struggle." In 1934 she had left Poland for Brussels. She was a Communist, involved in worker issues, photographing strikes, working for small news agencies, an active member of the Resistance in Brussels, in France, and, later, in Poland. Three decades after the war when she visited her former Polish village, she saw her house but did not knock. She recognized the climate that had developed through and after the war towards Jews, their families mostly dead, their properties confiscated and sometimes occupied by Polish families. She had remembered the violence to her camera. What was once was no longer. Julia lived with that loss, cloaked in grief.

I do not think of writing as my weapon. I do not struggle in the way that Julia did. I was born into relative tranquility in my immediate childhood world, though in 1963 the world raged around me. Things happened in 1963, as they will in any year: the first woman went into space, a Russian; James Meredith was the first black American to graduate from University of Mississippi; in Saigon, the self-immolation of Buddhist monks in protest of the persecution of Buddhists by the South Vietnamese government, followed by a coup d'état later that year; the March on Washington; Nigeria became a republic; C.S. Lewis died; zip codes were introduced; the first push button telephone appeared in American homes; Kenya gained independence; the assassination of President John Kennedy; the release of The Beatles' "I Wanna Hold Your Hand." I was born, the first of two children, the only girl, to white, middle class parents, both from modest backgrounds. I arrived home from the hospital into a duplex, but within a few years lived in upwardly mobile suburban neighborhoods in detached houses with large lawns and trees, neighborhoods for the most part lacking in diversity of people and cultures. In that 1970s milieu, it was socially assumed everyone was the same because of shared economic status and geographic location.

My father was familiar with poverty, frequent migration and dislocation, abuse in the house, and his father's alcoholism. He worked diligently to give me something

---

[147] Krystyna Dabrowska's essay appears in the Jewish Historical Institute's (Warsaw) exhibition catalogue entitled *Julia Pirotte: Faces and Hands*, in Polish, *Twarze i dłonie*.
[148] Gross, *Fear: Anti-Semitism in Poland After Auschwitz*, 2006.

safe and sure. He succeeded, and, yet, I lost things because of his diligence. Mine was a world where secrets lurked just outside the front doors, of not knowing that many things existed. Shards of suffering, war, injustice entered my house through television and radio news, images in the background, distant voices and sounds that hinted at unrest and suffering. Yet, I wanted to know. I could see and feel things. No conversations in our home, our family addressed these events. There were things to which I wanted proximity, but I had no knowledge of the route, or how to even begin the movement towards them.

Julia Pirotte (née Diament). Self-portrait, Marseille, 1942.
Source: Wikimedia Commons, Public Domain, 2009

Every museum exhibit of war and Jewish history in Poland comes from those people who donated items and collections. Things were destroyed in Poland in the wars, disappeared, taken, and disappeared even further through the years of communism. What remains, the collections of historical documents, maps, photos at historical institutes, the various small museums in former synagogues, has been assembled and opened to the public painstakingly and after much work of collection, personal donation, and time passed where history comes to meet the present. Poland has begun in the past twenty years, and with increasing focus over the past decade, to claim and create a history disallowed under communism. The work of historical institutes is often retrospective in character. Whereas the work of museums, such as the Warsaw Uprising Museum, opened in 2004, is technologically interactive and experiential in character. For Pirotte, there was a box: press clippings, photos, folk songs in Yiddish, poems by Jewish poets in Polish translations (all of them about the Holocaust)— "carefully selected and something about you you'd rather not disclose. Besides her photographs, this folder with poems is the most personal testimony [she] left behind," writes curator and historican Krystyna Dabrowska in *Julia Pirotte: Faces and Hands*, in Polish, *Twarze i dłonie*.[149]

"Why are you interested in Pirotte?" our guide Maciek inquires of me. I hear myself saying, "She is a woman and a photographer. I feel compelled by her work." Still, I'm unsure how I'm drawn to her during my time in Poland, just that I am. She has stories to tell through her work, hidden behind her photos, and I want to know. I also know I'm drawn to women who have come before me and who have created with risk in the world. Julia is a spirit I want to follow and her photos that I first encountered in *Fear* drew me into her world, the world she knew having been born Jewish in Poland in 1908. She was after all in Kielce on the heels of a pogrom in 1946 when Jews were cautiously returning to Poland from the Russia and the Ukraine en route to somewhere else, mostly Israel and the United States. She was in Kielce at the Jewish Committee building on 7 Planty Street.[150] She was sent from Warsaw as a photographer to record the aftermath of events by the chief editor of *Zołnierz Polski*. She was in that apartment building, accompanied by a bodyguard, herself a Jewish woman originally from Poland, taking photos, placing her body in the midst of murder, thinking not of herself but of the necessary documentation to tell the world beyond Kielce, beyond Poland, of the murder of Jews as they returned to Poland in the dangerous period immediately after the war.[151] I go looking for photographs by Pirotte because she was a woman who took chances with her camera, compelled by something larger than herself. I want to see what and who spoke to her and who she was through and behind her camera.

A direct gaze is too much. Too much gets revealed and she had to shelter things within herself not only because she was Jewish and Polish in the early and mid-twentieth century but also because she had seen the direct violence of the world inflicted on the subjects of her photographs. And, the subjects of our photographs are always ourselves, if we consider that we are everyone and no one all at the same time. When we look out and gaze at the world we risk losing some of ourselves. If you have lived here for a while and/or experienced trauma firsthand or second-handedly, or both, you know that the world—the others in it who do not have your best intentions at heart—will take from you. So, the downturned gaze is one way to avert malintent and to save something inside. You want your art or your writing to express for you. The eyes become their own kind of sketch or painting or book or poem. They speak and echo and project and contain great pools of experience and dark caves of emotion. We therefore protect our eyes.

I'm seeking, looking, listening, attentive and attuned. I'm quiet in the hallways of museums. I want introspection, space, and solitude and, so, find myself alone as often as possible in Poland. The late afternoons stretch toward evenings. In small spaces I

---

[149] *Julia Pirotte: Faces and Hands*.
[150] Jan Gross in *Fear* details the events of the Kielce Pogrom on July 4, 1946. There were at least forty-two dead and over forty wounded on that day in Kielce. The anti-Jewish mob began killing at the Jewish Committee's building at 7 Planty Street. Random acts of violence against Jews living in Kielce at that time, many of them Holocaust survivors, spread and continued throughout the day.
[151] *Julia Pirotte: Faces and Hands*.

enter into other times and places that suddenly exist here now. Those places with attention and stillness return quietly in pieces, never whole. Lives, histories, tracings are all around me. I look for them and stay with them for a while. They linger, penetrate, and change me, when and where they find me. This is mystery. This is how body denies the parameters of time and space. This is how consciousness finds another world in the work of a woman.

2.7 ONE BOX

What would it mean to have a box? To whittle one's possessions down to their essence, to leave a single trace in the form of a box whatever its contents? Through the early years of adulthood, through my thirties, my mother required me to clean my closets and to rid our home spaces of my stuff—yearbooks, photos from dances, camps, and pool parties, a Bible from my high school years, underlined and annotated, first teeth, a locket of hair, a cedar box in the shape of a semicircle that my grandfather made for my mother when she was a child. There was an ivory box lined with crushed red velvet containing playing cards my mother had had as a child. Things that had been mine and things passed down to me—keepsakes, mementos, artifacts, both from my childhood and my mother's, pieces of her childhood now mine for the keeping.

I was thirty-one and moving to Chicago. Among other things, I threw away yearbooks, high school photos, and the Bible, dropping them into a dark green garbage bag. The Bible meant little to me. I felt no contrition. My act was one of absolution. I paged through it, paused, read the inscription—a gift from my parents at Easter, 1980 my sophomore year of high school, and then placed it in the bag. I was cleaning, but, too, I was erasing the personal inscriptions of religion—my family's particular strain, evangelical Christianity. I wanted to forget high school. I had feelings of wanting to break out, to leave the affluent suburb where my parents had bought a house in the hills. I was dissatisfied with the Baptist church in which I had been raised, led by male pastors who told their congregational how to live and think. Yes, it was beautiful. But that kind of beauty came with the cost of insularity.

The photos did not matter. I ridded myself of yearbooks, their volumes of individual class photos and football games and popularity contests. Yet, tenaciously, I kept the photos of Europe, the years in Italy (1984, 1985, 1986), the images of my lover, Michele, the wet streets of Florence, of my two roommates with our student friends, cooking in the sparse kitchen and dining together in the cold *sala*. The photos helped me to recall the physical feeling of Italian space—marble, tile, wood, fluorescent lights, and high ceilings, neighbors walking overhead, their lives made auditory in arguing, peeing, flushing, and snoring, the morning roar of Vespa at the curb—the press of life in Italy. Now, I had the quiet accumulation of life in California and an increasingly empty closet. I moved to Chicago and my mother moved three months later to a small condominium blocks from the Pacific Ocean. The end of the family home had come—my father remarried, my mother left our home to begin a life of her own, and then for her a succession of small rental spaces, travel, and finally a house by the beach.

By 2015 the boxes had been reduced to two and were stacked in the corner of my room. Two plastic bins packed with journals, the European photos, photobooks from the years in Chicago where I had lived with John. The journals stopped in when I left Chicago for California, and then had met and dated a man and became pregnant with my son. I was momentarily stunned into silence by the life ahead and the gravity of my half-conscious decision to have a child.

Annie Darwin died at the age of ten in the spring of 1851. She had a fever and Randal Keynes, great-great-grandson of Charles Darwin, writes that she left a single box, a brown leather writing case, containing items that reflected her young self, tracks of the life she had lived.[152] There were stationary papers, stamps, and fountain pens. How difficult to lose a child first? Keynes writes of the box that Annie's mother, Emma Darwin, kept it in a drawer for the forty-five remaining years of her life. She took it out and fingered its contents, but once Emma died the writing case was largely forgotten in its drawer. It is now on public display at Downs House, the former Darwin family house in Kent. In a glass case resides the writing case and its tiny implements that allowed Annie to imprint life to paper.

What do I want to leave when I die? I have left the journals to my mother's care, my mother who is now seventy-five. Who will care for my journals when my mother and I have both died? Those journals may be for my son. He may be a writer. Or, perhaps I will burn them. They chart a portion of my single life, a not exemplary life. They are not writings to be discovered and published posthumously, as were Franz Kafka's by his friend Max Brod. The photos? Those are fine and good. But, perhaps I should explain them to my son and eliminate the ones that do not have vivid meaning, the landscapes I do not remember, that I cannot locate. A feather, the petal of a flower, a rock, shell, or leaf. These things my son can find in the world. What I have collected, what moved me in the moment of encounter may not move him. He will have his own discoveries.

There are files, too, full of letters and manuscripts, typewritten poems, journals, and essays. Files from courses taken, graduate work, astrology readings, letters from my dear poet friend, Mary Ann, in Massachusetts. I will tell my son to toss these things, or tell my mother to recycle or burn them in a ceremony of my life. Perhaps she should return the letters and packages of poems and news articles to Mary Ann, the one friend with whom I've shared nearly all my poems. Keep my poems, the ones I wrote when Elias was young and I was sometimes lonely, in love with the new growing boy in my life and hungry for the passion of a man. They are my poems of desire and the beginning of a new life with a very young child, my heat, the poems of early motherhood. Burn the poems with me. Cremate the poems, for they are the cellular reflection of who I've been and who I was once becoming. Burn me with that struggle, burn me with the aching heart, burn me with the newness of life and the fear of losing the old, burn me with the poems of desire.

---

[152] Keynes, *Annie's Box: Darwin, His Daughter, and Human Evolution*, 2002.

2.8 A LIFE IN BOOKS

My mother and I share a house where we have raised my son in the nearly twelve years since his birth. This late morning, we are in separate rooms—she in her den, I in my large room which doubles as a bedroom and office—cleaning our bookshelves—dusting, going through each of our collections, rearranging books, and putting some in boxes to trade later this week at Logos, a used bookstore in Santa Cruz. I'm careful which books I choose to give away. I've done this several times, perhaps many, over the years and have not infrequently given away too many books. Later I had looked for certain volumes and could not find them. I had either loaned or traded them and they were now gone. I caution my mother of this tendency when I enter her den and see the accumulation of books on the floor. She has a dust rag in her hand and she looks delightfully happy sitting on the Afghan rug under sun pouring through the skylight. She offers me some books on the Second World War, especially on Poland and on the Holocaust.

I've just created a shelf dedicated to these subjects in my room, made of books that I'm using in the project to write a memoir of my travels to Poland. The shelf vibrates with energy: most of my Primo Levi books are here, as are the writings by and about Hannah Arendt. There are books from the Auschwitz Jewish Fellows program: *The Jewish Book of Why* by Alfred Kolatch and *Fear* by Jan Gross; *Rethinking Poles and Jews*, edited by Annamaria Orla-Bukowska, Sociology professor at Jagiellonian University. The volumes of poems are here too: Zbigniew Herbert, Julia Hartwig, Anne Michaels, Czesław Miłosz, Wisława Szymborska. There are some theoretical books on collective and prosthetic memory, as well as philosophical works: *Relating Narratives* by Italian philosopher Adriana Cavarero, Maurice Blanchot's *The Space of Literature* and *The Writing of Disaster*, and, essays by Jean Améry.

There are certain books that are so much a part of me that if they went missing it would be as if I'd lost an arm. Jean Améry's *At the Mind's Limits: Contemplations by a Survivor on Auschwitz and Its Realities* is one such book. I read his essay "Torture" at a meditation retreat. Elias was a toddler. I was in the throes of motherhood, practicing a dedicated spiritual path with teachings, and compelled to academia, to attaining a doctorate but the timing had not yet been right. Two hundred students in a practice group of which I'd been a part for five years sat inside a hall meditating for an hour. I sat in the lobby reading Améry's essay, "Torture." This reading at this particular moment *was* my meditation. There was sense in these words, "Whoever was tortured, stays tortured. Torture was the total inversion of the social world. That one's fellow man was experienced as the antiman remains in the tortured person as accumulated horror."[153] It was 2006. I had been teaching Levi's memoir for a year to my students in critical thinking courses. Levi's appeal in his first memoir embodied a logical, cautious, even scientific approach to his memories of deportation and camp life and death. Levi was an observer, even while in the midst of great suffering

---

[153] Améry, *At the Mind's Limits*, 34.

imposed (by other men) in highly adverse circumstances. His seemingly objective tone did not lack pathos. Through his narrative, in memories of encounters and interactions with fellow prisoners, he conveys a sense of care for human relations, for ethics, and for the ability of people to remain human amidst severe degradation and depravation. His belief in the world as it once was outside the camp allows him to cautiously hope for a life beyond Auschwitz, though he knows his survival is in large part determined by fate or random chance. There were no two men who could provide me with more truth. With Améry and Levi's works, I was in the presence of immense wisdom, tempered through intellect and the order that writing imposes. I felt the silence of things said, the whoosh of breath near my body, the painful words that must be uttered. I was stunned, and realized that engaging these words, allowing them to become integral to my own humanity, was a necessity.

Within a few weeks I had resigned from the group and the spiritual school and had decided that it was now time to further study cultural theory, philosophy, history, ethics, and literature. Looking back on it now, it's not more than a little ironic that my response to Améry's writings, essays that argue the mind's limitations through the experience of grave violence, compelled my return to graduate school. But rather than sit and meditate, I actively wanted to study books and ideas again; hence, my presence in the lobby and my separation from the group, which would soon become a formal separation. Just over a year later, I would begin doctoral studies.

On my shelf with *At the Mind's Limits* stands Améry's last work, *On Suicide: A Discourse on Voluntary Death*, composed two years before the author's death by overdose. In that book, he argues that a certain inner experience leads one to choose voluntary death (his term for suicide) as an act of freedom. The book is an exploration through philosophy and psychology of the logic of voluntary death. His metaphors— leap, open road, laying hands on, belonging to oneself—potentially bring the reader into an empathic understanding with self-determined death. It was with compassion and attentiveness to Améry's stops and starts, his tentative tone in finding a path for himself through the discourse and desire of (voluntary) death, that I read the work. I sought knowledge of the reasons and feelings that motivate one to want to end the tedious terrestrial reality of everyday relations, which largely includes engagement in language and the need to make oneself heard and understood. With an accumulation of life experiences, coupled with individual response to that accretion and the fact of biological aging—deterioration of physical ability, of the nervous system, the brain, the organs, of memory—one may conceivably and in good faith make a choice for death.

Scattered around my room are other important books. Delbo's *Auschwitz and After* on my desk and on my bedside table Marjorie Agosín's *Of Earth and Sea*, a memoir of growing up in Chile with Jewish immigrant parents and through the murder of socialist president Salvador Allende and the seventeen years of the Pinochet regime during which the writer and her family moved to the United States. It is summer and I'm dabbling in the pages of several books. I can feel the rich world of writers' minds around me and like the order taking shape as I rearrange and order the bookshelves. Michael Chorost's confession, factual and unapologetic in his memoir, *Rebuilt*, that just after he graduated with his doctorate he donated half his books to the library has stayed with me. I was in graduate school when I read his words. I had spent a good deal of money on books and thought that I would not part with those volumes of theory and critical thought. I would want to refer to them later. Chorost conceptualizes the experience as "casting off the apparatus of grad school," and continues, "*Shakespeare and the Popular Voice*—gone. *Surprised by Sin: The Reader in Paradise Lost*—gone."[154] Of course, those particular book titles held no meaning for me. Rather, I was shaken by the word *gone*. Given away, traded, never to be seen or engaged again. The knowledge imbibed in reading, responding to, and engaging with texts organically becomes part of the mind and consciousness. The knowledge that stays finds expression in one's thinking, writing, and action according to the idiosyncratic ways of the self it inhabits. The rest falls away. I understand Chorost's *gone* now and the freedom of unburdening oneself of artifacts, moving into a new phase of life, of knowledge and interaction, study, and love, of being human in a rich world that arises of knowledge and the delight of stories we cannot stop telling.

The lineage of books that passes through a reader's life reveals those things that have compelled and engaged, periods of obsession and interest. To give away a book is no small task. My mother removes a book from the box. "You would really like this." She's right. But reading is highly personal endeavor and increasingly an act of freedom once one has left school. I have other books waiting, books that call to me, Poland on my mind after last summer's travels, compelled to write about the writers that will never leave my shelves, unless their words are in my warm hands as I read. "Put it back in the box. I'm trying to get rid of books, not add to my collection!" Even as I clean the shelves a new book arrives in the mail—*The Self Comes to Mind* by Antonio Damasio. My particular interest is the autobiographical self, the one we create in imagining and inventing ourselves, fashioning the self as we want it to appear in the world. This self-design, of course, narrates itself in what we love. Books are mirrors of that love. No wonder I do not give them away easily. The books have become me.

---

[154] Chorost, *Rebuilt*, 194.

After Poland

CHAPTER 3

Undercurrents

3.1 EVERY MOMENT

One cannot live with Auschwitz at every moment. One does, in fact, live with it every moment. There is no moment once the journey is taken without the fact and the stories and the silences and the absences and the indomitable presences of Auschwitz and all the universes that have spun from that ground and its memory. Polish poet Zbigniew Herbert (1924-1998) wrote poems that were partly about loss. From Poland, I learn what it means to live with loss.

> What will happen
>
> when hands
>
> fall away from poems
>
> when in the other mountains
>
> I drink dry water
>
> this should not matter
>
> but it does

Here this reader thinks that what matters must fall away but refuses. The poet is still afraid of death. He fears not engaging with life as he has known and loved it. So it is that we learn to live with loss, even as we know what we love.

> what will poems become
>
> when the breath departs
>
> and the grace of speaking
>
> is rejected

will I leave the table?

and descend into the valley

where there resounds

new laughter

by a dark forest[155]

He asks questions, absent of question marks. Accordingly, the stanzas gather in a collective statement of knowing—without stop—to close the poem.

Death humanizes being and "without it abject fear returns."[156] In other words, it is the fact of death, its nearness, and the demand of confrontation with it that makes us human. He writes not of death's absurdity, as the existentialists wrote, but the absurdity of its exclusion, its loss. Without death, the descent into Herbert's "other mountains" where the water is dry, poetry would not be so rare and necessary, one's hands falling away, as it were, from the act of committing one's interior to paper in response to the world. With Herbert's poems I find lines and cannot find them again. Lines disappear. Words remain, conjured of my own memory, or perhaps the poet's.

Archeology.

Leg.

Head.

Cup.

Window.

Ash.

Murderous.

Alone.

---

[155] In *Zbigniew Herbert: The Collected Poems 1956-1998.*
[156] Sandor Goodhart, "The War to End All Wars: Mimetic Theory and 'Mounting to the Extremes' in a Time of Disaster."

Herbert knew at death that life would not change, that people would continue their violent behavior, discord, and betrayal of eons. Yet. To have lived as best one could under difficult, often oppressive circumstances. Yet. To have loved one's home—wartime and then Communist Poland—despite the lack of abundance, the gray, the depression and despair. Yet. To have returned because one was called. Poet Adam Zagajewski, born in 1945 in Lwów, writes how Herbert did not receive prizes or major recognition. He was relegated to live in various cities—Berlin, Paris—and in countries like Italy and the United States, and his outstanding work did not receive the recognition in the literary world it deserved.[157] Though he did not grow bitter, he sometimes fell into depressed states as he struggled through exile with illness and aging and a lack of recognition. Still, his poems reveal that he did not accept betrayal, but acknowledged the vicissitudes of historical circumstance and continued to live well—true to his heart, in relationship to others. Yet. To have cherished small things—a cup, snow, a particular window, certain rooms, and larger things—a friend, memory of a brother, parents, aging, the vulnerability love imposes. These actions and intelligences make a poet—in life, and beyond for his readers.

3.2 AN ARTIST'S INNER LABYRINTH

Two Selves Remember

Our guides through Poland have introduced the fellows to a rich history that includes Jewish and Catholic experiences of the Second World War. Maciek has told us relatively little about Marian Kołodziej whose work we are about to see. However, he has sent us a link to a website where we can view some of the artist's drawings prior to our viewing. I click on the link and strange, otherworldly drawings appear. They are etched in black on white, with an emphasis on light and shadow. The lines are precise with fine detail, and at the same time they convey an urgent and frenetic energy. The lines themselves are a structure, an insistent labyrinth that will urge me into the stories these pictures tell. I see that two men exist in relationship: the young prisoner and the aging man—an artist who has survived the camps. These two are entwined in memory, burdened by a private and collective historical past, a grossly traumatic past, as it manifests in the personal present. As I read Kołodziej's story, this layering of selves startles and compels me. What secrets did this artist harbor inside? How did he see the experience of the camps, the annihilation of those around him, and the Jewish genocide? He saw severe violence and once free did not speak of it. Some fifty years later his memories arose. I am preparing for this outpouring.

In the olish town of Harmęże, just a few kilometers from what had been Auschwitz, Kołodziej worked as a forced laborer under German command. He was born in 1921 as Poland regained independence. He grew up outside Ostrów, a place of resistance during the partition periods of Poland and through the First and Second

---

[157] Zagajewski, "Beginning to Remember," in *A Defense of Ardor*.

World Wars.[158] He became involved in resistance activities when he was seventeen. He wanted to capture and keep this naiveté and its loss in his drawings.[159] A Polish priest encouraged him to join the Polish resistance and after only a few weeks he was arrested, deported to Kraków, and imprisoned in Montelupich, an interrogation and detention facility used by the Gestapo. Later he was transferred to a prison in Tarnów.

In June 1940 he was on the first transport to [KL] Auschwitz. Over five years he was imprisoned in Auschwitz, Buchenwald, Groß–Rosen, and, for the last five months of the war, Mauthausen. While most Jewish prisoners survived only a few weeks, or less frequently for a few months, Kołodziej was imprisoned and labored in the camps for five years; the fact that he was a political prisoner helped him to survive. He continued to assist the resistance movement from inside the camps. When his subversive activities were discovered at the sub-camp of Blechhammer he received a death sentence and was transferred to Auschwitz and imprisoned for a time in Block 11.

After the war, he attended the Academy of Fine Arts in Kraków in the faculty of painting. He graduated with a specialization in scenography and took a job as a set designer in the avant-garde "Wybrzeże" (Coast) Theatre in Gdańsk, the city where the Solidarity movement took root with shipyard strikes in the 1980s. He collaborated with other theatres in the country and abroad, as well as in the realization of thirty feature films. In the painting, drawing, and sculpture he produced he never returned to his camp experiences.[160] Yet, he acknowledged that the camp experience remained a negation within him:

> I was in Auschwitz. I was actually building Auschwitz, because I was brought there in the first transport. The truth is that I didn't talk about Auschwitz for almost fifty years. But for all that time Auschwitz was present in everything I did. Not literally, though. My theatrical work could be regarded as a protest against what I experienced there. So, Auschwitz has always been present—but as its negation. I did not trust literalism. The concentration camp cannot be told about literally.[161]

---

[158] Poland, a nation state between the tenth and fourteenth centuries, underwent a series of partitions between 1772 and in 1795. The nation was divided between Russia Empire, Prussia (the German Empire), and the Austro-Hungarian (Habsburg Dynasty) Empire. In November 1918 Poland celebrated its second republican independence. In the interwar period, people lived for twenty-one years with a relative sense of nationalistic pride and hope for an independent government. In 1939, as it had been in the First World War, the country was occupied by the Germans. Poland remained an occupied territory into the early part of 1945. The years from 1945 to 1948 marked the end of German occupation and Russian takeover of the country.

[159] *The Labyrinth: The Testimony of Marian Kołodziej.*

[160] "432. Marian Kołodziej. Magister vitae." *Auschwitz-Birkenau News.*

[161] *The Labyrinth: The Testimony of Marian Kołodziej.*

Entering the Labyrinth

In the basement of Franciscan church and monastery Saint Maximilian Kolbe Centre the artist's drawings have been arranged to fit his concept of memory as labyrinth.[162] He conceptualized the permanent installation of his work as photographic plates of memory.[163] It was his intention that viewers consider his drawings a permanent impression on the brain's memory. In his testimony he explains, "This is not an exhibition, nor art. These are not pictures. These are words locked in drawings. I propose a journey by way of this labyrinth marked by the experience of the fabric of death. It is a rendering of honor to all those who have vanished in ashes."[164] The visitor descends into a mnemonic world that depicts, with very little distance the punishing desperation of the camps. This is a world of the dead. The process of dying comes from all directions, at every angle: the sinking body, the rising body, the mind and spirit leaving its body.

These are canvases of departure. The struggle to resist that departure imposed as a crushing weight on to those imprisoned and killed at Auschwitz. I have the sense in witnessing the artist's interior world that he remains astounded by the sheer volume of bodies and souls that have been forced into the compressed violence of this space, this concentrationary universe.[165] In one drawing men sing in a choir with eyes of terror. In another drawing a child mouth open, screams with no sound, eyes crying but without tears. In encountering these "words locked in drawings" that unfurl in the labyrinth before me, I absorb this shock. Here is a moment of acute visual detail, largely metaphorical and intensely physical, exact in its anatomical depiction of emotion, pain, and terror.

Drawings extend the length of passageways and arch across the ceilings of subterranean rooms. Yellow bulbs cast shadows. In a central room, small rocks have been arranged at the base of drawings. I am reminded of Jewish memorial sites where rocks are totems to the dead. The piles also recall the slave labor of prisoners made to carry heavy objects. Bunks have been designed to recall the barracks. Wooden ladders run floor to ceiling. These materials assault the viewer and pull her into an underground existence.

Kołodziej was a set and costume designer. He was known in Poland for avant-garde set designs. The rooms in Harmęże resemble a stage set. They represent a brain with its cerebral cortex and neural passageways. The viewer is asked to capitulate to the artist's subconscious. Kołodziej asserts, "Here, every room has its designation, its

---

[162] Marian Kołodziej first exhibited his drawings of imprisonment in the *Konzentrationslager* (KL) Auschwitz in April 1995 at the Holy Trinity Church in Gdańsk, and then in 1996 in Essen, Germany. From January 1998, the artist's work has been permanently installed at the Church of the Saint Maximilian Kolbe Centre at the Franciscan monastery in Harmęże near Oświęcim, Poland. See *Auschwitz-Birkenau Memorial and Museum News* for 9 October 2013.
[163] This was name of the installation at St. Maximilian Kolbe Centre in Harmęże at the time of the author's visit with the Auschwitz Jewish Center Fellows in July 2014.
[164] *The Labyrinth: The Testimony of Marian Kołodziej*.
[165] David Rousset's first used this phrase to describe the world of concentration camps in his 1946 memoir, *L'Univers concentrationnaire*.

own emotional charge."[166] There is a creative mania on display. Sketches crowd one another. Canvases compete for wall space. Drawings of eyes follow visitors through passages. The eyes are those of the artist and perhaps his fellow prisoners. Some eyes express fear, some wariness, some resistance coupled with surprise. The shape of each forehead, nose, and brow differs. The methodology of the camps was designed to reduce men to skeletons and to erase each person's humanness; yet, each prisoner awash in the degradation and reduction of the camps remains in these drawings unique and singular. The eyes stay with the artist and he draws them into our own consciousness. We are watched, followed, asked to remember.

Father Kolbe and Transcendence

In Kołodziej's drawings of Father Kolbe he focuses on an individual. This man made a choice to save a fellow prisoner. During the Second World War Kolbe provided shelter to refugees from Greater Poland, including 2,000 Jews whom he hid from Nazi persecution in his friary in Niepokalanów. He was active as a radio amateur, critical of Nazi activities through his reports. In February 1941 he was arrested by the German Gestapo and imprisoned in Pawiak Prison. In late May of that year he was transferred to Auschwitz as prisoner 16670.[167] Kolbe voluntarily chose punishment in exchange for another prisoner who pleaded not to die because he had a wife and children. He was imprisoned in a starvation cell. After three weeks, during which time he led his fellow prisoners in song and prayer, he died by an enforced shot of carbolic acid. His body was burned in the camp crematorium. The prisoner in whose place he died lived to see liberation.

Father Maximilian Kolbe prior to the Second World War.
Source: www.huffingtonpost.co.uk

---

[166] Marian Kołodziej in conversation with Paweł Sawicki, *Oś*, 14.
[167] "Maximilian Kolbe." *Jewish Virtual Library*.

In Kołodziej's drawings Kolbe takes on the persona of a saint. In fact, the Catholic Church canonized Kolbe in 1982. The artist's fascination with Kolbe extends beyond religious faith. His drawings of the priest and political activist depict the bodily disintegration of a man who was once healthy and robust. The viewer understands that the process of starvation deprived the priest of his physical and intellectual powers, leaving him gaunt and near-death, but, as a result, increasingly luminous, almost transparent with an energy that looked beyond physical reality. The viewer finds Kolbe as he attains a new level of wisdom and knowing, reflected in luminosity. This light, the artist implies, is denied to the survivor who has not undergone transformation through the sacrifice exacted in giving one's life to rescue another. At the same time the outline of the former man exists in the drawings, evidence that a human being may, if he survives, reemerge. If Kolbe were to have lived, he would have likely been tainted with shame, marked by injustice and its requisite horrors, as were so many survivors. Instead, Kołodziej carries those shameful memories. He rescues himself as he paints Kolbe and remembers the possibility for goodness in the world.

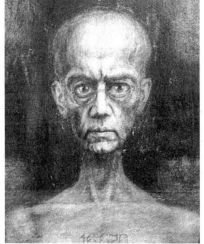

Marian Kołodziej's rendering of Father Kolbe as he might have looked through his imprisonment in the starvation cell at Auschwitz.
Source: http://thelabyrinthdocumentary.com

For Kołodziej, Kolbe is a Christ figure, representing hope for humanity's potential to choose ethically. The survivor of the camps seeks out examples of human connection and ethical behavior. Those who remember them deify such exemplars. Their lives and, as in the case of Kolbe, their deaths reveal that ethics of the highest caliber require self-sacrifice in the interest of others. Primo Levi in his memoirs of Auschwitz remembers Lorenzo, an Italian bricklayer conscripted by the Germans to work at the Buna. In part, because he was not imprisoned within the camp, Lorenzo represented for Levi hope of an untainted humanity. Lorenzo gave Levi courage to survive, not necessarily because he brought food to Levi and sent news to his mother in Torino, but more so because, "Lorenzo was a man; his humanity was pure and uncontaminated, he was outside the world of negation. Thanks to Lorenzo, I managed not to forget that I myself was a man."[168]

In the same way, Kołodziej transforms Kolbe into an ethical figure that assures the continuity of human feeling for and in response to others. There is an element of transcendence, even religiosity, if one wants to translate these signs and symbols through the artist's Catholicism. He creates at the mercy of memory. His hand is responsive to those affective images that press their way to the surface of consciousness. Whereas the viewer may want to see these drawings as art, as the skill is apparent and the meanings literally and metaphorically profuse, Kołodziej frames his work otherwise. "You cannot call this art. I thought about how to begin this; and started with my own growing up and rescuing my own humanity."[169] The drawings began and continued as a project of rehabilitation. As he created along that guiding line, drawings came with force and insistence.

In *The Labyrinth* he suggests that his traumatic history was always present as an unarticulated absence. Even through his years working in the theatre conceptualizing set design and in his work for film, the camp experiences were existent. The memories found alternative outlets of expression. Eventually his need for beauty in his artwork changed through aging and physical disability. Those changes allowed for a direct confrontation and reckoning with Auschwitz. Once he began the rehabilitative process, he unloosed a cyclone of images.

Justice takes on a special meaning to the survivor, said Kołodziej, much different from the scales of liberty and justice that democratic societies strive to implement. He painted the scales of justice depicting how justice in Auschwitz was grossly imbalanced and distorted. He represents the Kapo fat and heavy on one side of the scale and the emaciated prisoner, light and insubstantial, on the other.[170] This was "justice" in the concentrationary universe. A narrative implies order, structure, and a measure of coherence, which derives from the imposition of form onto experience and the processes of chronology (Κρόνος) or plot-driven movement (a logical sequence of actions). These drawings appear to have no such normative or cohering chronology or structure. Logos (Λόγος) has disappeared from these canvases. What remains is consumption. A devouring maw has descended upon experience and rendered obfuscation in its path. Horror arises in the absence of order and form and in technologies of killing. Journalist Chris Hedges argues "war is an enticing elixir" and, however tragically, it gives humans a resolve and a cause:

---

[168] Primo Levi, *Survival*, 122.

[169] Sawicki, *Oś*, 14.

[170] The Kapo was a trustee prisoner in the concentration and labor camps who was assigned by the SS to manage fellow prisoners. Kapos served as guards, administrative functionaries, and overseers of forced labor crews. They typically received special privileges or protections for supervising, often with brutality, other prisoners. Nikolaus Wachsmann writes in *KL* that "Just as the figure of the Muselmann is taken to symbolize the destruction of prisoners' bodies, the figure of the Kapo often stand for the corrosion of their souls" (512).

fundamental questions about the meaning, or meaninglessness, of our place on the planet are laid bare when we watch those around us sink to the lowest depths. War exposes the capacity for evil that lurks not far below the surface within all of us. And this is why once it is over war is so hard to discuss.[171]

In Kołodziej's drawings evil manifests as harm inflicted on fellow beings and the perpetrator's pleasure and purpose found in such power. Evil is a graphic depiction of love's murder. It is a failure of humanity to address the humanity of others. It is ultimately an ethical failure. It is this failure that Kołodziej asks viewers to address.

His subjects are the lice, the Kapo, the Nazis, the devoured men within the mouths of devouring men. The devouring man turned wrathful god parallels the wrathful deities of Tibetan (Vajrayana) Buddhism who represent the afflictive forces within and among humans that pull toward unethical behavior and cause humans to harm themselves and each other. Yet, the devouring gods in the concentration camps were very much embodied men and women to whose every whim and command the prisoners had to respond. The drawings forcefully portray prisoners literally consumed by the Kapo. Death surrounds the destroyer so that he becomes death itself—a conglomeration of curling corpses that, in turn, consume him. He is no longer human.

One kills his humanity in choosing violent power as his primary mode of interacting with others. The destroyer is reduced to parasite. He no longer sees that his fellows are human. He sees them as objects for his own benefit, to be disposed of. Certainly, prisoners in the camps suffered lice infestation, but the singularity and enormity of one terrorizing, devouring louse dominates a canvas and pronounces the parasite a source of death. It was a carrier of disease in the camps, a destroyer that cooperated with the Kapo in the work of annihilation. Thinking of the Kapo as devourer, the line between human and insect parasite blurs. Annihilation takes on an otherworldly dimension where the feast on others becomes profane ritual of destruction. Kołodziej transforms these memories into an expression that personifies greed. In the presence of these works each viewer confronts the degradation of humans by humans. This confrontation contributes to an expanding knowledge central to who we know ourselves to be in relationship to the history that has preceded us.[172]

In one of his most striking drawings, the older artist reaches over a field of numbers. The younger man, the Auschwitz prisoner, rides his back. The numbers on the canvas range between Kołodziej's assigned number—432—tattooed on his left forearm into six-digit numbers and into the hundred-thousands. The field falls off at the left corner of the canvas, disintegrating from a burnt edge into a pit of corpses. The Germans replaced names with numbers in an elaborate and constantly changing classification system designed to track thousands of prisoners through the

---

[171] Chris Hedges, *War Is a Force That Gives Us Meaning*, 3.

[172] This knowledge is postmodern in that it is post-Auschwitz. It is not after in that it is present, but its character is always a response to historical events. A number of writers have eloquently addressed the subject of the state of thought after Auschwitz, including Josh Cohen in *Interrupting Auschwitz: Art, Religion, and Philosophy* (2003).

concentration camp system across Europe during war. The prisoners lost, among many other things, their names in the camps.

Primo Levi writes, "My number is 174517; we have been baptized, we will carry the tattoo on our left arm until we die." [173] The tattoo was to be a mark of identification. He refers to the number as his name, "My name is," as we would in ordinary civilian life when we refer to ourselves and introduce ourselves to one another. His declaration conveys the terrible imposition of a permanent condition, indicative of a mechanized system of classification in which he is now a functionary. In a process intended to severe people from country, language, family and home, the tattoo attempted to enforce namelessness.

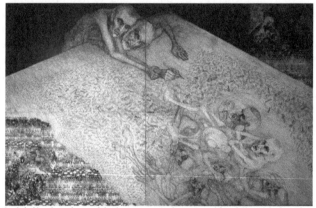

Kołodziej's drawing with the young prisoner-self guiding his hand.
Source: http://thelabyrinthdocumentary.com

Kołodziej's reference to a rehabilitative line might be read in two ways. The rehabilitation was physical and mental. First, the stroke mandated that Kołodziej confront his past and integrate it into his work. It was because of injury due to a serious stroke, a cerebral infarction that paralyzed the right side of his body, that he opened up and his memories began to drink light and breathe air. Second, the literal lines that bisect the drawings, creating planes of life and death, were his rehabilitation. He confessed that he did not find "a line" in art school. The line coiled inside him until circumstances colluded and there was a medical mandate to rehabilitate. It was then that memories manifested in the material world. With the opportunity to emerge that line became a visual panoply of personal historic memory.

Through imagining Kolbe's bodily change in starvation Kołodziej also recognizes for himself the dual selves he encompasses. These selves are rooted in historical and present time. Yet, in his drawings a dualistic representation emerges where two selves transcend past and present time. The selves meet and merge across binary divides—past and present, wholeness and disintegration, humanity and

---

[173] Primo Levi, *Survival*, 27.

sainthood. The layering of this past-present self is not simply a metaphoric device. It is viscerally physical in the drawings. There repeatedly appear in the drawings both the older artist and the emaciated, eyeless, husk of a prisoner, incessantly marked with his identifying number, 432. In some drawings he renders himself with a crown of thrones or crucified upon a cross; in another, his post-Auschwitz self carries the young, dying prisoner on a large metal plate. He offers this dying self to the viewer in a gesture of supplication and sadness. In another work the older man carries his prisoner self on his back, passing through barbed wire, ignoring the warning sign with skull and crossbones that reads, "HALT! STÓJ!"[174]

The older Kołodziej carrying the wounded prisoner self.
Source: http://thelabyrinthdocumentary.com

The symbiosis of the older man and his younger self reveals compassion, decency, dependence, and necessity. This layering I find most remarkable—the intimacy of prisoner and survivor selves. Art allows this viewing: the layering of selves; the bodies that have visited a particular human being through time; the way the face takes on lived experience, and, in this case, the nearness of death and one's resistance in its proximity. As a recipient of history, I recognize the coexistence of historical and contemporary selves. Though it is not often that I encounter startling visual representations of the relationship between selves. I teach my students, for example in

---

[174] Stop or halt in German and in Polish.

reading Levi's *Survival in Auschwitz*, to critically assess the relationship between the writer and the self he characterizes in his autobiographical work. They should note the distance between the (immediate) writing self and the (more remote) character self. But the students work with words and often do not make pictures of these selves in conversation. Hardly is the juxtaposition of selves, their very dependence on one another—especially potent in this vulnerable and tender relationship between prisoner and survivor—acknowledged with such immediate and assaultive visual force as evinced in Kołodziej's works.

Poetry and Courage

Halina Słojewska-Kołodziej, the artist's widow, has related that a particular poem initially encouraged her husband to share his camp memories.[175] Zbigniew Herbert (1924-1998) writes in the opening lines of "The Envoy of Mr. Cogito," "Go where those others went to the dark boundary/for the golden fleece of nothingness your last prize" (lines 1-2). The story of Jason's quest to gain the throne in apprehending the Golden Fleece is ultimately a tragic one, as Herbert's poem suggests.[176] This tragic narrative could be applied to Herbert's increasingly pessimistic view of Poland with the Nazi invasion and establishment of German extermination and labor camps in the country followed by the loss of a democratic Poland during four decades of totalitarian rule, and, finally, to his flailing hope for an ethical world of mutual respect and accountability between humans. The poet's consideration of these lived histories accounts for the despair in his words, "the golden fleece of nothingness."[177] Once having attained what you thought you had set out to attain you will find it is nothing. That will be your prize for giving testimony, Herbert's phrase implies.[178]

Who better than the poet through the experience of war and then under dictatorship to provide encouragement to the artist who finally emerges in the early nineties, after the success of Poland's Solidarity movement, to draw the memories of his camp years. Yet, the one telling should not expect to receive anything in return for giving story to the world. In fact, for his harrowing journey to the outer boundaries, to memories of violence and death, he should expect exactly the opposite: nothing. The

---

[175] Halina Słojewska-Kołodziej shared her memories at a talk and presentation devoted to the life and work of Marian Kołodziej in October 2013, organized by the International Centre for Education about Auschwitz and the Holocaust and the Saint Maximilian Kolbe Centre in Harmęże.

[176] Jason, raised by a centaur to whom his mother delivered him for safekeeping, emerges from hiding on the Mountain of Pelion to challenge his uncle Pelias, who had killed Jason's father and usurped power, to his right to rule. Pelias tells Jason he may accede the throne but that he must first set out on a journey by ship to find and return with the Golden Fleece from Colchis, the then-unknown world. Jason does so, passing a series of additional tests set out for him. Yet, in the end, he is unfaithful to his wife, Medea. Abandoned, he dies grief-stricken, sitting under his decaying ship, the Argo, when a beam falls and strikes his head.

[177] Herbert, "The Envoy of Mr. Cogito."

[178] In fact, Herbert's life was one of returning to Poland between periods of exile. He won few prizes during his lifetime but, as poet Adam Zagajewski relates, "Herbert chose to do odd jobs over living the life of a privileged writer so as not to compromise his artistic stance during the years of repression in Poland" (*Solidarity* 173).

poet attests that we live with meaning and try to attain goodness, a degree of enlightenment, maybe even sublimity, but we recognize we will not. Life is action, effort, and living manifests in doing and trying. Our ethics should be that the means (writing, art) is the journey; it is the only end. This is the envoy of the thinking man and woman. There is no salvation, no God or fleece to be attained. There will never be a utopia attained through stories expressed in literary and artistic creations. The work is the ethic lived.

Jason gains the Golden Fleece, accedes to the throne but later suffers because of betrayal and loss. He suffers despair, loneliness, and death by injury to his head, a fatal blow to his thinking mind. He is knocked eternally unconscious. The Fleece of Nothingness, as Herbert reminds his readers for their pains. Still, the writer and the artist make the journey; they follow through. Action becomes an ethical response to suffering in the world. Action not only defines humanness; it constitutes humanness. But to make the journey for the poet and for the artist is to remember, to enter knowledge (however buried), to confer language, and to give material form to psychic content. Kołodziej had witnessed the trauma of violence both as an individual and as a collective human being of his age. Reward? Denied. Fleece? Nothing. Finally, one must live life for the living itself. Poet Adam Zagajewski writes his own ethical response to life in concluding, "to be able not to answer the most difficult questions, and keep living anyway."[179]

Kołodziej responded to Herbert's challenge to venture to the dark boundary when he began to draw his camp memories. The lines of poetry that most emboldened the artist to finally draw his experiences were these: "you were saved not in order to live/you have little time you must give testimony."[180] The work created in his testimony becomes his *raison d'etre*. Life matures in the act of giving testimony. The journey of the thinking man (Mr. Cogito in Herbert's version) in the wake of totalitarian regimes of the twentieth century has a special diplomatic mission to fulfill: giving testimony. The artist asks the visitor to listen, look, and interact with his drawings and the visual narratives that arise of them.

However, these narratives are fragmentary bits of memory. A maze frequently does not make sense because the sojourner lacks distance that gives perspective. If narrative structure lends coherence to a situation, no matter how traumatic, are these drawings, these plates of memory, narratives? Certainly, they reveal stories (the "words locked in pictures") to the reader. Yet, further still the drawings and the style in which they are exhibited suggest how this artist accessed memory, its labyrinthine nature for him. We inhabit these drawings as moments contained within an architectural structure—labyrinth as a dwelling of memory. We move through rooms wherein whole worlds of the artist's brain, his memory, and the historic situations depicted emerge and rush toward us. There is a center to which we are directed. Here stones are piled around a central canvas. Once we reach the center, we must find our way out again. There is no map, only memory and its artwork. His memories are

---

[179] Zagajewski, *Another Beauty*, 203.
[180] Zbigniew Herbert, "The Envoy of Mr. Cogito."

contained in an underground space, a crypt, the subconscious brain. Above, ordinary life goes on. Light reflects in arches of summer sky and gathering clouds. The air is humid, the breeze warm. Below, the smell of earth and rotting things. The visitor descends. She has entered the labyrinth.

Halina Słojewska shared that her husband "lived for the beauty of the theatre, art, and life." Once he became very ill and was paralyzed on the right side of his body, the doctor told him to rehabilitate his right hand and he begin to draw. [He] "attached tiny pencils to his fingers and tried to draw on tiny pieces of paper."[181] He had to learn to manipulate the pencils. The physical work and the mental concentration needed to learn to utilize the paretic hand again became for the artist an experience that forced him inward. Memory has its own logic and time. Kołodziej provided the space for it to manifest and the tools, literally at/on his fingertips, for its expression. He had now to train his movements. In Herbert's poem he recalled the lines about giving testimony. He found strength, resolve, and the will to move forward while moving into the past.

In the field of neuroaesthetics, researchers have found that after stroke some artists experience a change in their artistic style and production. Those artists with left hemispheric damage, where the right side of the body experiences paralysis, have exhibited, among other traits, increased production of artwork, repetition of images, predominant themes, fluid lines, minimal color, and a preponderance of symbolism.[182] In the act of drawing, the process of remembering is imbued with physicality. The hand rubs against canvas as it shapes line, space, light and shadow through art's tools. Still, Kołodziej rejects the reference to his work as "art" per se. "I do not do art," he says. "Art always goes in the direction of aestheticism, and all of this is quite brutal and quite cruel."[183] Aestheticism signifies a style unique to the artist and, perhaps, a statement that pleases the audience with representational or interpretative meaning. In a turn from his earlier work where he had embraced the beauty of theatre and art, the later work insists on the fact of brutality and cruelty. Kołodziej was creating outside of artistic paradigms and traditions as those parameters were established in his time. The aesthetics in which he found refuge in his professional work through decades of communism was inverted in the works from about 1993 to the time of his death in 2009. He was creating and exhibiting for the public scenes of extreme suffering.

In the 1980s Poland moved into a period of new freedom with the expansion of an organized Solidarity movement and with democratic openings in Eastern Europe during the period of Mikael Gorbachev's Perestroika. By 1989 Central and Eastern European nations under communism were undergoing a radical opening and integration with Western Europe and the world at-large. The Berlin Wall was officially demolished in 1990. Democratic reforms began in earnest. These collective shifts influenced, in part, the creation of art within Polish society. The social and political openings in Poland also created new spaces to remember, conceptualize, and

---

[181] *Auschwitz-Birkenau News.*
[182] Quantitative systems of measurement are needed to formalize the study of neurological damage on artists' work, as Anjan Chatterjee argues in *The Neuropsychology of Art* (2015).
[183] Kołodziej, "I Was Rescuing My Own Humanity," *Oś*, 14.

narrate history in ways that under communism had been largely prohibitive. Kołodziej was creating material markedly divergent from the set and costume designs of his professional years and, before that, in his struggle to define a personal style in art school. The illustrations created in the late years of his life were dark, strange, and foreign to his ideas of art and its aesthetic purposes. Zagajewski speaks to the predicament of being an artist in a totalitarian state when he writes, "Beauty in the totalitarian state is a special problem."[184] Beauty, or as Zagajewski discusses it, metaphysics, was mediated by the stringent dictates of communist social reality.

Disintegration and the Courage of Memory

Writer Terry Tempest Williams in *Leap* details a year at the Museo del Prado in Madrid where she considered the subject of Hieronymus Bosch's painting, "The Garden of Earthly Delights," painted in the early sixteenth century. She queries what each triptych tells us about who we are. What kind of world we have created? What kind of world do we want? Bosch depicts hell, a futuristic nightmare of the evils of invented technologies used to malefic purposes that create suffering on earth. These technologies emerged through the Age of Reason, the Age of Enlightenment. As in Herbert's "Mr. Cogito," nihilism and despair induced in part by technologies and ideologies of war threaten to destroy the thinking person of the twentieth century.

In Bosch's image of hell, people lose their human appearance. They fight and maim one another. They become unrecognizable, a maelstrom of human and animal forms. After weeks observing the painting, Williams feels decomposition, *desintegración*, overtake her. "*Yo soy la desintegración.*"[185] A contemplative and attentive viewer engaged in developing an ethical view from what the painting teaches, Williams becomes the very processes she observes in the painting. The ethical call to art causes us to feel the disintegration of our humanness even as we strive to shore up and strengthen it. In relationship with the painting, Williams merges with the artist. She notes that Bosch brings the unsatisfactory, partially human, and the inhuman into conversation through visual narrative. In Kołodziej's work disintegration exists in his depiction of himself as an aging, frail man who carries upon his body the physical memory of the camps. He makes the shadows of suppression into a shared story. This duty Kołodziej calls an "obligation of memory."[186] Horror and denigration find expression in the world; they move and open others as a part of that story.

The artist chose to be interred at Saint Maximilian Kolbe Centre, his body in a crypt amidst his collection of drawings. In the final part of his life he surrounded himself with memories that he buried over five decades. The years of dissociation when he corralled traumatic memories into small, forgotten spaces of the brain ended after a stroke. His drawings reveal an effort to remember as a means of reentering the

---

[184] Adam Zagajewski, *In Defense of Ardor*, 14.

[185] I am disintegration. Williams' words are suggestive of Frida Kahlo's painting in a personal diary in which Kahlo inscribed, "*Yo soy la desintegración.*"

[186] Kołodziej, "I Was Rescuing My Own Humanity," *Oś*, 14.

world and living at the dark boundary that, not paradoxically, also enlightened his understanding of the twentieth century world in which he lived.

I begin to feel the artist's work permeate my present as I drive home one day from work. The California foothills unfurl in autumn colors of dark green and dusty brown. I feel the spaciousness of the land. The sky matches it, rain clouds stretching over yellow sycamores, wind blowing leaves onto the highway, lavender light angled. There is space here in this Western landscape. The vivid courage and emotional outpouring of the drawings appear before my mind's eye. I recognize the faces and bodies that spill onto the space in my vision. Paralleling this landscape is Kołodziej's in-scape, images peopled with memories of comrades and prisoners he did not know, whom he saw just once or perhaps daily, and whose faces he remembered. In the midst of these drawings, this viewer feels time populated with beings, spilling into a spatial plane that canvas could barely contain. What once belonged to Poland and to a man who held his secrets for fifty years now inhabits me. These remembered beings float on California sky, as if to people this second life here without boundary of time or space, just before cherished rain in another drought year.

Herbert writes in his thinking man's poem, "be courageous when the mind deceives you be courageous/in the final account only this is important."[187] Recording the harrowing journey of the thinking man through the twentieth century, Herbert writes his own story. He had been a poet-activist from his early years. He wrote within Poland and, as borders gradually opened after the revolts and initial liberalization in 1956, he wrote from Berlin, California, Paris, and Siena. Inexorably, he was drawn back to Poland. He could not leave for good and, so, in his poems he struggles to come to terms with what history has given him, a Polish man, a poet who both loved and hated his century.

Herbert reminds the survivor to give testimony amidst those who have turned away. He tells himself and his listener to have courage, even when the mind believes that nothing is possible. Let anger flow, do not let it reify and become a solid core from which you exist. The natural world will provide respite from crazed humanness. Look to the created world around you, not to find consolation but to exist. Repeat the stories and myths. Chant the narratives, a mantra to remember the good though which you will attain insight. Follow the ancestors because you must, because you have no choice, because you can only act in this way if you choose to live honestly in the world, given the world as it is and given your time. Return to the act of creating, the small pencils fastened to the end of fingers on the right hand. Return to the rehabilitative journey. The Golden Fleece is elusive and in itself no guarantee of meaning. Kołodziej made his envoy, his final labyrinthine opus testifying to his refusal to suppress memory. It is clear in these rooms that circumstances and choice brought this artist to confront the burden of personal and collective history.

---

[187] Herbert, "The Envoy of Mr. Cogito."

3.3 WHAT DAMAGES MUST WE KEEP?

I had long wanted to visit Auschwitz. It sounds strange to write of "visiting" Auschwitz-Birkenau, but that's what it is. It is a memorial now and it's a place that people go to, a museum with artifacts. Tour buses unload people. In March 2015 more people visited the camp than ever before—82,000 visitors. On average, that is 2,645 people per day.[188] The busloads of people from Kraków are much criticized by our academic tour guides, but most people are there because they have chosen to be there.

There is something, even if unarticulated, unformulated, that we want there at the camps. There is some knowledge or sense of things that each visitor feels she is missing. It may be true that some go unwillingly, because they are with another who wants to go to the camps, but most are there harboring some reason, sentiment, or need coupled with sorrow or uneasy belief. The Holocaust is now a permanent part of many people's awareness and their worldview; Auschwitz is one of the major representations of that event and prominently symbolizes its memory and how we interact with history of the Second World War and the situations and events that preceded and followed it.

The memorialization of Auschwitz-Birkenau might become history lesson, a sightseeing tour, or an academic study of artifacts more than a place to be present with the atrocity and grave violence that occurred here. There is hardly time for any ardently expressed or savage grief, and, as our guide has argued the memorial is not a place for that. Our guide wants to suppress an "internal narrative," which he views as an obstacle to experiencing and seeing the camps in an historical context.

My own writing immediately post-fellowship was to begin to respond to that official sense of things regarding visitation at Auschwitz. I felt, and continue to feel, that there must be space for one to think, reflect, and simply sit at Auschwitz. There have to be benches and shrines and offerings everywhere. There have to be personal stories and blank pages, unwritten stories, reminders of stories everywhere at the camps. It could be messy, it could be wildly variant and uneven, it could be political and perhaps strange and inappropriate, but that would have to be navigated because grief takes many forms. The official staff at the museum would not police remembrance as much as they might like. There always has to be some restraint on that policing, even as the memorial is preserved and cared for and maintained. In Poland there are small rocks everywhere, in piles, interspersed with ribbons, candles, small sayings, and other totems. They comprise memorials, solidity for the dead. They tell us something about vast numbers, sheer quantities of people murdered, and they remind us of individuality, distinct human uniqueness, the totality of a life and the way its ending—an ending that never ends—should shatter us.

---

[188] *The Auschwitz Report* (Auschwitz-Birkenau Memorial and Museum) for 2015 indicates approximately 1,725,700 visitors in 2015. In the 21st century annual visitation rates have grown exponentially. Some of the increase is due to media and online presence, but there continues to be a growing global awareness of human rights and the consequences of war. As such, Auschwitz-Birkenau is a symbol of destruction and the human need to seek peace through a confrontation with history. There is a strong educational component to the work of the museum and memorial, and a demand for the body of knowledge provided by that education.

I went to New York and Poland to study Jewish and Polish history pre-war, post-war, and through communism into its current development into a new socialist-capitalist society. This journey involved more than four weeks of travel. I begin to read and study for my travels in April 2014. I am still writing and reading about Poland. It seems that the permutations of my fellowship will stretch over the years of my life. Poland is like a blanket for me. I'm wrapped in it. It is inside me, and all around me.

There was very little time to feel in Poland. I would have to feel later. It was the usual academic tour with many sites to visit and histories to discuss. At the same time, we were meeting with Poles who work to bring the changes brought about by the war into present times through museums, restoration of synagogues, educational programs, school curriculum, and memorialization. Of course, the heavy content weighed on participants. As we moved around the country meeting with survivors, with rescuers, with writers, professors, and museum curators, small moments allowed notes in a journal, written on the van or at a bench in the garden of an inn where we stayed.

The second night in Poland the younger students were out in small groups. I relished a few moments to myself and took my notebook with me. I found the old market square, Rynek Główny, the largest in Europe, elegant and beautiful. It was a warm summer evening. People of all ages ambled in the square. Others enjoyed beer and food under umbrellas at restaurants bordering the square. Adam Zagajewski, who was raised in Gliwice after the war and attended Jagiellonian University in Kraków in the 1960s, writes of the city's architecture reflecting two layers, the heavy dark red bricks of Western Gothic style, imported by Polish kings and princelings from Germany, and the nobility's later taste for the Italian Renaissance—slim spires, stylish loggias, and vertiginously upright arches. With a poet's feel for his adopted city as a young college student in newly Communist Poland he describes both the lightness and heaviness of Kraków: "It was as if someone had tied dozens of ether-filled balloons to a massive Gothic trunk and then waited for the stout city, that stony paperweight, to make its way skyward toward the Italian azure." Though during those years, the poet found the city dark, cold, and ugly. Piles of coal, ready for winter, covered the sidewalk. Everything was dying—chestnuts rotting, gray rain streaking dull yellow buildings. "Everything was geared toward survival, vegetation."[189] During Nazi occupation the square was named Adolf Hitler-Platz. This is not the Kraków I experienced. My Kraków was summer, sensate, and superficial, seen through the intoxicated eyes of a tourist, a scholar on fellowship to take in the present and the past as it presented itself through apparent surfaces. The air was humid and cooling with summer rains. Linden trees blew lightly in the wind and the sky darkened with gray. Tourists filled the square.

One late afternoon the fellows walked through the main square to Massolit Books, an English language bookstore. From the moment we arrive, I want to live in there. It is intimate and warmly inviting, in a residential section of old Kraków,

---

[189] Zagajewski, *Another Beauty*, 33.

through a door and up a few stone steps into a room with sunken hardwood floors and dark bookshelves packed tight with English language and Polish editions. We meet in the back room, settling in with iced coffee and cake. Our speaker today is Mirosława Gruszczyńska, who had been awarded the status of Righteous Gentile, or Righteous of the Nations, by Yad Vashem. Mirosława begins to tell the story of a time her mother gave shelter to thirteen-year-old Jewish girl whose mother had been a friend of hers. To pass as a Catholic, Anna assumed the name Marysia. A priest drew up false papers to certify her baptism in the Church. Yet, someone recognized her on the street and she had to go into hiding in the apartment in case anyone recognized her. The city was occupied by the German army in the first week of September 1939. Governor General of Poland, Hans Frank, who had been legal counsel to the Nazi Party, established his headquarters in the Wawel Castle. The castle became the designated capital of the Generalgouvernement. The girls existed within this environment of occupation. Jews were expelled from Kraków. Those who remained were forced into a ghetto, created in March 1941 in Podgórze, a district located across the river, rather than in Kazimierz, a quarter where Jews had lived for over two centuries.[190]

The girls were the nearly same age. They shared a room and became friends. They told anyone who asked that they were cousins. Anna remained with Mirosława's family until the end of the war. Her mother was killed but she was able to reunite with her father and with her brother who had been a prisoner of war under Russians. Together they were able to find Róża, Anna's twin sister. The twins migrated to Israel, and their father and brother eventually joined them there.

Mirosława and Anna maintained their connection between Poland and Israel. Through four decades (the 1950s, 1960s, 1970s, and 1980s) it was difficult to correspond under communist censorship. Mirosława did not travel and Anna did not come to Poland. My guide Maciek informs me that for Poles it was hard to travel from behind the Iron Curtain to Western Europe, North America, and Israel. As part of the Soviet bloc, Poland did not support Israel from 1967 onward.[191] In the late eighties the two women began to meet in person. In 1990, Mirosława, along with her mother Helena Przebindowska (who died in 1969) and her sister Urszula Sławomirska, was awarded by Yad Vashem the title of Righteous Among Nations.[192] After our meeting, I spend an hour in the fiction section, then purchase two Polish novels and a journal, *New Eastern Europe*.[193] I leave the bookstore in a light rain and make my way through narrow streets in search of a space that will allow me to delve into the new journal.

When I travel in Europe I seek a small table, where I settle in with a glass of wine and my notebook, to watch life in the new place, often a city, and to feel the pulse of streets, the weather, and the people who make the life of the city. I learned this art of

---

[190] United States Holocaust and Memorial Museum, *Holocaust Encyclopedia*, "Krakow."

[191] Maciek Zabierowski in personal communication with the author.

[192] Auschwitz Jewish Center Fellows, 2014 Speakers Bios (Kraków).

[193] *New Eastern Europe*, a biweekly journal published since 2011, focuses on contemporary Central and Eastern European literature and politics. The project is a collaboration between the City of Gdansk, the European Solidarity Center and the Jan Nowak-Jezioranski College of Eastern Europe.

living in Florence and then traveling alone through Europe in my twenties. I draw near through reading, eating, the taste of wine, and the quiet space of a table from which to watch the city or town's rhythm, it's sensual movements as day slides into night. I settle into a high table at a restaurant-bar just off the market square, where I delve into the new magazine. Lech Wałesa says that young Poles must not look to the past but to the future. "I look to the future. What happened in the past is now history; the future is important." He explains that Poland has had a geopolitical position between Russia and Germany that had caused the people to "keep up their guard." This, he suggests, has contributed to the Poles ability to "foresee things." [194] Historically, the Poles have developed keen awareness of the possibility of being attacked and in the past have warned the world of war to come. He suggests that these abilities will assist Poles in activity creating democratic, representative government and in their relations with Russia and the Ukraine at present. Poland has been a European Union nation since 2004, and it is thriving. "We are building new state–Europe." [195] Poland is gradually becoming a full-fledged democracy, increasingly integrated into a commercial, capitalist, and unified Europe. This stage, he says, requires for Poland young leaders with a vision for the future. But capitalism must be tamed and disciplined, asserts Walesa.[196]

One concern for Poles continues to be its position in relationship to Russia. At the time of this writing in 2016, Russia points its nuclear warheads toward Poland. Poland's position is precarious in a changing Europe where Russia still threatens to the east. During the Nazi occupation, the years of the Second World War, Jewish and non-Jewish Poles lost territory, loved ones, nationhood, and the exercise of collective and individual rights through occupation. In 1945 Poland's government, exiled during the war in London, and the Polish people on the ground felt betrayed by American and British relinquishment of Polish territories to Stalin at the Yalta Conference, effectively transforming Poland into a Russian communist satellite within three short years (1945-1948). Poland, a nation state between the tenth and fourteenth centuries, underwent a series of partitions between 1772 and 1795. The nation was divided between the Russia Empire, Prussia (the German Empire), and the Austro-Hungarian (Habsburg Dynasty) Empire. In November 1918 Poland celebrated its second republican independence. In the interwar period, people lived for eighteen years with a relative sense of nationalistic pride and hope for an independent government. In 1939, as it had been in the First World War, the country was occupied by the Germans. Poland remained an occupied territory into the early part of 1945. The years from 1945 to 1948 marked the end of German occupation and Russian takeover of the country.[197] Poland felt that the West had betrayed the country's government in exile to Stalin. By the early 1980s the Solidarity trade union began to exert political pressure

---

[194] "Only When Forced Do I Look to the Past," a conversation with Lech Wałesa in *New Eastern Europe*, July-August 2014, 7-8.

[195] Wałesa, 9.

[196] Ibid, 12.

[197] Norman Davies provides a detailed history of Poland's struggle for independence in *God's Playground: A History of Poland Volume II: 1795 to the Present*, 1982. See in particular pages 279-321.

on Russia for worker's rights and for labor unions that would freely represent Polish shipyard workers in Gdansk. An opening to democratic reforms followed in the late eighties and early nineties. In 2014, Walesa wanted the younger generations to hold a vision of Poland's economic growth and thus inclusion in a Western world community. Walesa argues his philosophy that looking back to the violence and loss of wars, to the silence and depravation of Poles under communism may not move the country forward, which is the focus it now needs.[198] It is a past on which not to dwell. Yet, how can one resist remembering in Poland? Increasingly, Poles are called to remember. Walesa's conflict represents a larger underlying conflict in Polish society: how to envision a vibrant future while acknowledging and addressing a painful past best characterized by occupation and destruction?

Professor of Sociology Annamaria Orla-Bukowska notes what she calls "external visitors" to Poland have their own memories of the Second World War and the Holocaust, or the Jewish Genocide, as Poles have called it.[199] External input from visitors to the country forces Poles to confront non-Polish and, therefore, divergent and global representations of the Holocaust in Poland and the country's role in relation to Polish Jews. The external incoming influences challenge Polish notions of personal and national identity.

The country has made an art of memorialization and preservation. I was in Poland, with others of like mind, to study and encounter the remnants of the past. We went to the apartment building at 7 Planty Street where the Kielce pogrom occurred on July 4, 1946. It was just after the Second World War had ended and Jews were returning to Poland from Russia and the Ukraine en route to Palestine and the United States. Forty-six Jews were murdered here. Flower wreaths and candles adorned the front of the building just below a commemorative plaque. Bogdan Białek of the Jan Karski Society in Kielce met with us and explained that elementary school teachers in Kielce wanted more class time to teach their students Second World War history. He stressed the urgency that young Poles know their history to live with increasing knowledge and understanding in the present.[200]

One afternoon late in our trip we met at Auschwith Jewish Center (AJC) in Oświęcim with our museum guide, Paweł Sawicki. Maciek had called Paweł "the accidental guide," as we were to have another guide at Auschwitz-Birkenau, but she could not accommodate us to her schedule. We were fortunate that he hosted our group. Since 2009 Paweł has worked with the Auschwitz-Birkenau State Memorial and Museum Press Office. He writes press releases, manages social media publicity (a position that balloons in responsibility with each passing day!), serves as a point of contact for the outside press, handles negative publicity, and in his role as editor of *Oś*, the organization's official publication, conducts interviews, attends events, and

---

[198] See Wałesa in *New Eastern Europe*, July-August 2014, 7-8.

[199] Author notes from a lecture with Dr. Orla-Bukowska at Jagiellonian University, July 2014.

[200] Author notes from a visit with Bogdan Białek, Founder and President, Jan Karski Society, July 2014. Jan Karski was involved in Polish resistance to German occupation in World War II. He was an informer to the Polish government in exile in London and to the Allies. For more on his life, see "The Patron" at The Jan Karski Society's website. The organization's offices since November 2014 are located at 7 Planty Street.

writes articles. He tells us that the memorial-museum has 270 staff members and 250 guides. Individual companies also provide tour guides but all groups must tour with a guide. There are general tours, as well as educational tours, as was ours. The official staff is obligated by state law to deal with the history of Auschwitz. The staff partners with other organizations and can tailor tours to group's needs.

Oświęcim as a contemporary town has been overshadowed by the liminal and literal presence of the camps. Paweł points out to us the problems of linking the town and the museum. Many visitors do not realize that Oświęcim is a Polish town where people have lived for centuries. The town boasted a thriving Jewish community, numbering about 7,500, until the war. It is now home to nearly forty thousand Poles, none of whom are Jewish. The AJC was created in part to draw visitors to Auschwitz (the German transliteration of Oświęcim) into the town, both to learn the town's Jewish and Gentile history (Jews and Gentiles had lived and worked together in Oświęcim over centuries of cohabitation) and to consider the town as a vibrant space where contemporary Poles live.

Of course, people come here to visit the various Auschwitz compounds (there are four major sections of the camp). "People come to see artifacts," Paweł explains, "to see an authentic site." Conservation allows this possibility. "We have one of the most modern conservation labs in the world." [201] The universities at Kraków, Tarnów, and Warsaw send their conservators to the museum where they engage in work to preserve twentieth century materials: shoes, suitcases, toothbrushes, leather, fiber, paper, metal, wood. The conservatory efforts present particular challenges due to the range of materials found at the camp.

The conservation lab works closely with university conservation departments in Kraków, Tarnów, and Warsaw. In the case of the memorial and its artifacts, a conservation philosophy is essential. The philosophy at Auschwitz is "to not rebuild," but to preserve what remains and objects that are still being discovered. People come to see an authentic site, to see artifacts. At the Auschwitz state museum original is synonymous with authentic, new with inauthentic. The staff asks questions in the interest of conservation. What is the history of the object? What damages must we keep? Preservation is a science. In considering buildings and their spaces, a compromise occurs between conserving the original landscape and the original site. "We're not an emotional theme park," Paweł imparts the organization's philosophy of guiding tours. The guides are sensitive, trained in professional ethics, but the education they offer does not address the emotional impact of being at Auschwitz. The emphasis is on history. Guides make visitors aware of why things happen and their meaning and urge visitors to assume collective responsibility for the ethical implications of history, what he calls the "universal lesson" that evolves of reflection on and response to the events of the camps. "Israeli groups have their own narration," he continues. "We work together a lot. We travel to Yad Vashem and they travel here to Poland. Most Israeli groups have with them an Auschwitz museum guide and their

---

[201] Author's personal notes, July 2014.

own guide. It has been a long process of building trust and becoming friends," he tells us.[202]

Paweł's discussion with our group is momentous for me. How often does one meet in a small group with a man that comes to work every day to the old Auschwitz grounds and knows the place and its history intimately? Paweł is both a guide and a press officer at Auschwitz. He received his training to guide groups through the former camps over a period of several months. He took rigorous examinations to be able to guide educational groups. He had to speak at least one foreign language speak fluently. He also had to develop extensive knowledge of war and camp history, of conservation, and the reasons that motivate different cultural, religious, and national groups to visit the camps. Guides meet with survivors as a part of their training. They receive voice training and learn how to work with large groups of visitors. They also learn how to educate people about the camps, especially younger people, within the context of genocidal events on a global scale.

A professional at Auschwitz-Birkenau Museum and Memorial, Paweł of course holds a view about visitation to the camps very different from my own visitor's view. He emphasizes technology in his discussion, an area that will see exponential growth in the coming decades. Auschwitz-Birkenau Memorial, as of 2014, has a Facebook page with 13,000 "likes." It is ironic to "like" Auschwitz, but Paweł's tone is serious. An international group has been hired to maintain the Facebook page and travels to Poland for a training event. In the past fourteen years, the number of visitors to Auschwitz has tripled. There were over 1.53 million visitors in 2014. This number indicates the highest attendance in the history of European memorial sites. These numbers influence the memorial-museum's administrative approach to visitors. Paweł tells us, "Historical monuments should not be destroyed. They should be explained. For example, a place should explain the how and why of a particular choice of commemoration. So, as guides we both promote and defend this place. People write a diary and now they take selfies. We cannot dictate how people choose to represent their experience." Here is where the ongoing conversation of ethics in response to memory becomes vital. Perhaps selfies haven't replaced writing. All these responses exist together. Someone in our group mentions the noticeably loud presence of Israeli youth groups. "Loudness and other behaviors at the camp can be a defense mechanism," our guide suggests. The projection of an Israeli group's presence becomes a statement of survival and return.

Before we embarked on our travels in Poland, our New York coordinator cautioned us to be kind to one another. Three weeks of travel together and the demand of history in Poland would impinge on our relationships. I read her advice as a reminder to give one another mental and emotional space that the trip would logically require. One of our guides in Poland, though good-natured and kind, was sometimes at a loss for how to address the mounting tension of our group dynamics. The other guide was often quiet, an intellectual, emotionally distant, and did not engage in the

---

[202] German repatriation monies paid for my fellowship. These funds pay for educational programs, scholarships, fellowships, and conferences. For example, Volkswagen AG helped to fund a conference at the Auschwitz-Birkenau Memorial Museum, "Remembrance Has Not Matured in Us Yet."

group's internal struggles. I was happy to have a roommate who was thoughtful, considerate, and who, within a few years of my age, shared similar hours to my own. Each of us in our own way dealt with the psychic contents of our trip and tried to get along as best we could.

There are consequences to sharing thoughts and emotions, especially when one is considering the genocide of Polish Jews and the Polish implication and historical response to decimation. Feelings run high and come from a coiled place inside that can explode when it reaches the surface. At some point, conversation—no matter how intelligent, thought-driven, and historically grounded—has to stop. There is a place, an hour, a moment when one cannot say much of anything. Silence has to be the response. But, there was never enough silence. With nine students and two guides, and a number of guest speakers, someone was always speaking. Conversation was ceaseless, even relentless. I felt familiarly desirous of silence, drawn to walks alone, spaces for writing, and wandering away from the group.

Space was mostly not forthcoming. Yet, I found spaces on benches at hotels and wrote in my journal on the van to sites. In Poland, I felt inside history, absorbing the small villages and the networks of bigger cities— Kraków and Warsaw. Poland was strangely new. I did not know Polish and had never been to Eastern Europe. It had been twenty-four years since I had been in Europe. In that time, I had travelled through the United States, particularly in the intermountain and southwest regions, as well as to Southeast and Himalayan Asia, and to South America. I had had a child at forty and had been parenting now for ten years. I was well into my career as a community college English instructor, had just passed my dissertation defense, and awaited conferment of the doctorate. In the quarter century that had passed since I had set foot in Europe, the world had radically changed. I was no longer the twenty-five-year-old woman who had just graduated from the university, worked in high technology, dabbled in writing, and thought one day she would raise a child on her own. When I had last visited the European continent, it had been 1990. Europe had entered a period of rapid and shocking transformation as the Berlin Wall was demolished. Germany was opening through its reunification. Gorbachev's implementation of Perestroika, a restructuring of political and economic systems, and Glasnost, the opening of former restrictions on the Russian people, had initiated the disintegration of the Soviet republics. Poland was no longer under communist closure, the kind of inaccessible Poland with which I had grown up in the sixties and seventies, even into the eighties as Solidarity begin to make inroads to achieve worker rights, to unionize the trades, and then push its activism into democratic reforms.

Poland of 2014 was still newly democratized and riding the capitalist energy of a growing economy, increased education at all levels, and experiencing an increased standard of living. Subsequently, Poles have experienced increased satisfaction in their daily lives. All these changes have contributed to a growing tourist industry in Poland. This tourism, rooted largely in an interest in the country's Jewish history, as well as its early history through periods of partition, into the world wars, through Communism and into democratization, and now well into its post-Communist development, has found expression in new museums, restored synagogues, Jewish community centers and festivals, and new restaurants and remodeled hotels.

History lies under things. It is often quiet. One must look and listen for it. History infuses the Polish land: in swaying stalks of wildflowers and grasses undulating in meadows, in cobblestone streets rising to meet the arch of the foot, in the curve of a synagogue's ceiling and the angled light filtering through high temple windows, in the unwrapping and smoothing of a Torah scroll, in the crooked, dusty doors of former Jewish storefronts in a small Polish town. In Działoszyce the central door to the old Jewish store has been locked. Bricks the color of sand have been piled in front of the two side doors. Above each door floats a disc of concentric circles: the sefirot emanations related in Kabbalah teachings as manifestations of enlightenment or God-nature, carried down through angels and into humans. In Poland I was alert to things that caught my eye, but frequently in the moment did not apprehend the meanings embedded in those things, such as the sefirot. It is only later in writing and reflecting, looking at photographs, that I renew my observations and notice things previously hidden from my awareness.

A former Jewish storefront in Działoszyce, Poland.
Source: Author photo, 2014

In her short story, "Poland," Thaisa Frank writes of a poet who died in the midst of composing his last poem. Its subject was Poland, though he had never been. (His parents emigrated from Germany just before WWII). The country and its history haunted him. He wrote of its snowy plains and bare trees, people hiding in barns and eating "ice for bread," seeing these images through his rearview mirror. After his death his obsession transfers to his wife and she, too, begins to seek out things Polish.

Perhaps so that she can draw closer to him. Are we not inexorably drawn into a writer's life because we want something of his perception? Isn't it true that those closest to us are those we know least of all? Ultimately, reading is a beloved intimacy saturated with distance. "Poland stayed on her mind like a small, subliminal itch."[203] After the poet's death his second wife—who begins to see Poland in her own rearview mirror—sends the poem to the first wife. The first wife is angry. She has tried to rid herself of this man and his memory (perhaps as the poet tried to rid himself of Poland?). The second wife agrees but had obeyed the compulsion to send the poem to her anyway. The second wife has inherited the poem from her deceased poet-husband (previously she had neither read his poetry nor taken any interest in it). The image of Poland stays with her and she cannot dissolve it, even after she has sent the poem to the first wife.

What is it we keep giving to each other? In language, we force our history onto beings present and those to come. They may ingest our words and make a life in the present that includes places never seen and barely known but remembered in language. It is as if those lives in words that came before, those stories in countries we have never inhabited, now belong to us. Those countries have become our own. More than two years have passed since I traveled to Poland. But sometimes I feel Poland inside of me. It happens at random moments. In California I drive down the hill toward the ocean, the back of my Subaru filled with groceries, books, and student papers. I'm on my way to pick up my son at school. When the day is bright, mid-autumn, and the ocean refracts light like a fierce jewel, the time in Poland fills me and I feel hopeful. I remember that anything we thought was dead might come to life again. Beauty insists. Beauty wants recognition. What is it? It is a feeling of hope, the promise and inevitability of something new and purposeful after war. This feeling is both historical, potently appearing in the wake of war, and ahistorical, lingering through time, which for humans is ceaselessly ripe with the possibility of war. It is the distinct possibility of rebirth, the necessity of remembering. It is people who survived history and who have come through punishing hardship and partition and occupation and the closing down of a country under communist regime. Poland is the recovery of people through their community centers, Jewish centers, wall murals of color and hope, through the little pathways that wind into villages, the flowers and fence posts, chickens and blueberries.

I feel Poland as a history I never knew, a place that may return me to some part of myself that I lost in being born post-war, in this late twentieth century at the far Western edge of the North American continent. Poland is with me. I feel joy that it is more than memory. It is a country growing into its history, reaching out to the world to share its history and in the process revisioning its past. It comes out of shame and into dialogue with the world, largely, ironically, through its Jewish history. It is absence—the hole that exists where once a vibrant Jewish population thrived—that speaks in Poland. That absence is being cared for and discussed and brought into consciousness again. That absence takes the shapes of words. It settles in places that

---

[203] Frank, *A Brief History of Camouflage*, 94.

people populate with remembrances and horror and wonder and quietude. Poland returns to find itself. It reaches back to remember what it has been and how it has experienced. It is this insistence that Poland makes alive in me.

3.4 DREAMS IN THE MIDDLE OF POLAND

Four nights of snakes

A river, boat filled with water

Belongings submerged

Head above, torso below

Destroyed buildings,

my son, Elias, and I inside

he unafraid and pragmatic

leap to another dimension

we look at a house,

too expensive I cannot buy it

even with a co-buyer, with my mother

we cannot purchase it together

nothing is possible

everything destroyed.

3.5 ON THE WAY TO TREBLINKA

Fields green and yellow

Scots pine. Birch.

Bogs, stands of forests,

Rivers, ponies, storks in flight

Barns, tall grasses

Jersey cows grazing

A girl and a woman on bikes

Dirt road, hay

Northeast of Warsaw

toward Belorussian border

Small town

House with cornflowers and red poppies

Squash, cabbage

Yard with apple tree

short fences

Gray low clouds,

looks like rain

Wild yarrow on the roadside

Our van stops. Railroad tracks.

Waiting.

3.6 A SPACE OF INDETERMINACY

What is there and not there? Certain presences make the page but absences are often more telling. I am reading to piece together a mystery. What is there and not there? What has been told and what will never be told? Jean Améry's writings in *On Suicide* guide me in navigating, like a ship at sea, the facts—with some maps and a sextant— and the mysteries—mostly the silent moments of decision or indecision that led up to his fall—of Primo Levi's death. Elie Wiesel once commented, "Primo Levi died at

Auschwitz forty years later," a statement that evolves of his question, "Can one die in Auschwitz, after Auschwitz?"[204] Levi's death, for Wiesel, answered that question. Yet, another question might be: is there life after Auschwitz without Auschwitz? The answer has to be "no," both for survivors of the camps and for their descendants. I use the word descendants collectively. For humans living at the contemporary moment have inherited Auschwitz, and its consequences brought forward in time, as a symbolic and literal space of genocide.

"Can one die in Auschwitz, after Auschwitz?" is the same statement that literary scholar Sandor Goodhart claims "opens the interrogation from which our identity in the wake of disaster may be construed."[205] If we are to have an identity, a sense of self both personal and collective, it must arise, by default it does arise, of Auschwitz. From there, as Goodhart suggests, and only from there—that place, the space of genocide, the wake of events that crests over our heads, our hearts, our very bodies and threatens to engulf us—we may begin to sense who we have become because of the gravity of what has transpired. Why then am I compelled, even if objectively compelled, safely housed in scholarly distance, by Levi's death? Not so much because his death is my own but because his death becomes a statement, one among many such statements, of how he chose to live and how he might have determined to die.

I return now to Jean Améry the profound writer and philosopher, intellectual friend to Levi after their release from the camps, also imprisoned at Auschwitz (1943-1945), who wrote *On Suicide* as an apologia of suicide. The decision of suicide for him revolved around a wish to no longer participate in the absurdity, the language game, of the world. Améry consciously ended his life in 1978 at the age of sixty-five. In this final book he argues that suicide is an act of freedom and as such he calls it voluntary death. The word choice of voluntary signifies collusion between Améry and death. The author and death have negotiated and achieved a bargain. Death says, "It is time now and here's how you will do it, and here is the typewriter key pressing ink to paper and here's the letter." In the two remaining years of life he wrote his apologia as a conversation with death, a conversation, too, with his readers. Perhaps we—his readers—as participants in the language game, the deceits and delusions with which it blankets our minds and in which we bathe as warm water—are the reason he desires to leave the world once and for all. In his body live memories of torture at Fort Breendonk in northern Belgium, where the Gestapo had detained him. He had already been imprisoned at Gurs in southern France, had lost his young wife to heart ailment while in exile from the Nazis in Belgium, and would experience imprisonment at Auschwitz, including the labor camp Buna-Monowitz, Buchenwald, and, finally, Bergen-Belsen. There is for him under torture what is the terrible loss of agency, choice, self-control, and intellect. There are boots and bludgeons and shoulders tied and dislocated. There are essences inside him that were once only his and in torture have been raped and sullied. He carries a specific and particular shame he no longer wants to bear. He is kind in his writing. He is kind to the one who has determined to

---

[204] See Gambetta's "Primo Levi's Last Moments" in *Boston Review*.

[205] Goodhart, "The War to End All Wars: Mimetic Theory and Mounting to Extremes in a Time of Disaster."

take his own life. He unravels the ideas that readers may have about the suicide act, the attempts and accompanying desires. He crafts not explanations from the purview of psychology but exegeses from his personal experience and philosophical writings, as well as the experiences of others who chose voluntary death. He explores suicidal thoughts and actions that may ensue from that thinking.

I most urgently want to write of the association of suicide with the emotional experience of shame. Readers can never be certain that Levi purposely fell to his death when he fell over the balustrade. He fell from the spiraling staircase into the foyer of his Torino apartment building and crashed—jumped, blacked out—three floors to his death. In *November of the Soul: The Enigma of Suicide* George Howe Colt writes that there has been a reported rarity of suicides in the Nazi concentration camps. He quotes Levi writing in *If This Is a Man* who describes the need to survive in an environment of death and that in such a dire place there was no time to think of killing oneself. Yet, he continues, "Many survivors seemed to experience a delayed reaction in which a built-up residue of depression found expression only after the immediate threat of death was gone." He details Levi's return to Italy from Auschwitz with a few survivors from his original transport, and then writes, "Forty-two years later, at age sixty-seven, suffering from severe depression, the author threw himself down the stairwell of his fourth-floor apartment in Torino, one of numerous death-camp survivors who ultimately took their life."[206] Tracing suicide as a venture, an endeavor, means re-entering history to look at the social response to suicide. Tracing Levi's potential suicide in particular means thinking about why he may have chosen to keep quiet his decision to tumble over the balustrade, or perhaps why he made the decision in the course of just seconds and then acted on it.

In England of the mid-seventeenth century suicides were judged legally criminal if the individual was of age and sane, but were not criminal if the individual was determined to have been mentally deranged.[207] Those who had attempted suicide and were sane were mutilated by stake and given burial on highways, considered then a shamefully public place, until 1823. How ironic and defeating that one could make a voluntary decision for death and, if unsuccessful, undergo criminal punishment and enforced death at the hands of others. This is the reason that Améry—partisan and Holocaust survivor—argues suicide as an act of choice, one that may be particularly important for those who have unduly suffered violent acts imposed by others. Such violence appears to have haunted Améry through his life and robbed him of much of his agency and will to persist into the later years of his life. The English desire to link suicide to humiliation and shame represented in the public display of the corpse was to serve for the living as a deterrent to suicide. To dishonor life, even one's own, was to disregard fellow human beings and the offender would be justly punished. Offenders were denied Christian burial, therefore jeopardizing their souls, and they were deprived of property, memory, and respect.

---

[206] Colt, *November of the Soul*, 222.
[207] Bähr. "Between 'Self-Murder' and 'Suicide': The Modern Etymology of Self-Killing."

The word suicide originated under the influence of Enlightenment thought, as denunciation of the deed gradually gave way to empathy for the doer. In England this process began in the 1650s; in France and Germany it started in the second half of the eighteenth century, with German giving rise to the equivalent term *Selbstentleibung* ("self-disembodiment"). Andreas Bähr writes that the attendant decriminalization of self-killing turned self-murder into suicide.[208] With decriminalization, sinners and criminals became victims, patients, melancholics, and the mentally ill. Améry resists pathologizing suicide, a pathology he points out developed as the study of suicide was subsumed into psychological analysis and explanation. However, he argues that in psychoanalysis a scientific language of categorization and method morphed into compassion for victims to the detriment of thinking directly about the act of suicide and its conditions and consequences. Does compassion impede a deeper, more detailed, even curious, mode of thinking? Améry suggests that, in fact, it does. Compassion for victims proves an obstacle to critical analysis of how and why people choose voluntary death. The notion that compassion impedes reasoning highlights the fact that understanding suicide should not be an experience of feeling with the victim but an inquiry into possible meanings and implications of suicide. Exploration of the possible meanings of suicide and the person's choice as an agent of free will allows one to consider suicide as a philosophy, as a way of being. The choice of how and when death comes makes death an expression of being. If we focus solely on the act, then suicide becomes the demise of (a) life at one's own hands. On Améry's view, voluntary death and its implications shift the focus away from death to life decisions. Améry considers the thought processes foundational to death as choice; choice equates with freedom and exercise of personal will. These contemplative acts likely create the resolve that gives voluntary death its occasion.

Améry urges his readers to understand suicide, at least in his case, late in life, through the rich experiences of writing and thinking and participation in the resistance movements of World War II, as well as his ongoing struggles with cultural and religious identities. His mother was Catholic, his father Jewish. He was born in Vienna, Austria, a country that betrayed him and his fellow Jews and partisans, as Hans Chaim Mayer. Thus, his personal death constitutes a deliberate and considered decision; its subsequent actions initiated through the will result in a choice purposefully made. Rather than others taking one's life, or being at the mercy of medical technology, voluntary death allows determination of the method and time of ending one's life. One might read that statement through knowledge of the effects of depression on the brain and the draw to suicide that those with depression may experience—a draw that reflects desire to obliterate emotional pain and to end bodily entrapment to the material, relational world, which as we age can become increasingly the cause of disappointment, disillusionment, despair, and fatigue. Depression and trauma, and their many effects on the mind and body, may have also motivated Levi's voluntary death in later life, if indeed he chose his death moment.

---

[208] Bähr. "Between 'Self-Murder' and 'Suicide': The Modern Etymology of Self-Killing."

Suicide is finality. One may choose it over a lengthy period of consideration or within the space of a few seconds. It is desire to transcend embodiment, to depart human interaction and the interminable, insufferable difficulties of life. It is desire to cease an interior conversation of self-doubt, of fatigue with the aging body, with the mind, with others, with suffering, and, ironically, with death itself. Many can relate to the impulse or contemplation of life's cessation at one's own hands. There is in that impulse a strange kind of agency, a tremor of violence. How many do not succeed in carrying the act to completion, how many attempt it, and how many (and how often) contemplate it? For some, suicide remains a thought, a dream, an imagined possibility of unerring, tremulous proportions.

Shame makes us human. It preserves a sense of shared humanness in the social realm; certain things are not supposed to happen to and between humans. We look away. We feel ashamed for having seen, and thus carry with us events and their memories that defy language. These events taint our language and our sense of what it means to be human. Language was made for something else—for dreams and possibilities of ourselves. We make language stoop, force it to bend to horror, so that words enter the realm of human relations. Violence, too, must be included in the story of being human. This is the work writers perform to make the unspeakable spoken.

The implication of those writers who comment on Levi's suicide—journalists, biographers, and well-known writers like Elie Wiesel, Cynthia Ozick, and Carolyn Forché—is that Auschwitz killed Levi. Forché, poet and writer of human rights, in the anthology *Against Forgetting* writes in a perfunctory biography of Levi that he committed suicide.[209] This scenario of the writer's death is readily accepted and circulated in literary and journalistic circles. It is public knowledge. Where then are the questions? Where is the openness to other interpretations, or the simple: Primo Levi died in a fall from the stairs located within his apartment building? In all this assuredness of his quiet choice, his lingering depression—the police report indicates death by suicide, his wife's lament that she knew for some time that he would choose this end—I, far from objective reader, long for a space of indeterminacy.

Ozick argues in her essay "Primo Levi's Suicide Note" that Levi's final book, *The Drowned and the Saved*, was his suicide note.[210] Yet, this reader finds that final book both hopeful and pragmatic. In it, Levi acknowledges the ongoing political problems in the world—violence, war, suffering, mistreatment of human beings by their fellows; yet, he says that one must continue to study, think, know, and act in the world against violence and for peace and well-being. His essays in that last book are realistic in facing past and future injustices. His tone reminds me of another writer, James Baldwin, who in concluding his 1955 essay, "Notes of a Native Son," wrote that he accepted injustice while he would continue with all his power to fight it. Rage and bitterness had killed Baldwin's father. He did not want the legacy of injustice induced by the poisonous effects of slavery, racism and segregation to corrode and

---

[209] Forché writes, "Primo Levi committed suicide in his native Turin in April 1987," 373.
[210] See Ozick's "Primo Levi's Suicide Note" in *Metaphor and Memory*.

kill him. He sought to recover himself from hatred. Levi's efforts to save himself after Auschwitz were not dissimilar.

Ozick argues that the tight control Levi kept on his rage killed him. But, I think not. Perhaps she finds the book his "suicide note" because in that manuscript he finally allows himself to express the suppressed rage he has harbored for forty years toward the Germans. She writes that he hurled himself down the stairs from which he fell and that he leaped from the staircase. She knows neither circumstance as a certainty, and I remain firmly confounded by the leaps in her own language, from imagination to imposition on a supposed reality. In my own exploration of Levi's death, I find that I cannot know, but that I will not allow myself to refer to his death as a suicide. Rather, I address the possibility of suicide, the pull that gravity exerts on all enthralled to the human condition, embodied and headed for death. Levi places his reader firmly in the terrain of uncertainty as he details in "A Self-Interview" his response to what and who he would have been had he not been a prisoner in Auschwitz. "If a man sets out towards a crossroad and does not take the left-hand path, it is obvious that he will take the one on the right, but almost never are our choices between only two alternatives. Then, every choice is followed by others, all multiple, and so on, *ad infinitum*. Last of all, our future depends heavily on external factors, wholly extraneous to our deliberate choices, and on internal factors as well, of which we are, however, not aware."[211] He concludes that for these reasons a person knows neither his own future nor that of his neighbor. Accordingly, one cannot say what his past would have been like 'if.'"

In a documentary film, *La Strada di Primo Levi* (2006), the writer looks haunted; he is unhappy; Auschwitz stays with him. After viewing, I read one of his last interviews and its tone projects tiredness with the world, with publishers, with young people, with reading audiences, with America, with the demands of public life and being a renowned writer. Every writer gets tired of this public performance; some do it well, many do not. The reader should want only his language and narratives and perceptions. To ask for anything beyond that, for a life, for a biography is invasive and perhaps transcends the limits of literature. Yet, words are the path to the writer. Words lead readers to explore the life and the meaning residing just beneath the text.

I revisit *The Drowned and the Saved* repeatedly, looking for any sign of despair, any finality in Levi's tone that would indicate knowledge of his coming death. I find no such thing, though it does not mean it's not there, or elsewhere. I read the writer more than the human being who lived daily life quietly and in a personal time and space about which he wrote little and mostly left to his biographers to uncover. Instead, I find a sort of deepened sharing with the reader on the themes he explored through his autobiographical writing: memory (primarily of what he calls the offense); shame; his experience of the intellect while imprisoned at Auschwitz; the futility of violence; the moral ambiguities of the gray zone within the camps and in the world at war that lacked an ethical code that people had previously established in civil society; the notion that readers often had of escape from the camps being a sort

---

[211] Levi. *The Voice of Memory*, 205.

of redemption from one's imprisonment. It is in the chapter "Shame" that he writes "suicide is an act of man and not of the animal. It is a meditated act, a noninstinctive, unnatural choice, and in the Lager, there were few opportunities to choose."[212] Levi and Améry agree that suicide is meditated and thought out. It is not an instinctive action but based on a rational plan of action. However, Levi notes of the *Lager* the special circumstances that disallowed suicide, an environment of extreme physical and emotional deprivation that curtailed and damaged the options prisoners had.

Yet, in this final book Levi is fully participatory in the human dialogue. He is immersed in the language, in conversation with himself and his interested readers. He writes in the preface his motivation to write this particular work.

> This book means to contribute to the clarification of some aspects of the Lager phenomenon which still appear obscure. It also sets itself a more ambitious goal, to try to answer the most urgent questions, the question which torments all those who have happened to read our accounts: How much of the concentration camp world is dead and will not return. How much is back or is coming back? What can each of us do so that in this world pregnant with threats at least this threat will be nullified?[213]

These questions sit at the center of his first book, *If This Is a Man*. They are questions that drive his writing, questions for the future and its readers. The book speaks. The book is interlocutor.

Levi in this final published work during his lifetime has a goal, an ambitious one at that. There is urgency, immediacy, even demand. He offers up some answers as to what humans might do to eliminate threats that give rise to genocide. This is not a man ready to leave life by his own hand. His voice does not belie preoccupation with death and plans of departure. This language reveals a man engaged with the painful questions arisen of life experience in relationship to his readers. This voice lays out the questions in an exploratory manner. This consciousness listens for change. It has not yet tired of trying to imagine change and remains ever vigilant against the ripe possibilities of violence. This is Levi the writer whom I hear, perhaps more than Levi the human being who suffers silently and who keeps his interior life at a distance while he writes. The best writers must do so, I think. The best writers are those, like Levi, who know how to keep their subject matter at center and who, in the interest of their writing, hold personal struggle at bay. But I'm uncertain that this distance is more choice than necessity.

The problems that Levi discusses in 1986 and 1987 as he writes his final work are the problems that continue to manifest today. He writes of Vietnam, Cambodia, and Afghanistan. I think with him, toward his thoughts, too, as I read of Syrian, Israeli, and Palestinian suffering. I think how he might have written about Islamic violence in a bid for political recognition and social power in the world. How would he have

---

[212] Levi, *The Drowned and the Saved*, 76.
[213] Ibid, 20.

experienced the disintegration of Communism in 1989, just two and a half years after his death? He was reading writers and poets, giving interviews, writing, and looking at the world through the lens of his past from his vantage point in the present.

In the mid-1970s Levi retired from his work as a chemist. He had worked in an asbestos mine in his early twenties, just after graduating. He and his friend also had a lab in the basement of their apartment building where their experiments created noxious fumes. Over his career as a chemistry student, a prisoner in the IG Farben lab at Auschwitz, and a technical and, later, managing director of an industrial paint and varnish factory, he worked with potassium, lead, arsenic, benzene, and ammonium chloride. For over thirty years he worked at SIVA with chemical compounds in paints. His exposure to chemicals over a sustained period of time may well have affected his health. He suffered from prostate problems in his sixties and around the period of his death a friend reported he had experienced dizziness, possibly from anti-depressants which lower blood pressure. Environmental and health concerns failed to figure into police reports. Then, the statements that lack any doubt, of all certainty: Primo Levi committed suicide on April 11, 1987. Primo Levi was depressed, and, as Wiesel said, he died at Auschwitz forty years later.

It is because of Levi that I do not consider the world of the camps, and the obliteration of approximately sixty million people in the Second World War, "things of another time." Rather than Levi killing himself, could it be that Levi killed Auschwitz, the one he carried in memory? Or, that the burden of Auschwitz in a delayed manner of forty years overwhelmed Levi? Implied meaning: Levi could no longer live with Auschwitz. Suicide has not been uncommon among camp survivors (refugees as Wiesel calls them in his novel, *The Time of the Uprooted*). In fact, Levi did live with Auschwitz for forty years. It was his work and it became the basis of his work. He became, he confessed, a writer because of Auschwitz.

Levi's rabbi friend David Mendel who spoke with Levi prior to his death saw no sign, no indication of suicidal tendencies. His biographers depict Primo Levi as a secret and tortured man. What if he was none of these things and he decided simply that he was tired? What if he lost consciousness for one moment and fell forward enough so that the gravity tugged him downward? What if he wanted to give into the underworld, the devouring spirals of Dante's imagined inferno? What if he was eternally and suddenly very curious? What if his death was not because of torture but a moment of extreme freedom and lightness of being, momentarily heavy with falling and collision that he had never known before?

Levi was a man of facts. He labored to establish as facts the terrible psychological and physical conditions of the camps that contributed to the demise of his fellow humans. He was also a man of questions. His mind energized to labs where he mixed and measured elements. He knew how to wonder, how to observe complex interactions of matter, and how to find solutions. He knew to note and remember, to frame queries and look for answers. He knew that writing was limited. He could not answer everything (or anything) in his writing, but he could try. Perhaps Levi chose his own death, as Carole Angier in her biography of Levi concludes from her research, "Primo Levi's death is not part of his testimony, but only of his disease."[214] His death then was linked with depression and trauma. Still, I avoid making the possibly untrue statement: Levi committed suicide. As if a finality, as if no questions, as if a totality of a life or an action through which one views a life. I cannot know. For me, there is something else: an open, endless possibility of unknowing. It is from this possibility that I continue to read Levi's work, his voice streaming through the course of my own lifetime. One cannot live the same after Auschwitz—survivor, reader, human being (even one who knows little of Levi's life and death). Life is complicated. Decisions intersect and collide at any one moment. At this fatal intersection dare I ask, what if Levi fell against his will and with his whole desire?

3.7 MY NIGHTS

I had a dream that someone

loved Levi

not his possible suicide

or his daily depression—

probably germane to all writers—

but the fierce tenacity of survival

to live in the world

despite despair

in the company of writing.

I had a dream that someone

set a table for Levi

invited him to tell story

he did not fear that

---

[214] Angier, *The Double Bond: The Life of Primo Levi*, 726.

what was real appeared unreal,

or that others turned a deaf ear

words flowed, the language

made for disaster

each sentence giving joy in the wake of violence.

3.8 READING MIDRASHIC

Midrash extends a text materially by creating a new text in conversation with the primary one. Midrash is a response to a text where it is broken, incomplete, and seems to have left off. Humans are that text in the way that each is incomplete and wounded. Out of this suffering they join to create healing. Such healing is in and of itself a kind of completion, a new skin, a way of re-seeing that allows restoration. That restoration is never fully achieved but is always becoming, and that is the point. Restoration itself is a process. Interpretative work then is continuous and cyclical. People complete one another's ideas and stories. In those acts of attention and completion, humans gift one another with sight and alternative experience; they transcend historical time and widen each other's views beyond material constraints imposed by the body, which is always located in time and space. Humans don't need to be alive to give the gift. Writers and other documentarians extend the gift through text and in the archive. They don't need to exist in one another's geographical space.

What is the story that lingers silent within the story told? "Midrash," Sandor Goodhart writes, "does more than just respond to a perceived gap in the text; it performs that dislocation itself; it echoes the dislocation that is already a part of the primary narrative to which it is responding."[215] In appearing to fill in a gap the text offers, or does the work of offering. Midrashic interpretation extends text in a physical way since in the act of interpretation reader and text co-inhabit a physical and cognitive space. Readers are interactive with the text in their personal encounter with it. This is the encounter of reading where interaction becomes "a scene of instruction."[216]

Midrash always exists to serve a text other than itself. Interpretation is not text. It is response to, a certain quality of attention, sensitivity, a will to know and to imbibe, and to attend to meaning—both in the present of the text and in the present of the interpretative act. The notion of midrashic or textual interpretation as accountable and

---

[215] Goodhart. "A Land that Devours Its Inhabitants": *Midrashic Reading, Emmanuel Levinas, and Prophetic Exegesis*, 18.
[216] Ibid, 20.

in relationship to story proffers ethics as each human being's responsibility to his fellow other. Emmanuel Levinas centers the face-to-face encounter at the very heart of his ethical philosophy. Without the effort to see, hear, and be present with and to another, there can be no true relationship based on ethicality, grounded in a moral response to the very being (consciousness) and existence of another.

> It is this attention to the suffering of the Other that through the cruelties of our century (despite these cruelties, because of these cruelties) can be affirmed as the very nexus of human subjectivity, to the point of being raised to the level of supreme ethical principle—the only one it is possible to question—shaping the hopes and commanding the practical discipline of vast human groups. This attention and this action are so imperiously and directly incumbent on human beings (on their I's) that it makes awaiting them from an all-powerful God impossible without lowering ourselves. The consciousness of this inescapable obligation brings us close to God in a more difficult, but also more spiritual, way than does confidence in any kind of theodicy.[217]

This kind of relating—attention to the suffering of the other—lies at the very basis of humanity and defines it. If midrash is responsive to the wound in the other (the other is also the text) and exists to serve it, then wounding is a given of human embodiment. The wound resounds as a core basis of interpretation and thus shapes our relationship to each human being and to each text we engage.

Primo Levi asked his readers to serve as judges of the events that transpired at Auschwitz. He did not want to indulge in hatred of the Nazis and their co-conspirators. His sense was that future generations would have to learn and to judge. It would be their world and he would offer his account to them. As his reader, I have accepted the charge of judge. To judge, for me as a contemporary reader (and all the contingencies and conditions that constitute that contemporaneity), does not mean to preside over and to make determinations of guilt and blame. It means to determine what are my ethics, what kind of world do I want, what actions must I take over the course of my life to create the kinds of relating that support life? How do I work with and feel pain, as a sharp and immediate sensation, and suffering, as a sustained and uncomfortable condition, in a way that I do not cling to anger but learn from others, past and present, in continuing my work in responsibility to all life, to self and others? Hannah Arendt reminds her readers that judgment is made of discernment, evaluation, knowledge, and, ultimately, determination of values. Buddhist thought adds to Western notions of judgment, which provision thinking with evaluative criteria, the ongoing practice one engages in developing qualities of wisdom (discriminating awareness) and compassion (suffering with others in recognition of and kindness toward one's own suffering) as a response to and way of being in the world.

---

[217] Levinas, "Useless Suffering," 94.

Readers live in the midrashic wound, tear, or gap. The place of story and allegory is a space of human uncertainty coupled with desire for (as a movement toward) clarity and understanding. This is the longing to be in conversation, to be in relationship to and with others. We live in the wounded caesura; it makes us sad and vulnerable. Yet, we participate in creation of the wound just by being alive. The wound is complex and contradictory. It compels us to refuse the world when faced with violence, grief, and sadness. It causes us to love life as a hard beauty in the midst of our shared impermanence, the fact of suffering and death, inevitable and impending with which we live.

Midrash reminds us that humans want to live and must be heard. But, as Levinas asserts, humans must take care not to shame one another. There is an internal commandment, one that as a writer often plays out in my relationship to texts: to respect (fear to violate) and love the sanctity of the other human being, for the other is myself and cannot be separated from me. Levi counters the power of shaming others in his frequent affirmation of the dignity of each human being. Responding to a call to midrashic reading, I trust that the other human being shows me the possibilities (and the difficulties) of being human; and, I do the same for her. For those who came before me, some with whom my lifetime has intersected, I extend their stories into the future, which is the now present they did not know. For those who come after me, I hope they, too, will extend the same to their contemporaries.

In *If This Is a Man*, Levi did not include the comprehensive social and political history needed for a fuller understanding of his capture in December 1943, his internment in and deportation from Fossoli in February 1944, and his subsequent imprisonment in and repatriation from Auschwitz. It was in later work, in his essays and interviews and his general speaking appearances and further writing projects, that he began to discuss the larger history that contextualized his first and subsequent books regarding the experiences of European Jews during the war. His first story was narrow in that it was his story, an individual story. Though it included the stories of many others, it was not yet historical, or had not been fully historicized. Historicity comes after events and is composed of a multitude of personal experiences, as well as in subsequent research conducted by historians, social scientists, journalists, and interested others.

In his novel *If Not Now, When?* Levi narrates the stories of Russian, Ukrainian, and Polish Jewish partisans. Writing the novel helped him to understand Jewish resistance and life in Eastern Europe during and immediately after the Second World War. He knew Poland in a very specific way through imprisonment and hard labor, and then through the first weeks of a repatriation journey home to Italy. The novel is a way for him to tend a longing to know about the life of partisans in the East, a life previously remote to him as an Italian Jew. The story begins in July 1943 and ends two years later in August 1945. During this time period, the Germans occupied Italy (September 1943). Levi fled to the alpine mountains where he briefly participated in partisan activity. However, he was quickly detained, jailed, held in a transit camp, and then deported and imprisoned. To write of partisans who had not been captured, who existed deep in the woods and staged acts of sabotage against the Germans, must have been truly satisfying for him. Just after the war, some of the Jewish partisans arrived in Italy from Central and Eastern Europe en route to Palestine. Over the years he heard their stories, in particular one man's story, and decided to express the narrative and interior geographies of imagined characters through composition of a novel. It is July 1944 and a beautiful scene occurs where the partisans, a band of about forty-five of them, come into a Polish village. Their leader, Gedaleh tells the mayor, "we're content with water, silence, and if possible a roof under which we can sleep for a few nights." Like the villagers, they are tired of "war and walking, we're homesick for the tasks of peacetime."[218] They are willing to work. They reap, repair chicken coops, mend roofs, and tend to gardens. The narrator tell us, "Once the first distrust was overcome, it turned out that there were also potatoes to be dug, and it was these potatoes that acted as cement between the wandering Jews and the desperate Polish peasants, at evening, under the summer stars, when they were all seated in the farmyard, on the packed hard earth still warm from the sun."[219] Reading this passage, among others, one feels bare need, the hunger for food and for normal life. There is the warm quality of shared work, a summer evening, a moment of solace and company carved out on the plains of war.

As Levi put himself into the journey of the Jewish partisans from Russia, the Ukraine, and Poland, so too this reader-writer—born in 1963 and teaching composition and literature in the early twenty-first century—made a journey to Poland to experience a part of Levi's journey. I entered Auschwitz with great care and considered thought. My desire to know the story and to accordingly experience the places of that story could be what philosopher René Girard has termed mimetic desire, a desire that plays out in imitation. My desire to learn from a man of wisdom and of consummate ethics means that I want to inhabit the midrashic wound in this particular writer's work. It means that his ideas and experiences speak to me across and through the caesura. It is this centrality of standing amidst the restoration and ruin of one man's life, his deportation to and repatriation from Poland that has fostered mimesis.

The notion of anti-sacrificial reading comes from Numbers and Deuteronomy when God told the Israelites who had left in exodus from enslavement in Egypt that they must worship only one God and not confer elevated status to idols. In contemporary interpretations of the Bible, idols have been everything but God, anything that might usurp God's primacy in the human mind: ideas, people, places, ideologies, substances, a polytheism that substitutes the true God for a false one. One might dangerously worship those things, become addicted and enslaved to them, but one might also scapegoat and hate and substitute them to the point of committing violence upon them. One might find a substitute for God, an idol, and be enthralled to it in worship or in hatred. Sacrificing commentary evolves of God's command that Abraham sacrifice his son, Isaac, to him, and the trauma that ensues for humans as inheritors of that command. Yet, that trauma is not explored in the biblical text, which is instead a brief sketch of divine commandments and subsequent events wherein

---

[218] Levi, *If Not Now, When?* 209.
[219] Ibid, 210.

Abraham enacts God's directives. Finally, God interrupts his actions and expresses satisfaction that Abraham has indeed listened, obeyed, and believed.

Sacrificing commentary means to give up seeing and interacting with literature as a construct.[220] Instead, the work is to engage literature as a continuous conversation through reading. When we read from a distant and remote place, we sacrifice the work we engage. We name it "literature" and what we are doing "criticism," or "critique."[221] We do well to follow Abraham's example who was immediately present and engaged with his God. When the reader makes of story a construct, she distances and objectifies the text. This way of relating constitutes a sort of violence. Anti-sacrificial readings refuse to sacrifice the sanctity of face-to-face engagement. This kind of presence with text means that face-to-face becomes reader-to-work, I/Thou, fewer intermediaries between mind and language so that the reader is fully engaged and interrelating with another mind through the immediacy of story. We let the story perform its pathos on us. The words are not just words but a living consciousness, a blueprint of another's mind, with which I am in dynamic critical and communicative relation through subsequent readings.

In reading a story, humans share their humanness. The individual reader experiences and understands her profound humanity in the reading of another. Because Jews have been sacrificed for centuries (from Isaac forward in time) the notion of anti-sacrificial has special meaning. As such, sacrificial logic no longer sacrifices the presence of self in relationship with other that occurs so poignantly and acutely in reading. There is continuity, an almost cyclical nature between literature and criticism.

> Literature is both before criticism and after it, both the impetus as monstrous writing that triggers the sacrificial critical response and already itself a response to that subsequent critical gesture in the form of the sacrificial source from which it has come. And criticism, similarly, is both subsequent to literature and prior to it, both a differentiating gesture that appears independent of the writing it reads, and already contained by that writing both within the crisis at its center, and within the concluding trans figurative gesture by which that crisis gets 'critically' read.[222]

Anti-sacrificial readings engage the reading-thinking self in relationship with and to another. Anti-sacrificial readings are midrashic readings. The midrash (from *d'rash* in Hebrew, signifying "inquiry into" or "seeking out") is the story. It is the story of oneself and the practice of seeing oneself in the story. For instance, the rabbi studies the text and then sees himself, meta-cognitively, reading the text. He is both participatory in and integral to it. He witnesses and participates in the story as he studies it. Importantly, literature and criticism function differently. Criticism is a differentiating gesture—it exists because and independent of the writing it reads.

---

[220] Goodhart, "Reading After Auschwitz" in *Sacrificing Commentary*.

[221] Ibid.

[222] Ibid, 258.

Criticism is also a trans figurative gesture in its querying, pondering, and ultimately interpreting the crisis at the center of the literature it reads.

For a writer, to think of readers is a movement to sacrifice. One offers up his writing for imaginative engagement, for commentary and critical understanding. In a luminous passage in "On Obscure Writing" Levi vividly evokes the reader's steady and powerful presence.

> he has with good will chose my books and would experience irritation or pain if he did not understand line by line what I had written, indeed, have written *for him*: in fact, I write *for him* and not for the critics, not for the powerful of the Earth, nor for myself. If he did not understand me, he would feel unjustly humiliated, and I would be guilty of a breach of contract.[223]

Levi's metaphorical "contract" establishes the author's moral responsibility to his readers, his fellow human beings. The contract opens midrashic space. Here it is a space of inherent trust and basic good will, a space of exchange—an invitation to share pain and suffering in story as interpretative offering between writer and his reader. For Levi, story was prosthesis, an artificial limb of materiality and form between present self and his experience of Auschwitz. He also knew that experience contained impersonal and universal aspects. He wrote to and for a reader, in addition to writing that first book for his own sanity. What part of his body and his personality had gone missing for him at Auschwitz? What had been taken and severed from him? Certainly, the amputation was psychic. But it also had physical aspects. Levi's friends disappeared into the camp. The people he had met there, some of whom he had known prior to the camp, were forced to gas chambers, shot, beaten, marched to other camps through ice and snow, murdered daily. He had been made to witness public executions. The self he had known before his deportation and internment had been violently taken from him. Was he unrecognizable to himself? The twenty-four-year-old man had been replaced by a witness. He was a man bearing a sense of shame arisen of ethical violations, a man who would remake his life while embodying immeasurable loss. With induction into Auschwitz, he was sacrificed in who he was and eventually emergent as a being who found humanity again. The rediscovery of his humanity manifested as a life's work, a kind of purpose in writing that had not been available, or immediately evident, in his life before Auschwitz.

Levi wrote with an acute awareness of readers. How am I responding to the crisis contained at the center of his writing? His enormous courage that constituted a move to writing for him and that offered to the world novels, short stories, essays, poems, articles, and interviews triggers my critical response. What or who am I then sacrificing? As reader of his first autobiographical account, I open to Levi who entered that camp and was dismantled through his repeated daily encounters with calamity. I live in the now of my life in California, and, at the same time, am wholly vulnerable to how this book constantly changes me, leading me in a thousand

---

[223] Levi, *Other People's Trades*, 159.

directions, to new places, to travels, to myths, to other languages and countries that I had never imagined I would encounter. The book becomes a centerpiece of this one life, from the girl teaching herself to read a children's novel on the floor in a shadowed corner below a bookshelf to a young woman studying European politics and Italian language in Florence who would one-day travel to Poland as a mature adult just after writing a dissertation and in the midst of raising her young son. I have sacrificed any ideas of who I might be to read this book, to be changed by a writer's thoughts and experiences as they rupture into this coastal garden of the present twenty-first century moment.

The gap is the burnt offering, the parts of the story that have been left out, destroyed, forgotten, erased with time and death. What is the Isaac of Genesis 22? What is the sacrifice brought to the reading? In the biblical story, it is the ram and not Abraham's son Isaac that is killed. God will provide, says the text. Provisions were made. The son lived. What must be sacrificed to the story? What must readers offer to the story and in offering what do they open? For surely the story offers itself. Writers talk with pages, with traces of stories remembered and imagined, recorded, and left for others. Readers find the edges of the gap, places where story leaves off. They climb into and inhabit those breaking points. This is how humans heal. This is how they make life again, and again. This is how they refuse injustice, how to live in the world. Humanity (ours) lives in the wound.

3.9 THINGS UNDERGROUND

A whole life everything dead

alive there

pulsing under the skin of

everyday contemporary

a railroad as if with tracks

movement transgressing borders

crawling through tunnels

under sage and moon brighter than desert

milk canisters with letters and journals

bones clean and dusty

roots wet with worm's privilege of

decomposition

books big houses smashed skulls

burned bodies gone

gone rotten and mulching the soil

bone calcium a girl someone loved

hidden metaphorical classes and teachers

students printing presses candles dampened and pamphlets

plans made, traitors interrogated and shot

whole cities networks sewers with pallets

above the stench and little cooking pots and breathing

spaces apartments makeshift flats

knives with dull blades tins with cocaine

passed between bars a shoelace a cigarette in

exchange for a piece of depleted bread

3.10 DON'T TALK ABOUT POLAND

"I'm going to Poland," I tell a sixty-something German acquaintance at a party. "Poland's pretty," she replies, and the conversation is perfunctorily finished. "I went on fellowship to Poland this last summer," I carefully mention to an Israeli friend, father of my son's soccer teammate. "Why would you go there?" I'm unsurprised by his reaction. A while ago we had talked about the Holocaust and he said then he could not believe people visit Auschwitz. Didn't he think that memorials were important, that people should know what happened? "Why should the genocide of millions of Jews be a tourist attraction for the world? The camps should have all been destroyed." Maybe he's right. My mother attends a dinner party hosted by a German friend. She tells the guests that I'm writing about Poland and that I'll present a paper at the Jewish American and Holocaust Literature symposium next week. "Oh, that's nice," they say. Pass the soup. A Jewish friend has been to Auschwitz. But he'd rather mention his visit in Cambodia to Tuol Svay Prey High School, which became S-21, a torture and execution center outside of Phnom Penh. "Have you been?" Another Jewish friend knows I've been to Poland, but doesn't ask about it. She wants to talk about Jane Smiley's latest book. I oblige.

A few friends will talk about Poland. Two Dutch friends know of the war intimately from their parents. One's grandmother swallowed a list of names of local Jews, who were hidden away, just before police knocked at her door. Another friend wants to know my analysis of the beautifully rendered film, *Ida*, which won an Oscar for Best Foreign Language Film in 2015. The one who over the years of writing this book indulged my need to know and explore is a professor of English and Jewish Studies, a child of Polish Jews who immigrated to Pennsylvania before the world wars, and the two of us found energy and support in our conversations with one another. He reminded me that people who want to explore and study these things, "the scene of the disaster," he called it after Maurice Blanchot, gravitate towards circles of discussion where they find one another.

Perhaps one shouldn't expect the world to talk about murder? Perhaps those who visit these sites are just curious and horrified. Curiosity and horror are okay, even justified, as long as they are nested within an approach of inquiry, reflection, and a commitment to ethics, to live responsibly and with thoughtfulness, an ethics characterized by com-passion, as shared feeling with—being human with, or remembering with, or offering oneself as a witness to a long chain of human injustices that we perpetrate on one another. Instead, I turn to books.

Majorie Agosín in *Of Earth and Sea* intertwines her childhood memories of Chile, the land, the sky, the water, the mountains, her Jewish grandparents and parents, her rooms and their views, with the memory of the pogroms and wars that made life for Jews in Eastern Europe one of danger and persecution. She describes tales of odysseys to South America received through her maternal and paternal grandparents. She comes "from a family of nomads, of immigrants who fled the Holocaust as well as the pogroms of Eastern Europe."[224] It is a memory that she absorbs. It is because of these persecutions and the Holocaust that she was a child and grandchild of refugees in Chile. She also writes of being a young woman during the military coup d'état that installed General Augusto Pinochet Ugarte in power from 1973 to 1990. She writes in eulogistic, poetic prose of those friends, student activists, who disappeared during the early days of the military takeover.

When I was visiting Chile, I went to the houses of Pablo Neruda. I wanted to know where he had lived and written. I wanted to see the views to the sea that he had imbibed to feed his poetry. In Valparaíso the manager of my hotel had arranged a tour of the city for me with someone who had been an activist and survived through dictatorship. The woman was sick on the day we were to meet and the glimpse into the human rights situation and the invisible places of violation were to remain hidden to me. Sometimes I mentioned the years of Pinochet's regime, but not many people wanted to talk about that. I alluded to human rights violations, but few responded.

I stayed at La Candela, an inn in Isla Negra, just down a small street along the Pacific from Neruda's house. Charo was an activist, folk singer, guitarist, and a young

---

[224] Agosín, *Of Earth and Sea*, 1.

student and friend to Neruda in the seventies. Her husband, Hugo, with whom she managed the inn, was a filmmaker. He took me into the small theatre at the inn and played black and white films he had made of Neruda for Chilean television in 1971 and 1972, just a couple years before the poet's death. They talked about being with the poet at his bedside just before his death and their heartbreak as the promise of a socialist government, of address to the needs of poor and working people in Chile seemed imminent. Allende's death, Neruda's death, the installation of the Pinochet in power for seventeen years, and the abduction, torture, imprisonment, and execution of perhaps more than three thousand people silenced the possibility of change and drove many to despair and muteness.

What did I want? The truth. The whole of reality: the dramatic geographies between sea and mountains and desert and wild clear skies that drew me there; closeness to places where Neruda had struggled and celebrated life, where he had imagined and composed his poems. Filled with the novels and stories of Isabel Allende and Majorie Agosín, I wanted a deep understanding of the literary and journalistic traditions of Chile as well as the pain for thinkers and activists in the years under military rule.

Why do you want the darkness, I can hear someone asking me now? Why the pilgrimages to places of shadow and abuse, war, and murder? If one does not know the violence, if she does not look, if she does not honor the dead, the process of dying, the incumbency of death, then how is she to live? How can she survive? She lives within an opaque glass sphere. She dwells in the hope of nothingness. She nourishes herself on the ephemeral. My work has been to resist illusion without capitulating to disillusion. What do I have if not my connection to others that arises of a desire for truth? Where is the place where my experiences are not my own but shared with others? How can I unite with others in a community of struggle, inevitable misunderstanding, and pain to find joy and possibility in living? How does my knowledge of death affect my present? I must turn to that which has been hidden from public knowledge.

I must live with Charlotte Delbo's command. *Look. Just try to see.* I cannot always look, but I can remember the vulnerability we suffer with each other and how to best live given that vulnerability. In *Auschwitz and After* I find a brave woman who returned to Europe from Argentina where she was working on plays with theatre actor and producer Louis Jouvet. She longed to be with her husband Georges Dudach and to work in the French resistance. I look to her as a strong person who as a political prisoner lost her young husband, who was executed (they had worked together as couriers, printing and distributing anti-Nazi pamphlets). She was deported to Auschwitz in a convoy of 229 French women who had been imprisoned for resistance activities. This was all very courageous—this return to France, her work with her husband, the tenacious survival in and through Auschwitz—when she could have stayed in Buenos Aires and avoided the war all together. But she confessed she could not look others in the eye if she remained in Buenos Aires while her country was under siege. She knew many were fighting the Germans and their collaborators.

She didn't remarry. I admire that she worked and wrote and found her material in the trauma of the past and waited for twenty years to publish the memoir—a trilogy of books—so that people would be able to absorb, to try to understand, because nothing of what she says in those books is easy. The reader realizes that knowledge and love are depleted through what she has seen and what over the years she continued to remember as if it had occurred only a few days ago. For my part, I try to live among poems and poets and to honor those who desired the freedom that unburdened humanity brings.

Agosín guides readers into her book with a promise of memory's continuation despite its partial, even fragmentary, nature: "Each one of these collages, segments, vignettes should be read like little signs, omens, and secret incrustations, footprints that memory continues to leave."[225] Memory is fragile and fervent. It is small pieces of glass that persist in the corridors of the mind and the hallways of the heart.

3.11 CAFÉ BERGSON

Travel to Poland on fellowship means historical confrontation with the diverse lives Jews lived prior to the Second World War. It asks close consideration of forced removal from their cities and towns, sometimes into ghettos that took Jews out of their homes and into neighborhoods not their own. It means feeling the loss of their communities, their families, and, for those who survived, their exile from Poland. There were 3.5 million Jews living in Poland, including eastern areas of what is now the Ukraine and Belarus, prior to the Second World War.[226] The German invasion and occupation of Poland took place on September 1, 1939. The Germans quickly moved eastward into the interior of Poland, a country they had considered historically their own territory, and accomplished occupation of the country within a matter of weeks. Labor and extermination camps were built in the country between 1940 and 1943. Russian, Ukrainian, and Polish prisoners of war—as well as intellectuals, union leaders, those against the regime, those considered dangerous or deficient in some way—built camp barracks and outbuildings. Visual artist Marian Kołodziej said that he effectively built Auschwitz; he was deported there in the first transport of Polish political prisoners in June 1940. Some of the largest labor and extermination camps (now referred to as killing centers) were built in Poland. These included Auschwitz-Birkenau, Płaszów in Kraków, Treblinka, northeast of Warsaw, Chełmno outside of Łódź, Sobibór in eastern Poland outside of Lublin, Majdanek in Lublin, and Bełżec near the city of Lvov.[227] The network of camps and sub-camps in Poland during the war has been estimated at 457. Over five million Poles and Polish Jews were sent to camps. The Nazis created ghettos in German-occupied Polish cities to quarantine,

---

[225] Agosín, *Of Earth and Sea*, 3.

[226] Robert Cherry and Annamaria Orla-Bukowska in *Rethinking Poles and Jews* point out that in 1930 "World Jewry numbers 15,000,000 including 4 million in the United States, 3.5 million in Poland, and 2.7 million in the USSR" (xiv). See also Timothy Snyder in *Bloodlands*, "In 1939 about ten percent of the Polish population were Jews. In Warsaw and Łódź, the most important Jewish cities in Poland, Jews were about one third of the population," 122.

[227] In Polish it was also known as Lwów. After the war it was part of the Soviet Union and is now Lviv of independent Ukraine.

imprison, starve, and eventually deport Jews to extermination camps.[228] After the war, there were fewer than 400,000 Jews in the country. Some of those who survived made their way back to Poland from exile in Russia and from rural areas of Poland where they had been hiding, involved in the partisan movement, or just released from concentration camps. Most of those Jews found that their houses and communities no longer existed. Vacated Jewish houses and lands that had not been destroyed during the war came to be frequently occupied by Poles.

It is within this history that I consider Café Bergson in Oświęcim. The café where the Auschwitz Jewish Center fellows meet to eat, drink, converse was once a Jewish family house. Its naked exterior walls had been constructed of brick, one cemented upon another to protect the family from severe winters. There were beautiful things about the house: a mauve-red door carved with insets that resemble the doors of an ark for safekeeping of the Torah; and, a polished copper door of a furnace. The father sold chickens out of the basement, which doubled as a family store where neighbors and townspeople bought kosher birds. Three children of nine survived the war. They dispersed; all left Poland. Szymon Kluger returned from Sweden to Poland in the early 1960s. Oświęcim's last Jewish resident, in a town that had been predominantly Jewish prior to the Second World War, he moved back into the house 1962; his mother's family had owned the home since 1928. In Oświęcim he worked for the chemical factory (IG Farben in the very camp that had once interned him). He lived in the house until he died in 2000 and was buried in the town's Jewish cemetery.

At that time his home, situated on a crumbling hill behind the medieval Oświęcim Castle, was in disrepair. Earthquake damage threatened the stability of the hill. Auschwitz Jewish Center purchased the home in 2013 and restorations began. Café Bergson opened in May 2014 and has since been nominated one of the most beautiful cafés in Poland. In this former Jewish house, transformed into a center of culture, food, and sharing adjacent to the synagogue, students, community members, and visitors gather.

Immediately I note the name of the café—turquoise letters on a warm white exterior wall facing a garden courtyard. I wonder if the energy of the café and the people who come here reflect the philosophy and phenomenological ideas of Henri Bergson (1859-1941), a French philosopher whose father was from Warsaw and whose mother was from England. Some of the Bergson family remained in Poland. One of Bergson's descendants, Simon Bergson, a businessman and philanthropist in New York City, is a board member and supporter of the Center and provided funding to complete the café restoration and its opening.

Henri Bergson was raised in Paris and studied mathematics. He loved philosophy, in particular its conjunction with mathematics and science, and went on to author several books, *Time and Free Will, Matter and Memory, The Creative Mind, Two Sources of Morality and Religion,* and *Duration and Simultaneity.* He found himself living during a time in which Darwin's theory of evolution emerged. That

---

[228] Polish historian and guide Maciek Zabierowski comments that there is no consensus among scholars as to how many ghettos there were exactly in German-occupied Poland but the number exceeds by far 200.

development transitioned into a period of Social Darwinism that included the dangerously racist policies of eugenics that evolved of totalitarian governments. It was also an historical period in which Freud's science of psychology was gaining a foothold in how people thought about themselves, their desires and interior lives, as well as Einstein's theory of relativity, which increasingly influenced Bergson's notions of time, in his concept of duration and his ideas of matter and memory. He was fascinated by the conjunction of physical and imagined worlds, of exterior and interior worlds, and he explored these intersections in his ideas of the actual and the virtual. His thought also introduced the idea of multiplicity, which helped to establish notions of public life as plural, of human beings living in plurality, with attention to the simultaneous existence of sameness and difference human beings share.

Some of Bergson's thought is represented in the plurality of the café space. Tomasz Kuncewicz, Director of Auschwitz Jewish Center in Oświęcim, shares that the café has become a meeting place of people and ideas—visitors from Europe and abroad as well as locals. The focus of discussion and expression is both Jewish themes and universal, inclusive, progressive, anti-discrimination programs and events. The building is a site of Jewish heritage; through its programs and exhibits it promotes diversity and confronts the dangers of xenophobia. Many locals become aware through their exposure to the café of the Jewish heritage and history of Oświęcim. The new locals are not necessarily interested in Jewish history or culture but are drawn to the café because of its quality and the diversity of its cultural, educational programs. There are also visitors to the Jewish Museum and the Chevra Lomdei Mishnayot Synagogue. [229] Those visitors include journalists, writers, filmmakers, and musicians. Tomasz says that "because of the café they spend much more time here and have more time to get to know our place." [230]

Café Bergson is a refuge and reflective place. Our group of academic fellows spent a week in the small town of Oświęcim, with several visits to Auschwitz and surrounding historical and cultural sites. The café welcomes us with the scent of brewing coffee, iced for hot days, homemade cakes and tarts, and a cool interior of high stucco ceilings and large casement windows open to high blue summer sky. Inside, near the espresso bar, magazines and vases of irises and daisies decorate little tables. On the walls are hung the original doors of the Kluger house. This house was once buzzing with family activity. I don't necessarily feel that when I'm here but imagine that the life in and around the café brings respect and joy to the space and to the lives once carried out within these walls. Café Bergson is a place to remember and respect Jewish culture and the vital Jewish community that once constituted over half the population of Oświęcim.

---

[229] See Auschwitz Jewish Center website for a detailed history of the synagogue.
[230] Tomasz Kuncewicz in personal communication with the author.

The Kluger house during construction and restoration.
Source: Auschwitz Jewish Center

The restoration of the building respected original structures and design elements and has thus allowed for the sense of the Kluger family house, built in the late nineteenth and early twentieth centuries, to remain. Symcha Kluger was a teacher and provided religious commentary on Saturday afternoons at the Great Synagogue, just a short walk from the Kluger house. The Nazis destroyed the synagogue by fire on November 29, 1939. A portion of ruddy red wall shows through the new white stucco wall, a reminder of the original aspects of the house just under the surface of the new construction. Strata of history and the present coexist here.

In the evenings the fellows relax in canvas lounge chairs on the deck. Grasses, vines, and flowers edged the patio fences brilliant with color—hot pink and lavender cosmos, orange coneflowers. After dinner we watch contemporary films that confront Polish and Jewish history. Our viewings focus on the effects of this history as it intersects with contemporary life in Poland. What I recognize about my time in the café in retrospect is how it represents not only the intersection of past and present in Poland, but how it brings together people from all over the world and of many different ages and interests. We gather in one place because we want to learn together.

We are compelled by Poland as a place and how it relates with its own history, a history that, increasingly, it is coming to know in illuminating and not infrequently contentious ways as Poles and others from the global community discuss, debate, dialogue, and share. Annamaria Orla-Bukowska notes that external visitors come to Poland with their own memories of the Second World War and the Holocaust, or the Jewish Genocide, as Poles have called it. Their presence confronts Poles with external representations of the Holocaust in Poland and the country's role in relation to Polish

Jews. These perceptions challenge notions of personal and national identity. The country has made an art of memorialization and preservation and now comes into new relations with its history as it encounters visitors to sites of memory. Likewise, those of us who visit Poland come, in part, because we want to hear how Poles are conceptualizing, grieving, and memorializing their own history of the events and consequences of the Second World War, the occupation and destruction of their country, the loss of Jewish communities, the Jewish genocide, and forty-one years under Communist rule.

Funds were required to realize the vision of a cultural and educational gathering space. A Kickstarter campaign began through Auschwitz Jewish Center in Oświęcim and the Museum of Jewish Heritage in New York City and raised over \$28,000.[231] Repair work began. The foundation was shored up, the roof replaced, and new consoles and façade in the original nineteenth century style, common to southern Poland's Galicia region, were added. The grand opening took place in May 2014. The café was nominated for best interior design of a building in Poland. Shiri Sandler, former U.S. Director of Auschwitz Jewish Center, notes the building's unique combination of historic elements with modern function.[232] The minimalist café retains elements of the original house–over 100 years of front doors, interior doors, doorframes, wall fragments, and prewar tiles. The right front door jamb, as is the case with many formerly Jewish flats and houses of pre-war Poland, bears an imprint, a hole where a small decorative case with parchment inside called a *mezuzah* once nested. The scroll might contain verses from the Torah, specifically Deuteronomy.

Café Bergson opened in May 2014 as part of Auschwitz Jewish Center.
Source: Author photo, 2014

Tomasz enjoys the relaxed atmosphere of the café and the mix of people it attracts. The current exhibit, showing in the downstairs gallery, is "Tiles of Oświęcim." The

---

[231] *Auschwitz Jewish Center*, 2016.
[232] Ibid.

exhibit strives to preserve the details of authentic prewar buildings, focusing on a forgotten and often demolished element of prewar interiors. The variety of colors, forms, and textures of the floor and wall tiles speak to the richness and multiculturalism of prewar Oświęcim. On a tour of Tarnów, Tomasz was particularly passionate to take us into old Jewish buildings and point out details of Jewish architecture and design. In one entryway, a floor of granite marble revealed an intricate black, pink, and gray star. It had not been restored and was subject to constant foot traffic. I could feel his sadness in finding and then leading us to these spaces, these elements of a history seemingly abolished, the artifacts of a people driven from Poland. There is vindication in return to these things. There is reclamation and admiration of them in Tomasz's guidance. He writes to me about one exhibit at the café that "appeals to the viewer to save the last remnants of a vanished cultural heritage that can still be seen in neglected floor tiles, doors, and railings, which are often removed and replaced by economical modern equivalents. We were able to reuse beautiful prewar tiles from a demolished house in Oświęcim; with this exhibit, we hope to inspire more people to take notice of everyday artifacts around us."[233] Things have a life of their own. The tiles appear again through the wear of time as Tomasz makes them visible. A whole way of life was erased. His knowledge helps us listen and attend.

The art gallery and film space have also become spaces for learning. Tomasz shares that the downstairs is used for the English Café, weekly meetings run by volunteers, which provides opportunity for integration of the local community and raises awareness of Jewish heritage. A recent discussion centered on the refugee crisis in Europe and another on a documentary on the murder of Roma people in Hungary by neo-Nazis with a post-screening discussion with the film's director Eszter Hajd, moderated by Dagmara Mrozowska of the State College of Higher Education in Oświęcim.

The café reminds me to find a space—mental and physical—after days being at sites of memory, which have been sites of destruction. The old Kluger house is a gathering place of contemplation, friendship, and dialogue. It is a place of beauty and community in Oświęcim, a town once home to a thriving Jewish community. People meet here to feel a difficult history conjoined with a contemporary moment of knowledge, memory, and hope.

---

[233] Tomasz Kuncewicz in personal communication with the author.

CHAPTER 4

What Remains

4.1 THE OFFICE

Incredible in the world

to inhabit an office,

books shelves sun-lit

white walls and new office furniture

warm window reflecting a city

dry corner a file cabinet

clean ceiling desk surfaced with papers

unsoiled eyeglasses

room for photos wall hanging

glass-covered

reflective degrees framed

awards on plaques.

What kind of space to transform

the mind's reflection into a world?

A life well lived the interior of thoughts,

tangible evidence of what

matters, and the path taken to arrive there.

Virginia Woolf called it a room of one's own.

So much required so many resources

beauty of binding, craftsmanship of chairs

desks, green glass bottle blown to curvaceous

fireplace tiled, Persian rug, its designs

swirling the soles of suede shoes.

In a world of migration

dislocation displacement,

to inhabit a space for thinking

just outside

the world held at bay

a sliver of space where reflection finds form.

This miracle asks much

of every human being,

work and discipline, the agreement to allow

a thing we call privacy and privilege

so that mind can suck on silence

surrounded by words and beauty

return to us

all we have forgotten

we knew.

4.2 LIVING HAUNTED

More often than not I live in past rather than present time. These days it would be the twentieth century and in piano playing sometimes the eighteenth. My present is an umbilical cord to the past. It is in the past that my writer self is rooted. If I expose myself to things that came before, I will have a different and perhaps more complex view of my place and experience in this body at this moment on the planet. Haunting is necessary to a writer's life. I go to books because I want to live somewhere else while also living here. I go to writers because I want to be someone else in addition to this solitary self in which my consciousness shelters. I live haunted.

Reading Paul Auster essays, collected under the title *The Art of Hunger*, made me think consciously of haunting in the relationship writers have to history. I want to conduct a poetic exploration of the word haunting here. There are times when I am thankful for technological prowess. I turn to Google Books to seek out the word haunt in Auster's *The Art of Hunger*. The search reveals its usage in speaking of Laura Riding's poetry, in the exploration of William Bronk's poetry: "Bronk has an uncompromising approach to the things that haunt and obsess him that is in the end more salutary than depressing."[234] Bronk's work revolves around a few essential themes: the rift between our image of the world and the reality of the world, the force of desire, the agony of human relationships, and our perception of nature. These themes evoke haunting in every sense of the word for a writer. These themes, too, provide a short list of the purposes of my own compulsion to write. Agony is an intense word in this context. The *agony* of human relationships. Certainly, our relationships can be and often are agonizing. Agony arises both in conflicts that combust in our daily relations with one another and in the memories of those relations that have ended, whether in death or in some random or forced departure that severs communication. What remains? The lack of conclusions, the inability to understand why and how a separation has occurred, a dearth of knowledge with which to make inferences, to understand who the other is, what dwells in the gulf that has opened in separation, and, finally, the impossibility of extracting wisdom. Dreams begin, sometimes nightmares. Hauntings. In absentia, the beloved manifests when ego defenses sleep. Bronk, Auster writes, compels "us to stare ourselves in the face, he brings us closer to what we are. He wants, quite simply, to come to grips with the

---

[234] Auster, *The Art of Hunger*, 141.

given."[235] To come to grips with the given. Quite simply! Auster's use of irony is not lost here.

Therein lies the rift between what we imagine and the actuality of physical and emotional reality. I feel that rift more poignantly as I age. How many of my hours are given to preservation and creation of an ethical world, a world of connected relationships, only to feel desire as a fragile thread that emanates well-being and beauty but refuses the total world in all its violence and complexity and angst. The total world defies rationality and knowledge because one head, even many heads, cannot conceptualize and make meaning of its chaos. This is a postmodernist view, and Auster has been labeled a postmodernist, a nihilist, negative, an existentialist. Yet, the very haunting he suffers, that writers who travel back to the past suffer, shows its mark in his critique of Bronk's poetry. Auster writes that for Bronk the belief of an ordered, coherent world is a mere sham, a construct to "domesticate the unknowable." In this poet's view the world was "essentially that which cannot be mastered."[236] I read these descriptions as an ironic doctrine, one that allows for the incomprehension of a world that evolves because and in spite of human actions. Simultaneously, I hold within me James Baldwin's resolve that one may accept injustice but must also fight with all his will against it. Baldwin addresses the mind and body's ability to hold two contradictory ideas in tandem, to comprehend thr truth of two paradoxical ideas at the same time. The ability to withstand paradox may be a postmodern ability. It is what we do now, the thing that we must develop in an increasingly confusing and complex world: to realize and even embrace contradiction, for contradiction exudes a certain complementarity. Baldwin's "Notes of a Native Son" reveals his practice of beginning to live paradoxically. Auster comments in regards to his own writing that all his books are the same book, that they are "the story of my obsessions. The saga of the things that haunt me. Writing is no longer an act of free will for me, it's a matter of survival."[237]

The idea of haunting is pervasive throughout literary writing and criticism. Writers use it in reference to the past, to memory, to things and people that will not release our consciousness. We use it to refer to a kind of possession by the subjects that demand our words to live in the world. Writing might be then an awakening of the dead, the buried, the long-since-put-to-sleep for those who do not want to remember and who want a life freed of haunting. It is because writers think certain things with such force of repetition, things that grow in emotional resonance and weight as we allow them to become the terrain of our in-scape, that we write. Is writing then a sort of trauma when it emanates of haunting? It is an obligatory act, a passionate answer to the past. Writing calls and inhabits us with memory. Writing makes past experience alive, here, now, vital within us. There is also the present and its experiences and things that fill us with desire. Desire is haunting. I open to a collection of poems by Pablo Neruda.

---

[235] Auster, *The Art of Hunger*, 141.
[236] Auster, 142.
[237] Ibid, 295.

Sweet, loud, harsh-voiced frogs,

I have always wanted to be

a frog, I have loved the pools

and the leaves, thin as filaments,

the green world of the watercress

with the frogs, queens of the sky.

The serenade of the frog

Rises in my dream and excites it,

Rises like a climbing vine

To the balconies of my childhood,

to the budding nipples of my cousin,

to the astronomic jasmine

of the black night of the South,

and now so much time has passed,

don't ask me about the sky:

I feel that I haven't yet learned

the harsh-voiced idiom of the frogs.

Neruda's desire grows. Out of the immediacy of frogs he is carried through dream to his past, to the high memories of growing and sensual things. Beside the harsh deep voices of frogs, time haunts him. It is ceaseless and burdens the poet with the (unsaid) end of things. He pushes on.

If this is so, how am I a poet?

What do I know of the multiplied

geography of the night?

He is haunted by the reminder of the frogs who make him remember his lack of knowledge in the world. How much he has to learn! How impossible he is to teach! He is forgetful, distracted, inattentive. Yet, he listens now and softens to the possibility of all things that he has in his hurried humanness and his temporality ignored.

> In this world that rushes and grows calm
>
> I want more communications
>
> other languages, other signs,
>
> to be intimate with this world.[238]

He makes a bold statement and excuses himself from the busy world of human affairs that interrupts his space and his ability to hear.

> *Yo quiero hablar con muchas cosas*
>
> *Y no me iré de este planeta*
>
> *sin saber qué vine a buscar*
>
> *sin averiguar este asunto,*
>
> *y no me bastan las personas,*
>
> *yo tengo que ir mucho más lejos*
>
> *yo tengo que ir mucho más cerca.*[239]

People are not enough, I have to go much farther, I have to get much closer. The longing is the haunting, the awakening and joy that comes from recognizing what is real, what matters. The frogs help to wake him up. They remind him that he has to move in the direction of what he loves.

---

[238] Translation my own. In thinking largely about Neruda's meanings, I want to suggest that languages might also be "tongues," and intimate may also signify "to know."

[239] Neruda, "Bestiary" in *Full Woman, Fleshly Apple, Hot Moon: Selected Poems of Pablo Neruda*, edited by Stephen Mitchell.

4.3 WRITER AT THE PERIPHERY

In January, six months after returning home from a four-week fellowship in Poland where I had studied Polish and Jewish history, I found myself at Books, Inc. on Chestnut Street in San Francisco's Marina. There I happened upon a gathering of noticeably thick books in the fiction section, *My Struggle*, by Karl Ove Knausgaard, one of a four, five, now six-volume series, by the Norwegian novelist about his ordinary and sometimes traumatic struggles through his daily life(time). The books stood out visually, as they are black and white, and each volume's spine has a different color mixed in with the black—lime green, burnt orange, dusty violet. The four books together looked like a small army standing. Now I think they were, and are, a mnemonic army, a battalion of memory as it surges and flows through the writer's mind and body, through this manic hand as he crafts his life in thousands of pages.

The title *My Struggle* recalls Adolf Hitler's infamous book. Perhaps this was an attention-grabbing gesture on Knausgaard's part, but once he has our focus he begins re-engineering what we recall when we hear that phrase *mein kampf*, or, in Norwegian, *min kamp*. Reviews of the writer's work read like this: "For Proust, style was a struggle, a way to be, in the parenthetical richness of his sentence, as complicated a person as he was in life. For Knausgaard, the struggle is actual. His is a struggle with family and the deadening quality of certain family routines. It is the struggle to retain the scintillated consciousness this book celebrates in its rush of detail." How can we not relate, those of us, at least, in midlife? Immediately, I was fascinated with the idea of logging everything, as if it was potentially important and mattered, at least to the writer. There was some sort of wild, even narcissistic faith in that, and I admired the guts and courage of the writer. Perhaps self-importance coupled with the self-indulgent drive of personal narrative, particularly when based upon past and current successes of the writer, transforms what might otherwise be stupidity in its degree of painfully detailed disclosure, into a brave, artistic adventure.

How to begin? At the public library in Santa Cruz, I checked out the second of Knausgaard's books. There was a waiting list for most volumes. But upon arriving home and cracking open the novel that first night, that first introduction into the Knausgaardian world, I was unwilling to read much. I read in fits and starts, suffering the narrative details of a stormy and semi-functional relationship with his second wife, Linda Böstrom: the problems with children, his braggadocio about writing awards and prizes (which he claimed to think were stupid), and his fascination with his personal scatology. He wanted to be a writer, was a successful one, but—of course, in the interest of his theme—he struggled continuously against Linda and their three young children to find time to write. His depiction of his wife is not complimentary. She seems impossibly tedious, depressed, insecure, and demanding. A number of male writers have portrayed women that way without querying the reasons for their partner's behavior. This is not to say that their interpretations are without truth. Rather it is to state that men's behavior frequently fuels women's insecurities and their veiled requests for attention, listening, and love. She's a writer, too; yet, there are three children—and then a fourth—for whom to care. Why does he have to expose all his frustrations, animosities, and psychological castrations to the reader when he is not able to talk with his wife about them? Why should the reader know the autobiographical details of his interior monologue when his wife is not privy to those same details? Why didn't they just talk to each other and work through things? Why was I subjected to their one-way, myopic drama of hurt feelings, misunderstandings, and silences? Why did she want so many kids with him? That ruins a marriage of writers, puts enormous stress on it, and makes one or both of the partners resentful. Why, why, why? My questions were relentless, something like accusations. Quiet down, I told myself. Shut up and begin to read. Then your rhetoric will turn into something more like reading and maybe, eventually, understanding.

I began to read. Writing for Karl superseded everything. He could never be enough for her, enough of a father. He wanted to run off to some quiet room or island and write. Who could blame him? This is the drama of the narrative, pocked with thousands of daily scenes from his life as a husband, father, and writer. He strives to capture the difficulties and insecurities of the writing life on the page. He succeeds. Clearly, he's a brilliant writer. But, he demands of the reader interest in things that may be purely interesting only to him. Just as his attitude was "screw the writing award and all the people who are bestowing it upon me," it is also "screw you, the reader, if you don't like what I write."[240] The result is a lack of trust between the reader and writer. Yes, reviewers have compared his memoirs to Proust, an ordinary, working class Proust. (Levi disliked Proust's writing. It was full of insignificant detail and a bore, he said. Perhaps he'd think the same of Knausgaard's autofiction.) Yet, with each book his writing develops, becomes increasingly lucid, riddled with brilliant passages of poetry rendered in prose. He becomes more and more aware of a reader and in doing so begins to write conscious of the need for drama, suspense, sexuality, fear, joy—all things the reader of the novel wants and understands. She wants to live her life through the life the writer offers her on the page. She wants to understand her life through the lens he turns on his own. In this way, Knausgaard delivers with each book a certain drive that begins to lend fuel and urgency to the growing multi-volume autobiography.

Where Primo Levi became my inspiration for a tone and a voice, measured, compassionate, considerate of the reader, taking her into his confidence, careful with and respectful of her time and attention, Knausgaard's process became immediately an inspiration for a project of daily writing and logging. The differences in their writing styles and the approaches to each of their narrative material signifies, in part, the degree to which autobiographical, even fictional writing, has changed between the mid-twentieth century and the early twenty-first century. Levi wrote in 1946, just after the Second World War had ended. He wrote primarily not to reveal his interior life in relationship to the physical world but to document the memory of his life in the Auschwitz camp and one of its subcamps, Buna-Monowitz. In his capacity as witness, he wrote also to remember to the page the people he had met in the camps. In the second volume of his memoir, *The Truce*, he wrote to record the narrative of events and people he had met over the months of his repatriation to Italy. He was a private man, reserved, as his biographers, particularly Carole Angier, have reflected. His

---

[240] My (admittedly) interpolated reading of a section from Knausgaard's *Book 2*.

double bond (Angier's term) was navigating the public persona of the writer with the basic urge of the human being who writes to hear himself think. The problem is people respond. People want more. People fall in love. They are hungry for the writer and the knowledge of his life and the root of his story. Why, why, why, they relentlessly ask, and the writer tries to hide, he shelters and withdraws, but at the same time there is the hungry part of him that needs and wants readers, that writes for a public. Levi does not record in his first memoir the details of his life prior to his capture and internment. When my students read the book, I preface his narrative with a few details about his life—where he lived, for how long he had lived there, his background as a Jew in Italy, his family situation, the relationship with his younger sister, Anna Maria, with whom he was very close, his friends at the time of his capture. These details, I believe, enrich the story, and provide a foundation for his narrative. I also talk about Poland, now that I've been, and some of the history of that country in terms of the German invasion, Levi's deportation there, the geographic distance between Italy and Poland, the number of Jews murdered in Poland and the status of the Jewish population there during the war in comparison with the situation of Jews in Italy during that time. In writing of Auschwitz, he utilized both his scientific and literary training. He refrains from excessive emotion and relies heavily on a rational, calm, even sober voice. He tells us that his account constitutes a study of the human mind. He recognized that his reader has a life, perhaps very different from his own; yet, he strove to reveal his consciousness and his mind, his thinking world, to the reader.

The topic of consideration in Levi's works is not so much "my struggle," but what it means to be a human being, to think, and live in the mid-twentieth century from the perspective of an educated, cultivated Italian Jewish man. Educated and cultivated, ethical and thoughtful, but with a recognition that culture and its products are frequently construed to the purposes of power, and that one must revisit and refine his ethics through the situations and historical conditions he has encountered and that have been imposed upon him. For Levi, that defining event was the Second World War, which importantly for him included the racial laws spreading through Europe in the 1930s, the partisan movements, and the extermination camps. However, it has been hypothesized that over the years Levi found relief and refuge in writing—from the management of the paint factory where he worked to family life in a large flat in Torino, where he had grown up and that he later shared with this wife, mother, and children. In this way, writing served for him the same function that it does for Knausgaard. Writing is a reprieve from the daily churning of life, the ordinary events and the mundane demands of living. Karl Ove calls it his non-narrative quotidian existence, the life outside the book, writing, "That's how I experience life, as an ocean of quotidian existence in which meaning is diffuse and difficult to grasp, and then comes death with its unprecedented concentration of meaning, or else love or birth."[241]

---

[241] Knausgaard, "The Shame of Writing About Myself."

In the twenty-first century we have blurred the genre boundaries between fiction and memoir, so much so that a new category of autofiction has developed, wherein the writer may write his life with the actual names and places of people that constitute his story but write them as if a novel, as if characters. Invention is no longer a necessary component of fiction. Nor, in that way, is truth a necessary component of autobiography. Readers expect mostly truth, but we also know that memory is an act of embroidery, a hodgepodge of imagination and recall. In fact, Knausgaard begins the third book of *My Struggle* with a comment on the elusive and ephemeral nature of memory, "It is never the demand for truth that determines whether memory recalls an action accurately or not. It is self-interest that does. Memory is pragmatic, it is sly and artful, but not in any hostile or malicious way; on the contrary, it does everything it can to keep its host satisfied."[242] He talks about canonized memories and then body memories evoked sensorially and emotionally. From there, he begins to tell his story, taking the great leap into the memories that present themselves to him as he inhabits that child body of the mid-1970s. Would it have helped to understand or see Levi as a child in his writings? Would the reader have related to his nightmares in the camp if he had related early memories of the home he quietly, ardently missed in Torino? Perhaps. But, then, we have to go looking for those missing details, if we desire them. And, I did. In Knausgaard's work I need not seek out the details of his lifetime, as they compose the very story he writes. It is the process and act of writing, the foundational elements of all this production that I seek to understand as I read. I'm as much fascinated by the story as I am by the writing process and the physical space and intellectual terrain of the man who wrote it.

I wanted to further understand the writing process of the writer who composed *My Struggle*. What drove him to write? What did he find in writing that he had been unable to find elsewhere and with others? He lives an ordinary life in Malmö, Sweden with his wife, a poet, and four children and sequesters himself in his studio to write because he must. He just writes and writes, and admits that he doesn't have to have a particular subject, or even an interesting life, as for so long in America we've believed writers must. He writes of the everyday and the inner obsessions and the urgency to write. His writing style, both in tone and visually on the page, reflects this urgency. Over a decade he has written literally thousands of pages. Lately, he confessed that his final writings for volume six of the autobiography amounted to some 11, 000 pages. In an interview he divulges his desperate need to write.

> I have to write—maybe I can write for 20 more years, that's maybe four or five novels; and that's not much, so I can't waste my time. I know where my fascinations lie, I try to go there. You can write about anything—you don't need a subject or a story. You can just write, everything will show itself, the story will come and the things you are really interested in will be in the book, no matter what you are writing about. I'm not looking for something to write

---

[242] Knausgaard, *Book 3*, 11.

about, ever. If it is valuable, it will be inside of me, so I'll write about it one day.[243]

In these words, there is an inherent trust of the writing process to reveal the material and content of one's life on the page. He doesn't say it is the content that matters, that is most significant to a life (the four or five defining moments of a life), or that is most valuable maybe in terms of dramatic weight in a narrative. Instead, he talks of fascination. To what and to where does the energy draw him? These areas might be obsessions or that which most compels. What brings one to the writing place above all?

Sometimes, as writers, we don't even know why or what draws us to write. There is a certain trust inherent in the process, the compulsion to go to the space and write. Hélène Cixous talks eloquently in her essay, "Coming to Writing," about writing located in the body, writing embodied, specifically in a woman's body and its uniqueness.[244] Writing is a force to which we are compelled and towards which we are moved. Physical movement and mental intention allow creation to manifest. Sometimes I avoid that compulsion to write. I am here at the desk, it's morning, my best time to write, if I get to it right away, but I'm doing other things. For some reason I avoid writing, but just for the time being. Avoidance is momentary. I've learned over years to trust the need and to honor it, to pay attention and give it its due. As long as I put it off, the feeling to write lingers. It remains emplaced—in body, in mind. I have lit three candles and they flicker here on the desk. The space has been prepared. For a long time, over a period of years, I have lit candles as a symbol of settling down and into writing. Instead, I delay. Check and send email messages, little communications to and with others, check off items on my to-do list, submit student poems to the college writing awards. Still, I have to write. I can feel it. If I don't get to it, if I don't delay the need to complete tasks and get on with business, all that needs expression will coagulate inside me, storing up and needing release.

This need fascinates me as I track Knausgaard's writing life and his written work. On November 13, ten months after my first encounter with his work at the San Francisco bookstore, a day before I am to leave to present a paper at an academic conference in Miami, I go downtown for a pedicure, but first find myself at Santa Cruz Bookshop expressly to buy a couple volumes of *My Struggle*. I purchase *Book 1* and *Book 2*, and immediately begin reading as the young Vietnamese woman removes old polish from my toenails. I'm drawn into the daily records of the author's life, an account that begins when he is an eight-year-old boy. He begins with what happens in the body just after death, the blood pooling to the lowest point, the skin slightly bluish there, and how we hide dead bodies from our sight immediately after death—covering them, removing them on stretchers, in body bags and on gurneys. Why don't we just leave them there for a while, he asks. They are not harming anyone. This discussion

---

[243] Schillinger, "Why Karl Ove Knausgaard Can't Stop Writing."
[244] Cixous, *Coming to Writing and Other Essays*, 1992.

of death, the immediate entry into his thoughts, and how those thoughts might eventually connect with whatever story he will present to his reader, makes me want to know how he will end this first book. As I read, I habituate to his tone, his language, the cadence of his words. He is thoughtful and confessional as a writer, quietly rebellious as a boy and young teenager. He creates tension and mystery through the solitude and silence of his father, a volatile man in isolation who lacks the ability to function through daily life without his cheerful and compliant wife around. Karl Ove is freer, though never happy, around his mother. Even early in the book it seems that happiness eludes him.

High up in the polar regions closer to the Arctic Circle the terrain is dark, populated with spruce, granite mountains, snowcaps of ice, black water, and low gray sky. Such a physical environment encourages an inner reserve, a quiet loneliness and reflection. Is the environment then internalized and, in turn, reflected in the writer's very prose? His sentences are long, but not breathless, a series of commas splices that allow him generosity of voice and the play of voluminous sentences that spread across the page. Paragraphs amble and extend sometimes over pages. I notice new things about syntax and punctuation as I read him. Comma splices are now a common, even preferred, style of writing. Paragraphs are hardly necessary. Long paragraphs and rangy sentences are staples of contemporary literature. My students compose serpentine sentences, and rarely think to invent shorter ones. Few have a sense of paragraphing. They prefer commas rather than periods. Yet, few use commas after introductory clauses. Knausgaard obviously knows what he's doing, but one can feel the urgency to write and tell story here, to reveal and to confess the dark corridors of knowledge embedded in personal history, pushing the boundaries of the writer's consciousness to emerge into daylight, to the page, and, somewhere in the background, the vague sense of a public, an audience waiting to consume and imbibe one's words and narratives. He uses commas as one would periods. He omits commas after clauses. He never uses semicolons, as perhaps they are too formal or premeditated for him. I read cautiously, wary that I could end up sounding like him or could unconsciously mimic his style because his voice is distinct, unique, one I can almost hear aloud through the veneer of my silent reading. He's honest and intimate. He is aware of creating a narrative, a story, and I feel that awareness, which is ultimately an adherence to form, the literary conventions and the ability to play with, break and bend them. It is also a nod to the reader. I know you are there, that narrative voice suggests, and it is for you—just after me, the author/composer—that I write. I have capitulated. I will let him take me where he will.

In the same way I was compelled to Knausgaard's oeuvre, I was magnetized by Paul Auster's voice in a collection of essays, *The Art of Hunger*, which I discovered at Bear Pond Books in Montpelier, Vermont when attending graduate residency for an MFA. It was July and after the residency I took the book with me to Little Compton, Rhode Island where I vacationed for a week with my boyfriend's family at the shore. He was from a Catholic French-Canadian family, the youngest of seven kids, and almost all the kids (except us) had children, so that there were at least thirty people together that week at the beach, in the waves, eating dinners, playing cards and board games after dinner, and gathering on the lawn for a bonfire in the evenings. I had grown up with a younger brother in a big house and all that togetherness, all under the presiding matriarch, stifled me and drove me to seek solitude each morning and afternoon. It was in those interstices, in the morning when people are padding around their beach houses and just waking to the day and deciding what they are going to do or in the afternoon resting after a meal that I took off. I'd kiss John, my boyfriend, goodbye, hop on the bicycle, and ride out to the point where rocks edge Sakonnet River and its estuary that gives out to the wider ocean of Rhode Island Sound and where across the water sits Newport. In the mornings, I would ride to Olga's Cup and Saucer for cappuccino and a blueberry muffin (the blueberries were from the adjacent farm where Olga had opened her first café in 1988). Tatters of mist floated about the air. I sat with my breakfast at a small outside table under hardwoods.

At the café, or on the rocks at Sakonnet Point, I reached into my backpack, pulled out *The Art of Hunger*, savoring the print across cool pages and the spine revealing a writer's mind, and began to read Auster's essays of writers and painters and thinkers who had moved and changed him. Love affair essays. Interviews he had given, prefaces to books, and sections from his *Red Notebook*. The back cover of the book described the work as his reflections on his "need to break down the boundary between living and writing."[245] I wanted that! I took copious notes in the back of the book. Not that day but over days that became months and then a year and then years, those years I lived in Chicago with John and taught writing and finished my MFA and wrote my own things and began to become someone who would consider herself, and later even relate to herself as, a writer. The notes and words were new to me, literary and philosophical language that still I do not employ frequently in my writing, though they are no longer new: jocularity, paratactic, disquisition, neologism, aphorism, assonance, univocal, dialogic. The literary thinkers were new—Georges Bataille, Osip Mandelstam, Maurice Blanchot, Mikhail Bakhtin, Edmond Jabès, as were the poets—Laura Riding, George Oppen, William Bronk. The title of Auster's book, The Art of Hunger was inspired by Knut Hamsun's novel Hunger and by Franz Kafka's arresting short story, "The Hunger Artist." Writing of Kafka's letters in 1977,

---

[245] Auster, *The Art of Hunger*.

Auster unveils the writer gently through his recognition that "Little by little, we are beginning to know Kafka." He continues, "Like the hunger artist in one of his finest stories, Kafka's life and art were inseparable: to succeed in his art meant to consume himself as a human being. He wrote, not for recognition, but because his very life depended on it."[246] Kafka confessed in his letters that, for him, writing was a form of prayer.

It is for this reason Levi's work compels me. Levi was not a religious man. Nor was Kafka, but each identified with their Jewishness and, Levi, particularly (as many Jews) through the war and after Auschwitz had a maturing relationship with his Jewishness. For his part, Auster introduced me to a world of thinkers, primarily male, French, many Jewish and European, that would not entirely become my own world of thinkers, but which contributed significantly to the world I was forming through my independent studies and writing. I sought out these philosopher-writers as I lived in and through that hungry book. In subsequent months and years, I spent hours in the Harold Washington Library, nine floors in the middle of downtown Chicago, near John's work at the Board of Trade. I took the elevated from our outlying neighborhood, got off at LaSalle, read all morning on the sixth (philosophy) and seventh (literature) floors and made Auster's mind and his world my own. I told my writing students that to love a writer's work and his voice is to copulate with a writer's mind. They stirred in their chairs, smiled. I liked the vividness of the verb copulate that emphasized the eroticism embedded in literature, in intellectual life, and in aesthetics. I was beginning to fall in love with intellectual and literary life.

Was it only with attractive male writers that intellect and sexuality were connected for me? Was I dabbling in intersexuality rather than intertextuality? Did I feel this kind of desire with female writers? No, it was different. With, for example, Anaïs Nin, I felt awe coupled with respect and admiration. I wanted my life or my voice or my thinking to in some way emulate hers. My advisor in graduate school insisted that I stop reading Nin, through whose diaries I was working my way. I also read her fiction—*House of Incest, Winter of Artifice, Under the Glass Bell, A Spy in the House of Love*. I adored her sensuality and her incisive psychological portraits of those in her social milieu. Her ability to self-analyze and to detail her life as a writer and artist was even more compelling than her portraits of others. I studied, too, her persistence in developing the diary as a new genre of writing. The diaries straddled the line of fiction and autobiography, and those who had the ability to publish her work in the early and mid-twentieth century assumed that such writing did not constitute a valid genre, that there would be no audience for it. Henry Miller, her friend, lover, and fellow writer, advised her to stop writing the diaries, to write real fiction. Yet, she persisted, to the point where she began to print and publish her own writing. *The Novel of the Future*, Nin's vision of the novel, became the basis for my

---

[246] Auster, 135.

Master's thesis in which I examined the purposes and power of poetic language in four contemporary novels. Likewise, Auster and Knausgaard each do something in their writing that compels me. They combine feeling with observation and curiosity. At times they are the character, immersed in and colluding with story and, at other times, the objective witness, entirely capable of analysis, understanding the ramifications and implications of a situation. I wanted a man in my own life that could unite head and heart in a passionate embrace of life and of me. It is these writers, whom I do not now idealize, but in whom I perceive a philosophical quality of passion and perception, of emotion and sensing that stirs and moves me.

A year later, another November, this time 2016, I'm drawn to Knausgaard's review of *Submission*, a novel by French writer Michel Houellebecq.[247] Knausgaard begins the review with a confession that he avoided reading Houellebecq's work due to what he imagined as its much-lauded brilliance. He feared that he would feel "why write?" once he had read the French novelist's work and that his own work was mere imperfection in comparison. The opener to his review is the narrative of his own resistance, the breakdown of that resistance (this parallels my experience in relationship to his work!), beginning to read the novel and a related novel (which influenced the French novelist), and, poignantly, a scene he depicts when he reads the complex novel while sitting on the cold bleachers at his ten-year-old daughter's gymnastic practice. When he gets to the body of the review he is acute, perceptive, and visionary in his analysis. He's fascinated by the protagonist of *Submission*, who he describes as "an ordinary guy," a nihilist who has long since lost the thread of meaning in his life and ostracizes himself from society.

Of course, Knausgaard relates to this sort of protagonist. The description might fit him, too. *My Struggle* represents both his need to belong, to feel himself part of a society, family, country, and social group, as well as his need to go inward, to find space to hear himself think, to separate and differentiate himself through the articulation, creation, and production of his work. He argues that out of the general apathy of society, French society in this case, toward social and political decay comes a turn to religion, once again (as the decay and subsequent turn to religion was also acted out in the nineteenth century). The protagonist's turn to religion, his forced conversion to Islam as France becomes an Islamic state, lacks passion and conviction. The character, Francois, converts because he has to. He does not care one way or the other about the religious takeover of the state as harbinger of things to come—the inevitable and impending limitations to social and political freedoms. In the review, he explores disillusionment—personal and social—and the linkages between the two kinds of despair. Religion is the illusion that muffles, temporarily, disillusionment. The disillusion, detachment from society and from others, from relationships and the effort to create meaning, itself becomes an illusion. Religion replaces it—but, as Knausgaard provocatively suggests, it is ironically replaced again with pragmatic, dispassionate, and disconnected conversion. The irony? Even the passion of

---

[247] Knausgaard. "Michel Houellebecq's '*Submission*'."

conversion has been transmuted into an experience devoid of life because devoid of feeling, conviction, and, ultimately, meaning. Conversion then is just another act in a time when action has no consequence. He ranges over political history, literary history and figures, contemporary politics in France, global concerns in European societies with migration, immigration, inclusion, and submission of new cultures into dominant culture, and, even, the feminist sacrifices liberals make in anti-racism campaigns.

The result of this writing in review of *Submission* is a dense, personal, and astutely intellectual piece of literary analysis. He turns to a nineteenth century French novel, *Against the Grain*, by Joris-Karl Huysmans, the dissertation subject of the protagonist Francois in *Submission*. He reads that novel (to which he has also been in resistance) in tandem with his reading of *Submission*. In his resistance to both novels, and now utterly forced to them by *The New York Times* invitation, readers get not so much an immediate review, as the story of resistance in reading. We get two reviews, of two writers, two novels nested together as it were, rather than a single straightforward review of the novel under assignment. The strategy does not come off as a literary device or a rhetorical trick. It takes shape as a story into which the reader is inexorably drawn. Once the story concludes, I'm seamlessly carried away into the review, as if a lover had taken me there against my will—seduced, captivated, once again in literary love, and willing to go where he takes me.

Seduction is an art, one that Knausgaard does well, and likely without complete consciousness as he chain-smokes his way through writing sessions, the chaos and messiness of life around and in him. Likely I'm not only reader who feels this creeping allegiance. His intended six-volume autobiography has been selling madly in all corners of the planet, especially since its translation into English. We in the English-speaking world now await translation and release of the sixth volume. He is doing well, too well, and he sometimes regrets the fame and publicity. But, reading the review makes me not only want to read the French novel but to return to his memoirs. He's like a boyfriend, one I know isn't good for me but who inexorably I refuse to drop. He's complex and contradictory, as is my literary relationship with him. I've come to think of him as "the writer at the periphery," as his literary form and some of his writing philosophy were the impetus to propel me back into daily writing and the incipient makings of a book-length project.

Because of the encounter with *My Struggle* in the San Francisco bookstore, six months after my return from a fellowship in Poland, clouded with dull despair that I had been unable to lift in the wake of that trip, having just completed a dissertation and six years of graduate study while working and parenting, I began to write. I did not purchase his book that day, but I thought about his project as represented and revealed in the books. Eventually I purchased a book, or two, or more in the series. At home, I sat in bed with my laptop and begin to read about him—the interviews and articles. That night, January 25, I started the book that had been inside me, quietly and without my knowing, since Poland. I began immediately a routine of daily writing about Poland, about Primo Levi, about Auschwitz and what I felt and saw there. First, I wrote of Jewish graveyards and the dead and the markers of broken, smashed, and patched gravestones. It was from pieces of memory that the book, *After Poland*, began to emerge. I could hear the story, I could hear myself through Poland, because, in part,

Knausgaard had been forthcoming about his process and because, in part, I had been drawn to the volumes of his memoir-opus shelved together on one shelf at eye-level in the fiction section of Books, Inc., my mother browsing in another section of the store, my son in young adult literature.

His persistence in writing is utterly inspiring. It is a daily necessity and he finds the interstices in his life peopled with children, a house, and a wife. His living environment is messy, things in disarray, a trait I hardly tolerate in my own environment. Disarray makes me wince; I cherish beauty and will not apologize for that. My own satisfaction with beauty may be bourgeois, even naïve and superficial in making of it a refuge of meaning and a space of writing, but I derive deep joy from aesthetic pleasure and I feel unapologetic for this propensity. "I know where my fascinations lie," he writes. Self-knowledge and then the pointed intention, "I try to go there."[248] There is an unabated, unabashed quality, an incisive desire and obsession, a willingness to travel to what obsesses and drives one to write. The freedom resides in there not needing to be a story, or even a subject about which to write. The writing shows itself. There's so much permissiveness there to stream from the unconscious to the page. It is an informed and intelligent automatic writing, but one thinks for days and dreams, perhaps, what one is going to write. It brews and seeps and evolves into itself, now the writer a servant to content, to language and words coming to the surface. He says that memoir is not a tradition in Norwegian society, that the society does not have a habit of self-disclosure as we do in European and American societies. So, memoir is novel, as in new, and he does not have a Scandinavian tradition from which he is working. Rather, he seems to work within a European (perhaps French) tradition.

He had written a couple successful novels prior to writing *My Struggle* at forty, just after his first child was born and he had found the grinding quality of life raising an infant into a toddler. Then, another child and another. Personally, I struggled to raise one child, and could not have imagined having more. Was there some unquenchable longing to procreate, to heal over wounds, to bond through the manifestation and joint adoration of a child, two children, three children, now four children? Those early years caring for an infant and then a toddler were demanding. I felt I had lost my life. At just over fifty, twelve years after his birth, I'm living a life of routine—teaching college English for fifteen years, writing in the garden to the cries of the neighbors' young boy and the loud sucking of a vacuum as they clean house. In writing breaks, throwing laundry in the dryer, ensuring Elias practices piano and does his homework. Driving to away soccer games and twice weekly practices, tournaments, home games, a few piles of papers waiting on my desk for review and grading.

Oddly, I'm satisfied with my life. Then I think to January 2015 when I felt disillusioned with life, that pale despair descending on me somewhere in the inner terrain after Poland, after being at Auschwitz. Maybe that is why Knausgaard's title—

---

[248] Knausgaard. "Michel Houellebecq's '*Submission*'."

My Struggle pulled me to the shelf where his voluminous book sat. I saw he was my brother's age, born the same year as Eric (1968), five years younger than me, of my generation. Self-indulgent, perhaps, but enthralling from the middle pages where I cracked open the book and began to read there in the store. Okay, I confess now to my son, who writes at my desk while I sit with laptop in the November garden sunshine, "I've just ordered all five books in the *My Struggle* series." He smiles, a sort of vindicated pleasure. I'm exposed with him. "Watch your resistances, because they'll always reveal something about you," I say. I know where my fascinations lie, says Knausgaard, and, so, my own fascinations lie with this writer. I return to his work again and again, desirous to connect to the work of a contemporary writer as I grapple with the histories I've inherited. Knausgaard starts with his own resistances. I know where my own fascinations lie. That's where I am trying to go.

4.4 ANCESTRAL HISTORY

Every year on the night of November 10 I dream of my grandma. But this time it is after Poland. I'm thinking of archives and lost houses and dead families and the memories created by war. I remember that the day of her death approaches, but when it arrives I do not remember at all. Instead I feel her presence. I evoke her or she calls on me and there is some communication.

I dreamt of a house, with some outbuildings, at the edge of Pasadena in a wooded area off a major road. There had not been a road there when my mother was young, and my grandparents had owned the house. The house looked like a barn—rough, darkened wood—and had a dull (once bright) red door. The pines had shed many of their needles and looked ragged in the dark night, lit only in the headlights of passing cars. I stood across the road and lamented the abandoned house that had once held much life—the activities and interactions of my grandparents, their friends, visitors from the church my grandfather pastored, and the energies of their three children—my elder uncle, my mother, and their younger brother. Pasadena had been a small city then, parts of it rural, and I felt out of place and out of date standing there across the road with my dusty memories. An unfamiliar woman, aged about sixty, slipped into a downstairs side door of the house. Perhaps she lived there and could tell me of the history she knew? I crossed the road to follow her but once on the property could not find her.

I entered and explored the rooms. The place was abandoned, dilapidated, the sheer curtains ripped. There were boxes and loose things—frames, photos, and dishes—piled on the floor. Chairs and couches were uncovered and smothered in dust. The loss of my grandma felt total, complete. I found old photos in a pile and more in a little cedar box in the shape of a semicircle in a big downstairs room that felt more like a barn than a house, and I began to look through them. At some point my mother appeared by my side and explained to me who was in each photo and its location. The photos were of an even more remote past—one prior to my birth, memories that would never be mine but which somehow I was to imbibe: my grandma as a young child in Iowa, standing solemn before the camera (perhaps in 1919) in a pale white cotton dress; my grandfather as a tall, handsome young man climbing a ladder (he died at age sixty-one in a fall from a ladder while painting a house); my grandparents, just married and childless for a few years, at a dinner table, my grandpa's arm around his new wife. Some of these photos actually exist, such as the one of my grandma as a child, but most are a concoction of memories, jumbled and scrambled together with my desire for my grandparents and the imagination of what their life might have been. I notice they are smiling in the photos and seem happy. Yet, I am uncertain if I have a single photo of my grandparents together in which they are smiling. A smile for the camera is something more contemporary, perhaps American. It says, I am pleased, in the midst of pleasure, fulfilled and satisfied by life in this moment. The way I grew up a smile indicates supposed health and the privilege of being entertained. My grandparents grew up on farms in the middle of Iowa, each from a family of nine children. They did not have to display signs of happiness. Rather, I imagine they just were—in the midst of life, struggling with daily problems, loving each other, raising children, and, for my grandpa, pastoring a church and painting houses.

My mother knows all the relatives, the many siblings of each of my grandparents (her aunts and uncles and cousins). She even seems to remember her parents in photos that were taken prior to her birth. Those memories are hers not mine. Though, in this moment she's trying to give them to me, to make them closer. I struggle until I feel my grandma's spirit hovering about me, nearby, haunting the house, haunting this place. Not in the way that fills me with fear, but as a quiet, unobtrusive presence that lives here, in this house, in and about me now. I see nothing. There's no apparition, but she's here, everywhere. She wants me to know that and she wants me to understand the photos and the house. She wants to give me the history and to fill in all the holes in my memory. I have to carry the time before I was born, she seems to be telling me.

My mother is gone, and it is just grandma with me. I'm a little bit afraid after all. I don't know the house, and this isn't my place. She hovers and floats nearby. She has no language, so she cannot communicate directly with me. She has to teleport her remembrances to me. I fear my inability to comprehend their meanings. I also have the feeling that I've been the grandchild closest to her, so who else but me? I'm responsible and afraid. Not afraid of ghosts but afraid of memory. Not having enough, not knowing the things I'm supposed to recall. Not being able to speak anything else but the language of life, of living, the one exchanged on this plane between humans who share a geographic space and a contemporary time together.

My grandma has left that place. I'm afraid of an abyss into which human experience falls when everyone is gone, and new people come, and things lie in tatters, artifacts of another time, other lives that no one remembers and that decay in silence. I'm afraid because I recognize that objects erode quietly into their own kind of deaths when there's nothing and no one to remember anymore.

4.5 WE HAVE BEEN BAPTIZED

Primo Levi has become over the past four decades an increasingly international writer. His audience is global. His work may be more widely read in the United States than in

Italy, though Italians were his first audience. Lines from his first autobiographical narrative, *If This Is a Man*, are elemental to some of the exhibits at the United States Holocaust Memorial Museum in Washington, D.C. Below his words he is identified as "Italian Jewish Author, Auschwitz Survivor." I read his words in that museum and understand that Levi has become integral, even intrinsic to the canon of Jewish writers who wrote of the Holocaust as survivors of its catastrophic events. I have traveled to one European country, the one in which Levi was interned, and to three American cities to "find" the author through his experience as it manifested for him during and after the war. I have sought him through the story he first wrote and which over the years he shared with the world.

Levi's sincerity and his steady, measured tone undergirded with a passionate devotion to ethics and to the material, sensual things of the world drew me to New York and Poland on fellowship, to Miami for a literature symposium, and to Washington, D.C. to witness the archive and public memory of the Holocaust in the United States. These travels have permitted me a deep sense of the history and events surrounding Levi's capture as a partisan, his internment at a POW and transit camp at Fossoli di Carpi, his deportation to Poland with a group of 650 Italians, and his arrival and imprisonment at Auschwitz. These travels have also provided space to generously imagine Levi's life after Auschwitz, which included his repatriation journey home over a period of nine months, his writing and the career it became for him, his study of linguistics and of physical science, his attention to the relationship between the symbolic and material realms of existence, and, finally, his battle with depression and despair (normal to so many writers who have witnessed and experienced the imprint of violence and trauma through political repression, war, dislocation, imprisonment, and extensive loss) in the decades after the Second World War.

In the first open public space, the Hall of Witness, my mother is talking to a woman from Connecticut who has been to the museum once before. She knows very little about Holocaust history and has no idea who Primo Levi is. My mother is telling her about Levi, that I teach his work and have recently been on fellowship to Poland. As usual, I'm looking for signs of the writer. He might be easy to miss. Here are his words on a wall just above a photo mural created by French photographer Frédéric Brenner. Each photo features a survivor's forearm, blue numbers needled into flesh. The center photo taken in 1991 in Salonika (now Thessaloniki), Greece is of four men. Their eyes look directly at the viewer. Three of them pose with their arms outstretched and their hands clasped together around a single wooden pole. The fourth, slightly separate yet part of the group, rests his chin in his left hand. Each arm carries a tattoo—116 and 118 in the thousands. They would have been interned about the same time as Levi.[249] Levi's words come early in his account of Auschwitz, in the second chapter "On the Bottom." At the museum these words unfurl over the photos: "My number is 174517; we have been baptized, we will carry the tattoo on our left arm until we die."[250] The tattoo was to be a mark of identification. In the original

---

[249] Between March and August 1943, the Germans deported more than 45,000 Jews from Salonika to Auschwitz-Birkenau extermination camp. Most of the deportees were gassed on arrival in Auschwitz. (USHMM)

[250] Levi, *Survival*, 27.

Italian, Levi writes— *"Häftling: ho imparato che io sono uno Häftling. Il mio nome è 174 517; siamo stati battezzati, porteremo finché vivremo il marchio tatuato sul braccio sinistro."*[251] We have been baptized. He refers to the number as his name, "My name is," as we would in ordinary civilian life when we refer to ourselves and introduce ourselves to one another. His declaration conveys the terrible imposition of a permanent condition, indicative of a mechanized system of classification of which he is now a functionary.

In *Beyond Good and Evil* Friedrich Nietzsche at the cusp of the nineteenth and twentieth centuries criticizes philosophers for having placed inordinate value on certain formulations of knowledge. He writes that their beliefs are then baptized: "something that is finally baptized solemnly as 'the truth.'"[252] Philosophers have had, he argues, a tyrannical drive to understand, a will to power which causes them to "baptize" their prejudices as truths. Those prejudices are then put forward in the guise of truth as philosophy. However, when Levi declares of the incoming prisoners "we have been baptized," perhaps in allusion to Nietzsche's reference of knowledge as "baptized" into certain truths, solemnly, perhaps even sanctimoniously, Levi tells his readers something about what truth has become by the mid-twentieth century given the creation and implementation of genocide. The Nazi regime's implementation and plan of destruction in the will to power reduced truth to violent prejudice and murderous greed.

To be baptized is to be immersed in the Christian tradition. Jews have had their own traditions of purification, such as ritual bath in naturally sourced water in a mikvah. This tradition has been called Tvilah and could be repeated over the course of a Jewish convert's lifetime. Levi's reference to baptism alludes to Christian ritual. Baptism has been associated with the messianic tradition—Christ's baptism by John the Baptist—symbolic of redemptive immersion or dunking in water, a purification in the name of the Father, Son, and Holy Spirit. In Dante's *Inferno* the poet enters the lip of Hell's chasm, "The abyss's first engirding circle," with his guide Virgil.[253] There he encounters unbaptized children, men, and women who did not sin, yet have not been saved by God. To be saved one must be baptized; he must be a believer. There, too, are the poets: Homer, Horace, Lucan, and Ovid. Accordingly, Levi chooses a leaden and shocking word to describe the tattooing process upon entry into Auschwitz. Baptism of Jews here implies Christian imposition, branding or marking of grotesque proportions, a religious ritual of death to an old self and renewal in Christ, now perversely made into violation of a human being. This is baptism into a Christian hell. This "ritual," which would leave permanent markings on their bodies, allowed the Germans to maintain meticulous identity records of the imprisoned. In the process, this practice destroyed personhood, erasing and replacing one's personal name and life details with a tattooed number carried to death. Here in the museum is Levi's number, still extant in the world. Levi's body is gone but that particular

---

[251] Levi, *Se questo è un uomo*, 21. Prisoner. I have learned that I am a prisoner. My name is 174 517; we have been baptized, we will carry as long as we live the tattoo on our left arm. [Translation mine.]

[252] Nietzsche, *Beyond Good and Evil*, 10.

[253] *Inferno*, Canto IV, 35.

number now signifies the tattoo that he was to wear for the remainder of his life. For the period of his internment he was for all intents and purposes that number. 174517. His gravestone in Torino bears this number. In death the number remains. Baptism. Total immersion. The flesh and soul pierced with blue ink.

Standing before the photo mural, I am silent. The people to whom these arms belong are telling me something. I listen. All these beautiful limbs and the way the Jews of Salonika hold their arms and show the damage to the camera. I attempt to read (to intuit) the various relationships between arms and their numbers. How does one read what she cannot see? Where does the heart reside—with the arm, with the number, alone in some inner kingdom that shelters memory? Does the tattoo become one's own? How does a man or a woman, a child now grown, wear a tattoo enforced through trauma? Levi's number is a tattoo in my brain. I've memorized the way the numbers look: a pair of seventeens at either end and a middle forty-five, the year of the camp's liberation and Levi's release from the physical structures of Auschwitz. His number is a mantra. Sometimes I say it aloud. He transformed his relationship to that number. He became part of the number. He did not let his number haunt him silently. He did not try to hide it. Rather he wore it for others to see, to inquire, to wonder, to recoil from. But his words often brought closer those who would turn away.

Sometimes he wore short sleeves to make the tattoo evident. He would wear it as a memory and a reminder so that no one could forget what baptism meant. His biographer Ian Thomson relates how the writer attended a business dinner with Bayer Industries in Germany in July 1954. When questioned about the mark he told the electrical-insulation expert, Dr. Meckhbach, "It's a memento of Auschwitz."[254] Over the dinner, his daughter Lisa told Thomson, silence fell and forks clattered on plates. His biographer, addressing Levi's desire to travel to Germany on business in the first post-war decade, concludes that the chemist and writer did not want to understand the Germans, as he had professed, but to shame them. Maybe things were even more complicated. Perhaps shaming them was also a way of encouraging them to look and then to speak. Levi may not have been so successful on this account. In that post-war decade it is now common knowledge that many people did want to look back but desired forward movement. Yet, Levi's valuable teaching is that it is impossible to progress in a post-war situation when so many people are living with the legacy of war and genocide. The loss was total. Levi strives to represent that totality in the tattoo.

Then there were his children. Renzo, born in July 1957, was the youngest and Lisa his elder sister by nine years. When Renzo was three he asked his father, "Why have you been written on?" to which his father answered, "I was a prisoner once—that's what they used to do to us."[255] When I read this story, Renzo's age stands out. My son was also three when I was first teaching Levi's book in my college critical thinking courses. He asked me, "Mommy, what is Auschwitz?" Three is an age of

---

[254] Thomson, *Primo Levi: A Life*, 272.
[255] Thomson, 358.

discovery, of unmediated questions that come naturally and quickly, arising of a child's curiosity about the world and its phenomena. As Levi's son grew, he did not ask questions about the camp. Levi had tried to talk to both of his teenage children about his experience but neither wanted to hear. It is reported that Renzo fled the room in tears. Levi knew that he had a relation of distant affection with his children. He was a survivor, and he acknowledged that those in proximity to such survival feel the suffering, perhaps somehow feel the dead. Maybe the child is not ready, if ever, to know the violence and horror his father has seen, not until he is a full-grown adult, and by then the parent may be gone.

Both art installation and statement of horror, the spare black and white photos emphasize the centrality of the tattoo's presence and the partiality of the number. There is an embodied cosmology to which the arm belongs. Each arm represents a universe of knowledge, experience, and memory. The viewer does not see that unique self in each arm with its number. Rather, she intuits it. I stand at the wall observing the photos: the number against the modulations of flesh, the hue of skin, the shape, texture, and length of each arm, the manner in which each person holds their hand—high or low, closed or open, taut or flaccid, palm turned upward or downward. The Greek men central to the photo montage appear together. Yet, each possesses singularity: one tired, another defiant, one angry, another worried. They reveal multiple worlds contained within and streaming out from the tattoo. Still, they are a singular testament. In this collective way, the men remind me of Levi's assertion in *If This Is a Man* that he had taken a dark journey and was now witness to the gravity of that descent. This witness exists in the mark borne by each human being who returns from the underworld to the world of the living. Terrence Des Pres said of Elie Wiesel's writing that he "renders silence in ways that make it—and therefore what it embodies—present and meaningful to us."[256] In contemplating the legacy of the tattoo and considering the stories housed within the burden of each inked registration, silence speaks through the lives that have had to bear these marks.

4.6 THE PROMISE OF FRIENDSHIP

What did *the desert* mean to Hannah Arendt, who referred to that arid and seemingly uninhabitable geographic terrain of post-World War II in her political writings? She evoked the desert as a metaphor for the absence of a lush and verdant world that she must have known in the landscape of northern Europe (Germany and France) and in the cities and rural areas of North America (between New York and Chicago). But diligently and with great passion through wars, through political turmoil, through severe criticism of her written and public work, and, in friendships with fellow thinkers, writers, artists, and students she cultivated over her lifetime that lush world. She named in the desert a particular kind of wordlessness, which she described as, "the withering away of everything between us," and cautioned that the greatest danger of the modern age was human habituation to desert conditions. Those conditions in

---

[256] Des Pres, *Writing into the World*, 28.

the twentieth century were largely caused and perpetuated by totalitarian regimes, which with she was all too familiar. This was the great crime of the concentration camp that made people into desert inhabitants and deprived beings of belonging. Arendt argued that some, if they failed to imagine or hope for it, could not recognize their capitulation to the minimal and dehumanizing conditions that made their immediate world and the world beyond an endless, empty desert. She did not place blame on those who had suffered in the camps; rather, she thought the camps an ominous warning of human capacity to rob fellow humans of their worlds, worlds represented in the oases that nourish life and replenish human qualities.

Arendt makes a strong argument in her philosophizing to care for our abilities to know events and to judge and condemn them when they are unjust. She wrote that stories (at their very best) help humans to remember actions and feelings, conferring significance onto a string of events and delivering them with coherence, elegance, logic, and meaning into a shared common (and largely narrative) world. This world is the plurality within which politics emerges.

Arendt was born in 1906 into a German Jewish family in Königsberg, also birthplace of Immanuel Kant.[257] At the time of the first war she was seven; at the second war she was thirty-two. She studied philosophy with Martin Heidegger who was her thesis advisor at University of Marburg.[258] From her initial work with Heidegger she developed a way of thinking about ontology—the study of being or consciousness—that radically integrated the ontological into the public world. Her conceptualization of what had been a metaphysics into the public world brought being into relationship with politics and sought to elucidate linkages between the interior (private) and political (public) realms of human experience. Her idea was that reflection on being should not exist in an abstract world of higher thought but that one's interior life was inextricable from her life (appearance and participation) in the world. This fusion is more unique than it may appear to contemporary readers. In the early twentieth century few philosophers, and even fewer political theorists, linked the human psyche to the world of political events and institutions. However, for Arendt, that interior world was not as much emotional and psychological as it was based on a critical capacity to analyze, judge, and to conduct an ongoing monologue with oneself in determining one's relationship with and to the world. The thinking human being has to ask herself what actions she can live with. She has to ultimately determine if she wants to live an ethical life in relationship to self and others, and how she will do so. Arendt's particular experience as a German Jewish scholar, one of a very few women who studied at a top university in Germany and, additionally, studied with Martin Heidegger (who later would align himself ideologically with the National

---

[257] Kant was a moral philosopher of the Enlightenment period and author of, among many other works, *Critique of Pure Reason* (1781 and 1787). He was born in Königsberg on the Baltic Sea, a city which was then the capital of East Prussia. The city is now Kaliningrad, Russia. He attended the university in Königsberg and went on to become a lecturer and finally a chair in logic and metaphysics. See *Stanford Encyclopedia of Philosophy*.

[258] For a detailed discussion of Arendt's scholarly and personal relationship with Heidegger see *Hannah Arendt: For Love of the World* by Elisabeth Young-Bruehl.

Socialists), as well as her work in resistance activities in France after she fled Germany, followed by teaching in the United States and a large body of published work, made her a singular thinker.[259] Her political philosophy developed in response to exile from Germany and then from Europe, to the genocide of European Jews, to the phenomenon of totalitarianism, particularly as represented in the concentration camps and in the adjudication of Nazi war crimes, and through her writing and teaching during her years in the United States.

In *The Promise of Politics*, a collection of lectures Arendt gave at American universities (among them Notre Dame, Princeton, University of Chicago, and Berkeley) in the 1950s, she reveals her thinking about the great philosophers, among them her teacher Heidegger, and the German philosopher Nietzsche, as well as the ancient Greek philosophers Aristotle and Plato. She suggests that they had not fully considered the necessity of the human soul's need for spiritual and sensual nourishment as intrinsic to a thriving, functioning polis.

> The oases are those fields of life which exist independently, or largely so, from political conditions in the isolation of the artist, in the solitude of the philosopher, in the inherently wordless relationship between human beings as it exists in love and sometimes in friendship—when one heart reaches out directly to the other, as in friendship, or when the in-between, the world, goes up in flames, as in love. Without the intactness of these oases we would not know how to breathe, and political scientists should know this.[260]

The Promise of Politics spoke to a truth I had intuited but not yet articulated. This passage so caught me up that I began to consider intimate life as foundational to collective life, whereas before I had thought personal life, that is to say individual life, completely outside of and even demoted and ostracized by political life. *When one heart reaches out to the other the world goes up in flames.* It was measured, it was careful, but it was rhythmic, as if one heart were at this very moment reaching out to another.

This was a book on political theory. I looked at the cover. The Promise. Could politics promise something like love? Did politics inform love? Was the love I enacted in conjunction with another a hope for a sane world. Was love a hope for repairing a shattered collective space and for restoring that collective space? It was an ideal. But, certainly, it was beautiful. Every time I loved perhaps I was creating more space, more possibility in the world for politics, as an ethic of seeing and listening to the other. The world goes up. A flame. Not a flame of destruction, but a bonding of love, heat and connection between self and other. Suddenly, I recalled a room, sheer white curtains billowing at the open window. I was returned to Rome or Bologna, New York or San Francisco, Spoleto or Big Sur. Those moments of most knowing another, of bliss in love, of complete warmth and melting trust, however fleeting,

---

[259] Arendt's biographer Elisabeth Young-Bruehl describes Heidegger in the early 1930s as susceptible to Nazi propaganda. He became a member of the Nazi party in May 1933.

[260] Arendt, *The Promise of Politics*, 202.

extended a promise. Intimacy mattered, most obviously to personal relationships but also to a collectively shared world. What we do in private matters to the world we create with and for one another. It instills in us the value and vitality of deep connection with and to another human being. What other philosopher had spoken in this manner? This philosopher addressed with acuity the wordless relation between human beings. Out of the lacuna—the space between, felt but not visible—human life asserts itself against a tide of no-reason, a world of violence into which one may be forced through the vicissitudes of history to capitulate her humanity, even her very life. Here I read philosophy that spoke to the scene of one heart reaching toward another. Did these kinds of sensual thought interactions have validity in the world, and even more so in the political world? Continental philosophers such as Descartes and Spinoza had begun their treatises with God; others had moved away from God as axiom, moving instead toward the idea of an inner divinity or übermensch (Nietzsche's self-transcendent man). In Arendt's images a poet spoke. Could one write political theory with these words: fields of life, love, heart, flames? Could one write with this passion and ask me to judge history? It was my judgment, my faculty of wise and compassionate insight that would make me a student not of the desert but of the oases. Is judgment an act of love when rooted in one's passionate knowledge of the world? Is judgment an act of love when rooted in a value of shared life (present and past) among the world's inhabitants?

In Arendt's promise I found a way to frame Levi's creative opus, his memoirs, novels, essays, and poems. Like Levi, Arendt was largely a secular thinker and she overtly claimed her Jewishness as a political identity as Hitler came to power.[261] She spoke with reason and discipline as she gave voice to a renewed ethics in the twentieth century. Like Levi, she explored personal relationships as determinative of a collective ethics. Such an ethics would combat totalitarianism characterized by institutionalized violence that aimed to control human behavior and delimit freedom. In his account of Auschwitz, Levi narrates moments of connection with fellow inmates that clearly help him to survive physically and mentally his months of imprisonment. Even as he documents the dehumanization of people in the camps, he makes central the humanness in each encounter he has with his fellows, so that the story itself becomes an affirmation of humanness. However, he also shows us the destruction of that humanness and the adaptions people make to cleave to their dignity and to create chances for survival. With this complexity, no reader remains untouched. We know that Levi writes a story of tragic proportions. Terrence Des Pres details in his study of Holocaust survivors how those who were politically astute, who had been involved in political and/or resistance groups as Levi had, knew the

---

[261] In a 1964 interview with German journalist Günter Gaus, Arendt discussed becoming a political person in 1933: "When one is attacked as a Jew, one must defend oneself as a Jew. Not as a German, not as a world citizen, not as an upholder of the Rights of Man. But: What can I specifically do as a Jew?" See Arendt's *Essays in Understanding*, 12.

importance of camaraderie to survival in the camps.[262] Levi recognized that isolation brought danger and the strong possibility of death to an individual. He understood from resistance activities in northern Italy in the months before he was captured and deported to Auschwitz that relationships matter to survival. They matter in that cooperation with others not only increases survival chances but also allows one to feel human in the will to participate in a shared human world. Given the extreme conditions of the camps, as well as prior forms of imprisonment imposed on Jewish communities, such as ghettos, the environment of terror, and the imposition of isolation on individuals, survival increased to the degree that the individual was able to secure formal and informal communities of support, exchange, and help.

Levi wrote that just before and during the years of the Second World War Europeans existed in an atmosphere in which strangers were enemies. He writes in "Gold," a chapter in *The Periodic Table*, that Fascism had an effect on him and all his Italian friends. Though they tried to resist it, writing poetry and imagining stories, its undertow pulled them downward. "Writing sad, crepuscular poems, and not all that beautiful, while the world was in flames, did not seem to us either strange or shameful: we proclaimed ourselves the enemies of Fascism, but actually Fascism had had its effect on us, as on almost all Italians, alienating us and making us superficial, passive, and cynical."[263] He continues that they bore rationing and freezing in their houses without coal. Italians were humiliated. Each did his work, slackly, without believing in it, as happens to someone who knows he is not working for his own future. Purpose disappeared. In the wake of dictatorship, people no longer believed in the state to represent them and their interests. In this kind of climate, people lost their trust in others, in daily actions, and in meaningful work. Under a demolished state that looked out for its most powerful and allowed people to languish, humans became permanent skeptics. They live on the surface, and the interior world, as Levi attests, quietly consumed itself as cynicism formed a crust over the world of passion, feeling, and connection. Levi cautioned against this state—a cold acceptance coupled with rage, a cynicism that staved off despair—as a space in which humans, utterly disaffected, could remain. Arendt recognized this same danger in the years after the war. She thus counseled intimate relations, relations of trust and closeness, as bedrock to a sane and functioning collective life in a space of appearances, a public world wherein people worked together for good, a world she called politics.

In this way, Levi's writing concerning the effects of the war reveals the truth of Arendt's injunction to human connection as foundational to political life. Yet, he also explores in his writing the alienation and isolation of the individual under totalitarianism. Arendt considered political life to exist under the protections of a fair and democratic state that guaranteed and protected rights for its citizens. She envisioned such life occurring in collective spaces. These conditions did not describe Europe under Nazi occupation in the late 1930s and through most of the 1940s. Nor

---

[262] Des Pres, *The Survivor*. See in particular the chapter "Life in Death," where the author details the value of covert or underground resistance that operated among prisoners within the camps. Here he brilliantly explores the necessary coupling of obedience and resistance as dual means of survival.

[263] Levi, *The Periodic Table*, 128.

did those conditions describe Italian life under Mussolini's National Fascist Party. Arendt believed the work post-war was to create protections for human conditions.[264]

The oasis, Arendt writes, represents the "life-giving source" that lets us live in the desert without becoming reconciled to it. The oasis is where we find our nourishment—in solitude, in communion with self and others, in love, in creation, in impassioned thinking that leads to action. That single passage addressing how people create oasis in intimate space together had drawn me into her universe, a universe materialized in the knowledge of two wars, and in the 1950s and 60s, at the time of her writing, a nuclear arms race. Arendt suggests that spaces of mutual support and love that people imagine and labor to create among themselves resist withering. Such spaces can sustain people, mentally and emotionally, nourishing them to work in collaboration and with respect. This "love labor" helps resist the desert conditions of isolation, shame, silence, trauma, loss, distrust, ethical rupture, and persecution. At the time of her writing, Arendt had in mind the violence and corruption that characterized people's public lives over the years of the Second World War. As Jerome Kohn details in "Hannah Arendt's Jewish Experience," the great threat to human experience is that of loneliness, not belonging, being forced out of community. Therefore, she viewed the right to the human condition as the highest and most fundamental of rights, and she argued that this guarantee of human freedom occurred in a "comity of nations."[265] The friendly cooperation between nations seemed especially relevant at a crucial juncture when European Jews had been rendered through the war stateless and homeless with the imposition of racial laws, deportation from their homes, and total separation from their families and the societies in which they lived. Perhaps she foresaw a more robust role for the United Nations or the future of the European Union, however flawed those institutions have been. She may have been foregrounding a move to cosmopolitanism (a global culture shared through commerce, information and publishing, political alliances, trade, travel, and treaties) that has become increasingly important in a postmodern technological world—a cooperation of peoples across nations and ideologies for the benefit of all. As she wrote in *The Origins of Totalitarianism*, the highest right is the right of man to citizenship. Political equality creates between people a ground for working to envision and enact their nation's future. Such equality values difference and individual experience as formative of public and political space. It is, as Kohn writes, political inequality that is the foremost harbinger of loneliness.[266]

Have I capitulated to the desert at times in my life? Yes, of course. All beings have and do. When I begin writing this manuscript the desert pressed on me. It was attentiveness to meaning, desire for understanding, and engagement with my experience, despite momentary despair, that compelled me to begin writing six months after my return from Poland. I forged ahead without a sense of what I was

---

[264] *The Universal Declaration of Human Rights*, adopted by the United Nations in 1948, was one such protection.

[265] Kohn, *Thinking in Dark Times: Hannah Arendt on Ethics and Politics*, 189. I would also like to note that political equality must find its support in laws that protect the rights of all people, not just a select few.

[266] Ibid.

doing, recording my thoughts and memories of Poland and the various routes both literal and figurative by which I arrived there. Thus, I have found through direct experience that autobiographical writing matters in each person's personal relationship to history. Autobiography as one's story and its telling also nourish the spaces "in-between." These spaces are oases of personal relationship that help to create robust collective experience in the public sphere.

For Arendt, the public sphere was personal in the interest of the impersonal. That sphere existed, in particular after the Second World War, to build a public life that represented individuals in the interest of the collective good. It was from individual stories told within public space that she believed people could form a collective life that allowed sustainable conditions for all beings—whether citizens or stateless. Adriana Cavarero in *Relating Narratives* explores Arendt's political ontology as a basis of public life in which stories figure prominently, while also suggesting that autobiographical stories do, in fact, matter.[267] How a story is told is central to its reception; critical, interpretative responses to narrative are integral to the politics that form within public discursive space. Cavarero suggests that there were theoretical reasons for Arendt's particular view of narrative's role in public life. Arendt engaged not a focalized study of text in analysis of style or structural semiotics. Rather, Cavarero argues, the neglect of textual analysis revealed her intention toward the complex relations between beings, each life-story, and the specificities of the narrator of the story.

The initiatory movement into the space of appearance constitutes action. Arendt believed that life without speech and action, without appearance to others, is "literally dead to the world."[268] Ultimately, the self, or the "who" that Arendt concedes is an individual, is really nothing in public space without the company of others. The ability of speech and action to reveal that individual does not happen without people who are "with others and neither for nor against them [in] sheer human togetherness."[269] That the individual story can be told at any one point in a human life is true. Story exists at a personal level; this fact supersedes historical and political conditions. But it is the contribution of many stories that creates a complex weaving of shared human history and that, most importantly, creates politics. The self as the expression of one's particular and unique consciousness is expressive and relational; it is also external, in that it is social, entrusted to the attentive gaze and hearing of others. The attunement of another to our individual story signifies that story enters the collective and becomes, in turn, connected to, relational with, and, ultimately, the narrative tale of another.

This relationality posited through narrative is significant in its ability to weave an intricate discourse in public space.[270] Narrative exerts the ability to draw people together. Whether a piece of writing fits within or disrupts established literary forms,

---

[267] Cavarero, *Relating Narratives*, 2000.

[268] Arendt, *The Human Condition*, 176.

[269] Ibid, 180.

[270] This public space in a contemporary world vitally includes the virtual world wherein people share stories, photographs, postings, and events as they communicate instantaneously via technology.

regardless of its style and semiotics, narrative, as Arendt believed, serves as an impetus to appearance. Narrative possesses the potentiality of meaning and serves in acts of storytelling and interpretation as a portal into the world of human relations. The omission of style, voice, tone, and additional elements of craft in Arendt's analysis of narrative in public life means that narratives need not succeed or fail in their literary merits. Stories are not judged according to qualities of form or style. Importantly, this also means that she will be concerned not only with producing relations but elaborating what and how those relations are. Rather, she attended to the attachment we form to narratives and what relationship to history and to the possibility of judgment and politics those attachments suggest. Story does not only encourage connection between people as they listen and attend to others but becomes an antidote to the potentiality of abusive governments and other forms of world-destroying violence—motivating moral judgment, a kind of ethical decision making that forms a deliberative and discursive political engagement.[271]

The rhapsod, performer of epic poetry in ancient Greece, tells the story of Ulysses's journey. As Ulysses hears the events recounted, he recognizes it as his story. Hearing one's story in the mouth of another allows one to awaken to the events that have happened as story.[272] Ulysses hears his story and begins to cry. He begins to confess his own story. So, too, Levi begins to tell his tale, realizing even during his time of imprisonment in Auschwitz that the story is his and that to live means to tell and to exist because one's story is personal and collective. Yet, his tale is not entirely autobiographical (as no story is) because he tells the stories of others whose presence constitutes his very tale. He first tells the story as a deposition, a witness in the courts of post-war Italy to crimes of deportation and internment. He tells the story—a rhapsod for others who had perished in the camps and for those who had survived but would not be able to tell their stories. The first story is close to thirty-four pages. It was in relation to others, toward a juridical, testimonial, and social need for certain knowledge of violence and atrocity, crimes against humanity, that Levi wrote. He transformed personal experience from disparate happenings and observations into a historically and politically relevant narrative. He wrote a deposition [una deposizione], a legal document for the court to testify to deportation and to the conditions at Auschwitz and its sub-camps. This initial recording evolved into a longer story that conferred for generations of readers, as well as for the author, particular, acute meaning onto what had been a succession of loosely related events.

Levi's story evolved of a universe—swirling, wild feelings pocked with episodes of detachment, despair, and loss so heavy he no longer felt himself as human. In imagining that others would not listen, the fear, the nightmare of nonexistence arose in his dreams. One of my repetitive dreams involves someone I love intensely ignoring me, unable to hear me, mute and distracted to me, occupied with other things and people. I do not matter. I do not exist. I struggle to connect with the beloved but he is unavailable. I try to connect with the long-lost friend but she throws her hands

---

[271] See Seyla Benhabib's "Judgment and the Moral Foundations of Politics in Arendt's Thought" for a commentary on Arendt's notion of judgment in politics.

[272] Cavarero, "The Desire for One's Story" in *Relating Narratives*.

up and finally pushes me away. I am alone. I am unloved. There is a feeling of fear followed by slowly accumulating terror. Finally, groups of people tell me to go away or I risk bodily endangerment. I am no one. If I try to get the love I need, I will be humiliated, shamed, injured, even killed. I wake feeling that this is what it must have been like to be ostracized from one's community and one's nation. It is this terror that Levi tries to convey in his narrative.

Levi's work echoes a theme that resounds in my dreams. To be unheard is not to exist. To not exist means certain death. This death is the loss of an embodied self, enabled in its sensuality to connect with fellow beings, to speak as an act of love and an impulse of memory. To speak the story is to breathe into the collective mouth of life. There are others waiting for our speaking, others waiting to hear. This love act is the oasis. It waters the desert, a place absent human love relations, and makes a green ground on which we plant and grow that love. Humanness means having a story, having space for states of feeling—passion, grief, and love. To practice our humanness, we promise our presence to others. This attentiveness happens in the ability to hear and respond to one another's stories. In allowing ourselves to be changed by those stories we encounter, to be torn asunder in the words of another, we become the humans we are meant to be.

After Poland

REFERENCES

Agosín, Marjorie. *Of Earth and Sea: A Chilean Memoir*. Translated by Roberta Goldstein. Tuscon: University of Arizona Press, 2009.

Alighieri, Dante. *The Inferno of Dante*. Translated by Robert Pinsky. New York: Farrar, Straus, and Giroux, 1994.

Améry, Jean. *At the Mind's Limits: Contemplations by a Survivor on Auschwitz and Its Realities*. Translated by Sidney Rosenfeld and Stella P. Rosenfeld. Bloomington: Indiana University Press, 1980.

    On Suicide: *A Discourse on Voluntary Death*. Translated by John D. Barlow. Bloomington: Indiana University Press, 1999.

Angier, Carole. *The Double Bond: The Life of Primo Levi*. New York: Farrar, Straus, and Giroux, 2002.

Anissimov, Myriam. *Primo Levi: Tragedy of an Optimist*. Woodstock: Overlook Press, 2000.

Arendt, Hannah. *Essays in Understanding: 1930-1954*. Edited by Jerome Kohn. New York: Schocken Books, 1994.

    The Promise of Politics. Edited by Jerome Kohn. New York: Schocken Books, 2005.

Auschwitz Jewish Center. http://ajcf.pl/en/.

Auster, Paul. *The Art of Hunger*. New York: Penguin, 1997.

Bähr, Andreas. "Between 'Self-Murder' and 'Suicide': The Modern Etymology of Self-Killing" in *Journal of Social History* 46, no. 3 (2013): 620-632.

Baldwin, James. "Notes of a Native Son." *Notes of a Native Son*. Boston: Beacon Press, 1955.

Beauvoir, Simone de. *The Prime of Life*. Translated by Peter Green. New York: Paragon House, 1992.

Benhabib, Seyla. "Judgment and the Moral Foundations of Politics in Arendt's Thought." *Political Theory* 16, no. 1 (1988): 29-51.

Benjamin, Jessica. "The Changing Face of Feminist Psychology." *Psychology's Feminist Voices*. 2014. https://www.youtube.com/watch?v=KXxjgxlxhsY.

Brison, Susan J. *Aftermath: Violence and the Remaking of a Self*. Princeton: Princeton University Press, 2002.

"Carolyn Forché." Biography. *Poetry Foundation*. 2017. https://www.poetryfoundation.org/poems-and-poets/poets/detail/carolyn-forche.

Caruth, Cathy. *Unclaimed Experience: Trauma, Narrative, and History*. Baltimore: Johns Hopkins, 1996.

Cavarero, Adriana. *Relating Narratives: Storytelling and Selfhood*. Translated by Paul A. Kottman. London: Routledge, 2000.

Chatterjee, A. "The Neuropsychology of Visual Art." In *Art, Aesthetics, and the Brain*, edited by Joseph P. Huston, et al, 341-356. Oxford: Oxford University Press, 2015. https://repository.upenn.edu/neuroethics_pubs/140/.

Cherry, Robert and Annamaria Orla-Bukowska, eds. *Rethinking Poles and Jews: Troubled Past, Brighter Future*. Rowman and Littlefield, 2007.

Chorost, Michael. *Rebuilt: My Journey Back to the Hearing World*. New York: Mariner Books, 2006.

Christofidou, Andrea. *Self, Reason, and Freedom: A New Light on Descartes' Metaphysics*. London: Routledge, 2013.

Cixous, Hélène. *Coming to Writing and Other Essays*. Edited by Deborah Jenson. Boston: Harvard University Press, 1992.

Colt, George Howe. *November of the Soul: The Enigma of Suicide*. New York: Scribner, 2006.

Csikszentmihalyi, Mihaly. *Creativity: Flow and the Psychology of Discovery and Invention*. New York: HarperCollins, 1996.

    Flow: The Psychology of Optimal Experience. New York: Harper Perennial, 1990.

Delbo, Charlotte. *Auschwitz and After*. Translated by Rosette C. Lamont. New Haven: Yale University Press, 1995.

Des Pres, Terrence. *The Survivor: An Anatomy of Life in the Death Camps*. New York: Pocket Books, 1977.

Writing into the World: Essays 1973-1987. New York: Viking Penguin, 1991.

Descartes, René. *Discourse on Method and Meditations on First Philosophy*. 1637 and 1641. Translated by Donald A. Cress. Indianapolis: Hackett Publishing, 1998.

"The First Years of the Memorial." Auschwitz.org. Państwowe Muzeum Auschwitz-Birkenau. http://auschwitz.org/en/museum/history-of-the-memorial/the-first-years-of-the-memorial/.

Forché, Carolyn. *Against Forgetting: Twentieth Century Poetry of Witness*. New York: W.W. Norton, 1993.

Forché, Carolyn. "Reading the Living Archives: The Witness of Literary Art," *Poetry*, May 2011.

"432. Marian Kołodziej. Magister vitae." *Auschwitz-Birkenau News*. 2015. Państwowe Muzeum Auschwitz-Birkenau. 9 Oct 2013. auschwitz.org/en/museum/news/432-marian-kolodziej-magister-vitae-educational-session, 1047.html.

Frank, Thaisa. "Poland." *A Brief History of Camouflage*. Santa Rosa: Black Sparrow Press, 1993.

"Gallery: Marian's Artwork." *The Labyrinth: The Testimony of Marian Kołodziej*. http://thelabyrinth documentary.com.

Gambetta, Diego. "Primo Levi's Last Moments." *Boston Review*. Summer 1999.

Gaukroger, Stephen. *Descartes: An Intellectual Biography*. Oxford: Oxford University Press, 1995.

Goldstein, Rebecca. *Betraying Spinoza: The Renegade Jew Who Gave Us Modernity*. New York: Schocken Books, 2006.

Goodhart, Sandor. "'A Land that Devours Its Inhabitants': Midrashic Reading, Emmanuel Levinas, and Prophetic Exegesis." *Shofar* 26, no. 4, (Summer 2008), 13-35.

    Sacrificing Commentary: Reading the End of Literature. Baltimore: Johns Hopkins UP, 1996.

    "'The War to End All Wars': Mimetic Theory and 'Mounting to the Extremes' in a Time of Disaster." *Does Religion Cause Violence? Multidisciplinary Perspectives on Violence and Religion in The Modern World*. Edited by Joel Hodge, Scott Cowdell, Chris Fleming, and Carly Osborn. London: Bloomsbury Publishing, 2017.

Gross, Jan T. *Fear: Anti-Semitism in Poland After Auschwitz*. New York: Random House, 2007.

Halifax, Joan. "Meditation: Tonglen or Giving and Receiving: A Practice of Great Mercy." *Upaya Zen Center*. 2017. https://www.upaya.org/dox/Tonglen.pdf.

Heaney, Seamus. "An Herbal." *Human Chain*. New York: Farrar, Straus, and Giroux, 2010.

Hedges, Chris. *War Is a Force That Gives Us Meaning*. New York: Anchor Books, 2002.

Herbert, Zbigniew. "The Envoy of Mr. Cogito." *The Collected Poems: 1956-1998*. Translated by Alisa Valles, Ecco, 2008.

Jamison, Kay Redfield. *Touched with Fire: Manic-Depressive Illness and the Artistic Temperament*. New York: Free Press, 1993.

The Jan Karski Society. http://en.jankarski.org.pl.

Joseph, Eve. "How a stroke changed how writer Eve Joseph views herself." *The Globe and Mail*, 9 Jan. 2015. https://www.theglobeandmail.com/life/health-and-fitness/health/how-a-stroke-changed-how-writer-eve-joseph-views-herself/article22390532/.

    In the Slender Margin: The Intimate Strangeness of Death and Dying. New York: Arcade Publishing, 2016.

Julia Pirotte: Twarze i dłonie (Faces and Hands). Exhibition Catalogue. Jewish Historical Institute (Warsaw).

Kaufmann, William. *Existentialism from Dostoevsky to Sartre*. New York: New American Library, 1975.

Knausgaard, Karl Ove. "Michel Houellebecq's 'Submission'." *The New York Times Book Review*. 2 Nov. 2015.

    My Struggle. Translated by Don Bartlett. New York: Farrar, Straus, and Giroux, 2014.

    Book 1. 2013.

    Book 2: A Man in Love. 2014.

    Book 3. 2015.

    Book 4. 2016.

"The Shame of Writing About Myself." *The Guardian*. 26 Feb. 2016.

Kohn, Jerome. "Hannah Arendt's Jewish Experience: Thinking, Acting, Judging." *Thinking in Dark Times: Hannah Arendt on Ethics and Politics*. Edited by Roger Berkowitz, J. Katz, and T. Keenan. New York: Fordham University Press, 2010.

Kołodziej, Marian. "I Was Rescuing My Own Humanity." Interview with Paweł Sawicki. *Oś—Oświęcim, People, History, Culture Magazine*, no. 6. Jun. 2009. auschwitz.org/en/museum/news/osmonthly-magazine.

The Labyrinth: The Testimony of Marian Kołodziej. Directed by Jason A. Schmidt. December 2nd Productions, 2011.

Langbein, Hermann. *People in Auschwitz*. Translated by Harry Zohn. Chapel Hill: University of North Carolina Press, 2004.

Leake, Elizabeth. *After Words: Suicide and Authorship in Twentieth Century Italy*. Toronto: University of Toronto Press, 2011.

Leonard, John. "The Drowned and the Unsaved." *The Nation*. 1 Mar. 2001.

Levi, Primo. "A Self-Interview" (1976). *The Voice of Memory: Interviews 1961-1987*. Edited by Marco Belpoliti and Robert Gordon. New York: New Press, 2001.

    The Drowned and the Saved. Translated by Raymond Rosenthal. New York: Vintage, 1989.

    If Not Now, When? Translated by William Weaver. New York: Penguin, 1986.

    The Periodic Table. 1975. Translated by Raymond Rosenthal. New York: Schocken Books, 1984.

    Primo Levi: Opere: Volume Primo. (Se questo è un uomo.) Torino: Guilio Einaudi, 1987.

    The Reawakening. (The Truce). 1962. Translated by Stuart Woolf. New York: Simon & Schuster, 1995.

    Survival in Auschwitz. (If This Is a Man). 1958. Translated by Stuart Woolf. New York: Simon & Schuster,1996.

Levinas, Emmanuel. "Useless Suffering," *Entre Nous: Thinking-of-the-Other*. Translated by Michael B. Smith and Barbara Harshave. New York: Columbia University Press, 1998.

Luzzatto, Sergio. *Primo Levi's Resistance: Rebels and Collaborators in Occupied Italy*. New York: Metropolitan Books, 2016.

Maximilian Kolbe. *Jewish Virtual Library*. American-Israeli Cooperative Enterprise. 2016. jewishvirtual library.org/jsource/biography/Kolbe.html.

Michaels, Anne. *Fugitive Pieces*. New York: Vintage, 1996.

Miller, Nancy K. *Bequest, and Betrayal: Memoirs of a Parent's Death*. Bloomington: Indiana University Press, 1996.

    But Enough About Me: Why We Read Other People's Lives. New York: Columbia University Press, 2002.

Neruda, Pablo. *Full Woman, Fleshly Apple, Hot Moon: Selected Poems of Pablo Neruda*. Translated by Stephen Mitchell. New York: Harper Perennial, 1997.

Nietzsche, Friedrich. *Beyond Good and Evil: Prelude to a Philosophy of the Future*. Translated by Walter Kaufmann. New York: Vintage, 1966.

Orr, Gregory. *Poetry as Survival*. Athens: University of Georgia Press, 2002.

Ozick, Cynthia. *Metaphor and Memory*. New York: Knopf, 1989.

Rich, Adrienne. *Of Woman Born: Motherhood as Experience and Institution*. New York: W. W. Norton, 1995.

Rohlf, Michael. "Immanuel Kant." The Stanford Encyclopedia of Philosophy. Edited by Edward N. Zalta. Spring 2016. https://plato.stanford.edu/entries/kant/.

"Salonika." *Holocaust Encyclopedia*. United States Holocaust Memorial Museum. https://www.ushmm.org/wlc/en/article.php?ModuleId=10005422.005422.

Schillinger, Liesl. "Why Karl Ove Knausgaard Can't Stop Writing." *Wall Street Journal Magazine*. 4 Nov. 2015.15.

Silko, Leslie Marmon. *The Turquoise Ledge*. New York: Viking, 2009.

Snyder, Timothy. *Bloodlands: Europe Between Hitler and Stalin*. New York: Basic Books, 2010.

Synthos. http://synthosgroup.com/en.

Thomson, Ian. *Primo Levi: A Life*. New York: Picador, 2002.

Tompkins, Jane. "Me and My Shadow." *The Intimate Critique: Autobiographical Literary Criticism*. Edited by Diane P. Freedman, Olivia Frey, and Francis Murphy Zauhar. Durham: Duke University Press, 1993.

Wachsmann, Nikolaus. *KL: A History of the Nazi Concentration Camps*. New York: Farrar, Straus and Giroux, 2015.

Wałesa, Lech. "Only When Forced Do I Look to the Past," Our Revolutions. *New Eastern Europe*, July-August 2014. 7-13.

Wiesel, Elie. *The Time of the Uprooted*. New York: Schocken Books, 2007.

Williams, Terry Tempest. *Leap*. New York: Vintage, 2001.

Young-Bruehl, Elisabeth. *Hannah Arendt: For Love of the World*. New Haven: Yale University Press, 2004.

Zagajewski, Adam. "A Defense of Ardor." *A Defense of Ardor*. Translated by Clare Cavanagh. New York: Farrar, Straus, and Giroux, 2002.

 Another Beauty. Translated by Clare Cavanagh. New York: Farrar, Straus, and Giroux, 2000.

 Solidarity, Solitude. Translated by Adam Zagajewski and Lillian Vallee. New York: Ecco Press, 1990.

CPSIA information can be obtained
at www.ICGtesting.com
Printed in the USA
BVHW012020101118

532695BV00002B/3/P

9 781863 350075